The *Avatar* Television Franchise

The *Avatar* Television Franchise

Storytelling, Identity, Trauma, and Fandom

Edited by
Francis M. Agnoli

BLOOMSBURY ACADEMIC
NEW YORK • LONDON • OXFORD • NEW DELHI • SYDNEY

BLOOMSBURY ACADEMIC
Bloomsbury Publishing Inc
1385 Broadway, New York, NY 10018, USA
50 Bedford Square, London, WC1B 3DP, UK
29 Earlsfort Terrace, Dublin 2, Ireland

BLOOMSBURY, BLOOMSBURY ACADEMIC and the Diana logo
are trademarks of Bloomsbury Publishing Plc

First published in the United States of America 2023
Paperback edition published 2024

Volume Editor's Part of the Work © Francis M. Agnoli, 2023, 2024
Each chapter © of Contributors, 2023, 2024

Cover images © Getty Images; Alamy

All rights reserved. No part of this publication may be reproduced or
transmitted in any form or by any means, electronic or mechanical,
including photocopying, recording, or any information storage or retrieval
system, without prior permission in writing from the publishers.

Bloomsbury Publishing Inc does not have any control over, or responsibility for, any third-party websites referred to or in this book. All internet addresses given in this book were correct at the time of going to press. The author and publisher regret any inconvenience caused if addresses have changed or sites have ceased to exist, but can accept no responsibility for any such changes.

Library of Congress Cataloging-in-Publication Data
Names: Agnoli, Francis M., editor.
Title: The Avatar television franchise : storytelling, identity, trauma and fandom / edited by Francis M. Agnoli.
Description: New York : Bloomsbury Academic, 2023. | Includes bibliographical references and index. |
Summary: "This edited collection, the first of its kind on the Avatar franchise, applies a range of scholarly theories and topics to readings of the two series"– Provided by publisher.
Identifiers: LCCN 2022025152 (print) | LCCN 2022025153 (ebook) | ISBN 9781501387173 (hardback) | ISBN 9781501387210 (paperback) | ISBN 9781501387180 (epub) | ISBN 9781501387197 (pdf) | ISBN 9781501387203
Subjects: LCSH: Avatar, the last airbender (Television program) | Legend of Korra (Television program) | Animated television programs. | LCGFT: Television criticism and reviews.
Classification: LCC PN1992.77.A922 A83 2023 (print) | LCC PN1992.77.A922 (ebook) | DDC 791.45/75–dc23/eng/20220811
LC record available at https://lccn.loc.gov/2022025152
LC ebook record available at https://lccn.loc.gov/2022025153

ISBN:	HB:	978-1-5013-8717-3
	PB:	978-1-5013-8721-0
	ePDF:	978-1-5013-8719-7
	eBook:	978-1-5013-8718-0

Typeset by Integra Software Services Pvt. Ltd.

To find out more about our authors and books visit www.bloomsbury.com
and sign up for our newsletters.

CONTENTS

List of Figures   vii

Introduction   *Francis M. Agnoli*   1

Part One   Storytelling

1. Noble Lady's Beauty Parlor 貴婦美容院: Ba Sing Se Fashion and Coding   *Shuyin Yu*   11

2. Zuko Rides into the Sunset: *Avatar* and the Western Film Genre   *Francis M. Agnoli*   25

3. Environmental Bending: How *Avatar: The Last Airbender* Introduces Viewers to Environmentalism   *Gia Coturri Sorenson*   39

Part Two   Identity

4. Social Identity in *Avatar: The Last Airbender*   *Douglas Schulz*   59

5. "What Does Me Being a Girl Have to Do with Sewing?" Representations of Gender in *Avatar: The Last Airbender*   *Ruth Richards*   75

6. A Queer Relationship: Mapping *The Legend of Korra*'s Industrial Journey across Mediums   *Emily Baulch and Oliver Eklund*   95

7. Material-Spiritual Bodies: Posthuman Performativity of Avatars   *Şafak Horzum and Süleyman Bölükbaş*   115

Part Three Trauma

8 "Born in You, Along with All the Strife, Is the Power to Restore Balance to the World": Exploring Representations of Children's Experiences of Trauma through *Avatar: The Last Airbender* Joseph V. Giunta 135

9 Lessons from the Southern Air Temple: How *Avatar: The Last Airbender* Negotiates the Trauma of Imperialism Ryanne Kap 155

10 Far from the Last Airbender: Cultural Trauma Construction and Diasporic Reimaginings in *Avatar* and *Korra* Caleb Horowitz 171

Part Four Fandom and Reception

11 From Fan Blogs to Earth Rumble VI: Disability Discourse on *Avatar: The Last Airbender* Max Dosser 189

12 Ships at the Edge Ashley Hendricks 207

13 Fans, Gender, and the Sequel: Analyzing Audience Reaction to *The Legend of Korra* Brecken Hunter Wellborn 225

Episodes Index 240
Subject Index 242

FIGURES

1.1 Still from *Avatar: The Last Airbender*, "City of Walls and Secrets" (S2E14) 20
1.2 Still from *Avatar: The Last Airbender*, "Tales of Ba Sing Se" (S2E15) 22
2.1 Still from *Avatar: The Last Airbender*, "Zuko Alone" (S2E07) 29
2.2 Still from *Avatar: The Last Airbender*, "Zuko Alone" (S2E07) 35
3.1 Still from *Avatar: The Last Airbender*, "The Swamp" (S2E04) 43
3.2 Still from *Avatar: The Last Airbender*, "The Swamp" (S2E04) 48
5.1 Still from *Avatar: The Last Airbender*, "The Boy in the Iceberg" (S1E01) 86
5.2 Still from *Avatar: The Last Airbender*, "The Waterbending Master" (S1E18) 90
6.1 Still from *The Legend of Korra*, "Welcome to Republic City" (S1E01) 100
6.2 Still from *The Legend of Korra*, "The Last Stand" (S4E13) 101
7.1 Still from *The Legend of Korra*, "Harmonic Convergence" (S2E12) 117
8.1 Still from *Avatar: The Last Airbender*, "The Desert" (S2E11) 142
8.2 Still from *Avatar: The Last Airbender*, "Bitter Work" (S2E09) 147
9.1 Still from *Avatar: The Last Airbender*, "The Southern Air Temple" (S1E03) 165
9.2 Still from *Avatar: The Last Airbender*, "The Southern Air Temple" (S1E03) 168

11.1 Still from *Avatar: The Last Airbender*, "The Blind Bandit" (S2E06)   190
11.2 Still from *Avatar: The Last Airbender*, "The Blind Bandit" (S2E06)   193
11.3 Still from *Avatar: The Last Airbender*, "Sozin's Comet, Part 4: Avatar Aang" (S3E21)   199
12.1 Still from *Avatar: The Last Airbender*, "Sozin's Comet, Part 3: Into the Inferno" (S3E20)   213
12.2 Still from *The Legend of Korra*, "When Extremes Meet" (S1E08)   214

Introduction

Francis M. Agnoli

Water. Earth. Fire. Air

Nickelodeon's *Avatar: The Last Airbender* (2005–8) and its sequel *The Legend of Korra* (2012–14) are among the most acclaimed and influential animated television series of the twenty-first century.[1] Yet, despite their elevated status, they have rarely been the subject of academic publications. This book seeks to address this gap as the first edited collection on the *Avatar* television franchise, featuring chapters by an international group of scholars from a range of academic backgrounds. We have structured this book with an undergraduate readership in mind, providing a variety of analytical tools for future media scholars.

Introducing the *Avatar* Television Franchise

The *Avatar* television franchise is set in a high fantasy world divided into four nations—Water Tribe, Earth Kingdom, Fire Nation, and Air Nomads—with select members of each capable of "bending" their associated element. Every generation, the Avatar—a being capable of bending all four elements—is reincarnated in one of these four nations and is tasked with maintaining peace and balance between them. The first series, *Avatar*, takes place after a century of war instigated by the Fire Nation against the rest of the world. The Avatar has seemingly vanished until the Water Tribe siblings Katara and Sokka discover Aang, a twelve-year-old Air Nomad, frozen in an iceberg.

Along with their flying bison Appa and winged lemur Momo, they form Team Avatar. Across three seasons or "Books," the last airbender and his friends travel the world as he masters the four elements in order to defeat Fire Lord Ozai and end the war. Over time, they are joined by Toph, a blind earthbender, and Suki, leader of the Kyoshi Warriors. They are also pursued at various points by the banished Prince Zuko; his uncle, General Iroh; Commander and later Admiral Zhao; and eventually Princess Azula and her companions, Mai and Ty Lee. Set seventy years later, *Korra* follows the next reincarnation of the Avatar, the eponymous Korra, as she navigates an increasingly industrialized and fractured world. Whereas *Avatar* centered on a single conflict, *Korra* has a new antagonist each season: the anti-bender terrorist and leader of the Equalists, Amon; Korra's uncle and Chief of the Northern Water Tribe, Unalaq; the anarchist and head of the Red Lotus, Zaheer; and the fascist ruler of the Earth Empire, Kuvira. In her battles against these foes, Korra is aided by the new Team Avatar—brothers Mako and Bolin as well as non-bender Asami Sato—and by her mentor and Aang and Katara's son, Tenzin.

Both series have been met with critical acclaim and have been immensely popular with audiences.[2] In fact, their reputation has only grown over the years, especially after both series became available on Netflix in summer 2020. This extended lifespan can be seen in the various spinoffs and tie-ins associated with the *Avatar* franchise. In addition to comics, videogames, and action figures, the franchise has spawned two live-action adaptations of the first series, a 2010 theatrical release and an upcoming television show on Netflix. Furthermore, on February 24, 2021, Nickelodeon announced that they would be launching Avatar Studios, a new division devoted to creating original animated series and movies set in the *Avatar* world.[3] *Avatar* and *Korra* are rich and complex texts, ripe for scholarly analysis. Yet, despite the franchise's continued acclaim and influence, it has remained overlooked and undervalued within media studies.[4] This edited collection exists, in part, to remedy this lacuna.

Chapter Breakdown

This volume is designed with an undergraduate readership in mind. An instructor could assign any single chapter along with one or two corresponding episodes in order to satisfactorily introduce and explore a given topic. At the same time, these chapters exist in dialogue with one another, within and at times across the different parts. They complement, expand, and challenge each other's arguments and ideas, rewarding those who read through the whole collection. This edited collection is divided into four parts: (1) Storytelling, (2) Identity, (3) Trauma, and (4) Fandom and

Reception. Each contains three or four chapters that tackle their respective topic from different perspectives, illustrating different ways to approach not only the *Avatar* television franchise but also media studies in general.

Part One, "Storytelling," features close readings of select episodes of *Avatar*, analyzing how the visuals and narratives create meaning. The first chapter—"Noble Lady's Beauty Parlor 貴婦美容院: Ba Sing Se Fashion and Coding" by Shuyin Yu—analyzes character designs from the second season of *Avatar*, focusing on clothing and hairstyles from the Earth Kingdom, in general, and from the capital city of Ba Sing Se, in particular. Yu presents the idea that artists convey information through layers of coding, which contribute to worldbuilding and characterization. She thus decodes how the *Avatar* character designers evoked real-world historical and cultural contexts through direct references to the Qing dynasty and the Manchu ethnic minority in order to communicate information about fictional cultures and settings to an audience. The second chapter—"Zuko Rides into the Sunset: *Avatar* and the Western Film Genre" by Francis M. Agnoli—expands on these ideas, exploring how artists exploit audience knowledge by referencing specific texts or bodies of texts. In this case, Agnoli places *Avatar* within the corpus of the western film genre, deciphering how meaning was encoded into characters, settings, and storylines despite their limited screen time. He finishes the chapter with a close reading of "Zuko Alone" (*Avatar* S2E07), stressing the episode's parallels with the classic western *Shane* (1953). The first part concludes with the third chapter—"Environmental Bending: How *Avatar: The Last Airbender* Introduces Viewers to Environmentalism" by Gia Coturri Sorenson—which reads key scenes from the episode "The Swamp" (*Avatar* S2E04) through an ecocritical framework. Such an approach introduces and explores the topics of ecofeminism and environmental justice, anthropocentrism versus ecocentrism, as well as the limitations of pastoralism. Sorenson also demonstrates the value of implementing a specific theoretical lens to guide such a media analysis. Through ecocriticism, she addresses how *Avatar* conveys environmental awareness to a child audience as well as which narrative and visual elements produce those meanings.

Part Two, "Identity," applies major theories concerning the formation and production of identity to the *Avatar* television franchise. The fourth chapter—"Social Identity in *Avatar: The Last Airbender*" by Douglas Schulz—introduces a set of sociological concepts that can guide readings of fictional works. Utilizing social identity theory and the looking-glass self, Schulz analyzes how dialogue from key episodes of *Avatar* convey the identities of characters and their relationships to each other. This chapter thus sets the stage for the rest of the part, providing readers with the tools for studying identity within works of media. Subsequent chapters get more specific. The fifth chapter—"'What Does Me Being a Girl Have to Do with Sewing?' Representations of Gender in *Avatar: The Last Airbender*" by Ruth Richards—traces Katara's character arc across the first season of *Avatar*, performing close readings of key episodes through a feminist framework. In addition, this chapter situates *Avatar* within the history of gender representation in US children's animation, especially that produced by and for Nickelodeon. Richards then explores how this historical and industrial context influenced Katara's gendered identity. The sixth chapter—"A Queer Relationship: Mapping *The Legend of Korra*'s Industrial Journey across Mediums" by Emily Baulch and Oliver Eklund—also highlights the importance of recognizing such contexts. Baulch and Eklund chronicle how the "gender neutral" programming of Nickelodeon in the 1990s and 2000s gave way to a preference for "boy cartoons" in the 2010s. This shift affected how a show like *Korra* could depict its lead character in terms of gender and sexuality. The titular character's journey across timeslots, platforms, and mediums impacted how her identity was conveyed within the confines of children's media. Closing out this part, the seventh chapter—"Material-Spiritual Bodies: Posthuman Performativity of Avatar" by Şafak Horzum and Süleyman Bölükbaş—takes a step back and questions the apparent anthropocentrism of discussions of identity in the *Avatar* television franchise and within animated works in general. In fact, not only does the animation of *Avatar* and *Korra* illustrate posthumanist concepts, but the narratives of the series themselves demonstrate these arguments through the "posthuman subject" of the Avatar. Horzum and Bölükbaş trace the histories of three on-screen Avatars—Wan, the first Avatar, featured in "Beginnings, Part 1" (*Korra* S2E07) and "Beginnings, Part 2" (*Korra* S2E08); Aang, featured in *Avatar*; and Korra, featured in *Korra*—through a posthumanist lens, showing the value of this theoretical framework for studying animation and fantasy.

Part Three features chapters that read these series through the lens of trauma theory, a broad and growing field that offers a range of approaches to analyzing works of media.[5] Throughout the *Avatar* franchise, the Fire Nation's imperialist century-long war on the rest of the world has left deep scars on both an individual and collective level that continue into the sequel series, heavy subjects for children's cartoons. The eighth chapter—"'Born in You, Along with All the Strife, Is the Power to Restore Balance to the World': Exploring Representations of Children's Experiences of Trauma through *Avatar: The Last Airbender*" by Joseph V. Giunta—analyzes the serialized character arcs of Aang and Zuko through the lenses of trauma theory and childhood studies.[6] In doing so, Giunta highlights not only how this series depicts children experiencing trauma and posttraumatic growth but also how it presents these subjects to a child audience. By filtering ideas on the formation of identity through the lens of trauma studies, this chapter provides a basis for the rest of this part to go into greater depth on their chosen focus. The ninth chapter—"Lessons from the Southern Air Temple: How *Avatar: The Last Airbender* Negotiates the Trauma of Imperialism" by Ryanne Kap—forgoes serialized narratives and character arcs in order to focus on a single episode: "The Southern Air Temple" (*Avatar* S1E03), in which Aang returns home and learns that all of the other Air Nomads have been killed by the Fire Nation. Kap goes through this episode, scene-by-scene, performing a close reading of the text through the lens of trauma theory, abetted by vocabulary from semiotics and affect theory. She identifies the elements of the episode meant to evoke emotional responses within viewers, specifically within a presumed child audience. The tenth chapter—"Far from the Last Airbender: Cultural Trauma Construction and Diasporic Reimaginings in *Avatar* and *Korra*" by Caleb Horowitz—returns to a key concept from Yu's chapter, how meaning within a fictional text is created by evoking real-world cultural and historical contexts. In his account of the Air Nomads, as depicted in both of the television series and in the tie-in comics, Horowitz finds meaning not only through the fictional culture's parallels to Tibet but also through its parallels to his own American Jewish experiences. Through this reading of the *Avatar* franchise, he addresses topics such as cultural trauma, intergenerational trauma, and the diaspora.

As with most popular pieces of media, certain audiences are inspired or activated to produce their own original work. The fourth and final part, "Fandom and Reception," explores the different types of fan-generated content prompted by the *Avatar* television franchise. The eleventh chapter—"From Fan Blogs to Earth Rumble VI: Disability Discourse on *Avatar: The Last Airbender*" by Max Dosser—studies not only how disability is represented in *Avatar* but, more importantly, how fans have received and discussed representations of disability within the show. Using concepts like "supercrip" and "narrative prosthesis" from disability studies, Dosser analyzes how fans incorporate or do not incorporate academic terms in their reception of a text and in the production of fan works—namely, blog posts and comments. Thus, he argues that scholars should engage with how fans discuss these topics in order to better understand the representation of disability in media. The twelfth chapter—"Ships at the Edge" by Ashley Hendricks—presents fanfiction as a worthy topic for media studies as well as an Archive of Our Own (AO3) as a rich (re)source for academics. Hendricks examines how and why *Avatar* has inspired such a volume of fan works, even after all these years, exploring how the characterization, the world-building, and even the animation aesthetic created ellipses or gutters that invited viewers to fill in the gaps. She then identifies three pivotal episodes that have activated the generation of fanfiction, chronicling the "ships" that they inspired. The thirteenth and final chapter—"Fans, Gender, and The Sequel: Analyzing Audience Reaction to *The Legend of Korra*" by Brecken Hunter Wellborn—tackles a final type of fan work, "fan reviews." While less labor-intensive than a blog post or fanfiction, these works still reveal much about the fandom surrounding a text. In this case, by performing close readings of fan reviews posted on Rotten Tomatoes and the Internet Movie Database (IMDb), Wellborn explores the expectational standards that defined the reception of *Korra*, both in terms of gender representation and as a sequel to *Avatar*.

All thirteen of these chapters, in their own way, address the significance of the *Avatar* television franchise as (a) animation, (b) television, and (c) children's media. The fact that *Avatar* and *Korra* are animated objects impacts how they convey meaning to an audience. Close-readings of either series recognize differences from live-action filmmaking practices. Furthermore, animation itself challenges anthropocentric approaches to these texts, encouraging readers to instead adopt an ecocentric or posthumanist lens, as demonstrated in the chapters by Sorenson and by Horzum and Bölükbaş. By stressing the fact that *Avatar* is also a *television* franchise, this collection explores what it means to engage with serialized narratives academically. Some chapters focus on individual installments for their close readings, such as Agnoli with "Zuko Alone," Sorenson with "The Swamp," and Kap with "The Southern Air Temple." Other chapters track the development of serialized elements like character arcs, worldbuilding, or storylines across multiple installments, as illustrated by Yu on Earth Kingdom fashion, Richards on Katara, and Giunta on Aang and Zuko. Finally, a few chapters emphasize how these works fit into a larger franchise, as seen in the chapters by Horzum and Bölükbaş and by Horowitz. *Korra*'s status as a sequel to *Avatar* is a defining characteristic of the series; it has always existed in the shadow of *Avatar*, consistently viewed as part of a larger franchise rather than as its own separate entity. While many chapters in this collection explore *Avatar* in isolation, *Korra* is almost exclusively read in conjunction with its predecessor. The expectational burden placed on *Korra* as a sequel becomes a recurring theme, as seen in the chapters by Baulch and Eklund and by Wellborn. Finally, this edited collection stresses the importance of *Avatar* and *Korra* as children's media, a complex and nebulous designation, especially in conjunction to animation that Richards defines and contextualizes in her chapter. Many of these writers address how that presumed target audience affects the conveyance of meaning about and for children, especially when the franchise attempts to deal with "adult" subject matter, such as environmental awareness as explored by Sorenson, sexuality as explored by Baulch and Eklund, or genocide as explored by Giunta and Kap.

The *Avatar* television franchise is composed of complex texts that have inspired equally complex reactions. These series' approach to storytelling, identity, and trauma as well as the resulting fandom and reception are all rich areas of study, ones that deserve far greater attention than what one edited volume can provide. By directing these chapters at an undergraduate readership, we intend to impart to a new generation of media scholars the tools for critically approaching works like *Avatar* and *Korra*, so that they may continue to excavate the plethora of meanings and insights contained within such texts.

Notes

1   Throughout this volume, the titles of these shows will be abbreviated as *Avatar* and *Korra*, respectively. When referring to the franchise as a whole, we refer to it as "the *Avatar* franchise" or as "the *Avatar* television franchise."
2   During its original run, *Avatar* was consistently one of Nickelodeon's most watched programs, with the series finale reaching 5.6 million viewers. Jon Lafayette, "Nick Continues Saturday Streak; Cable Net Rules Daypart for Eight Consecutive Seasons," *Television Week*, June 6, 2005, 7; Denise Martino Hollywood, "Nick Sticks with 'Avatar' for 3rd Season," *Daily Variety* 293.57 (June 21, 2006), 8; "Nickelodeon Is Top Basic Cable Network in 3Q, Scores 54 Straight Quarters at Number One; Nickelodeon's Kids and Family Portfolio Posts Solid Gains for the Quarter," *PR Newswire* (October 1, 2008). The first episode of *Korra* was watched by 4.5 million people, but later seasons were released on nick.com. "Debut of Nickelodeon's 'The Legend of Korra' Draws 4.5 Million Viewers," *TVbytheNumbers*, April 17, 2012, http://tvbythenumbers.zap2it.com/network-press-releases/debut-of-nickelodeons-the-legend-of-korra-draws-4-5-million-viewers/; Adam W. Kepler, "New Animated Series Makes Inroads in Ratings," *New York Times*, September 14, 2012, https://artsbeat.blogs.nytimes.com/2012/09/14/new-animated-series-make-inroads-in-ratings/. In addition, *Avatar* won an Emmy, multiple Annie Awards, and a Peabody Award. *Korra* also won a Daytime Emmy and multiple Annie Awards.
3   Nickelodeon, "Nickelodeon Establishes Avatar Studios, Brand-New Content Division Devoted to Expanding the World of Avatar: Last Airbender and The Legend of Korra," press release, February 24, 2021, https://www.nickpress.com/press-releases/2021/02/24/nickelodeon-establishes-avatar-studios-brand-new-content-division-devoted-to-expanding-the-world-of-avatar-last-airbender-and-the-legend-of-korra.
4   Most academic writing on *Avatar* and *Korra* have been confined to master's theses and doctoral dissertations, including my own. Within peer-reviewed publications, there have only been a handful of articles and book chapters on the *Avatar* television franchise. For an incomplete list, see: Lori Kido Lopez, "Fan Activists and the Politics of Race in *The Last Airbender*," *International Journal of Cultural Studies* 15.5 (2012): 431–45; Fulya Icoz, "Regaining the Power to Say 'No': Imprisonment, Resistance and Freedom in Avatar the Last Airbender," *Interactions* 23.1–2 (spring–fall 2014): 113–22; Adolfo Aranjuez, "'The Legend of Korra' and Minority Representation," *Screen Education* 78 (2015): 24–7; Greg Langner, "The Discursive Implications of Sexuality in the Final Scene of *The Legend of Korra*," *Colloquy* 11 (2015): 23–43; Michal Daliot-Bul and Nissim Otmazgin, *The Anime Boom in the United States: Lessons for Global Creative Industries* (Harvard University Press, 2017), 21, 49, 114, 119; Bonnee Crawford and Shih-Wen Sue Chen, "'Be careful!': Child Safety and Empowerment in *The Legend of Korra*," in *Children, Youth, and American Television*, eds. Adrian Schober and Debbie Olson (Routledge, 2018), 241–59; Rukmini Pande, *Squee from the Margins: Fandom and Race*

(University of Iowa Press, 2018), 75–110; Francis M. Agnoli, "Building the Transcultural Fantasy World of Avatar," *Animation Studies (Special Issue: Transnational Animation)*, July 24, 2019, https://journal.animationstudies.org/francis-m-agnoli-building-the-transcultural-fantasy-world-of-avatar/; Cara Marta Messina, "Tracing Fan Uptakes: Tagging, Language, and Ideological Practices in *The Legend of Korra* fanfictions," *The Journal of Writing Analytics* 3 (2019): 151–82; Muhamad Azhar Abdullah and Nabilah Abdullah, "An Initial Attempt: A Synthesis of Cultural Adaptation and Representation in Animation," *International Journal of Academic Research in Business and Social Sciences* 10.12 (2020): 546–57; R. P. Aditya, "Decoding the Politics of the Whitewashing Phenomenon in Hollywood through M. Night Shyamalan's '*The Last Airbender*'," *International Journal of English and Studies* 3.4 (2021): 87–95; Lauren Chochinov, "'What's Going On with You Two?': Queerness, Fandom, and Adaptation in *The Legend of Korra* Franchise," in *Polyptych: Adaptation, Television, and Comics*, ed. Reginald Wiebe (Vernon Press, 2021), 111–34; Cindy Karina and Setefanus Suprajitno, "The Journey of Becoming a Hero in the *Avatar: The Last Airbender* Animated Series," *Kata Kita: Journal of Language, Literature, and Teaching* 9.3 (2021): 444–51; Xine Yao, "Arctic and Asian Indigeneities, Asian/North American Settler/Colonialism: Animating Intimacies and Counter-Intimacies in Avatar: The Last Airbender," *Journal of Asian American Studies* 24.3 (2021): 471–504.

5   For more on trauma and media studies, see: Anne E. Kaplan, *Trauma Culture: The Politics of Terror and Loss in Media and Literature* (Rutgers University Press, 2005); Allen Meek, *Trauma and Media: Theories, Histories, and Images* (Routledge, 2010); Peter Leese, Julia Barbara Köhne and Jason Crouthamel (eds.), *Langauges of Trauma: History, Memory, and Media* (University of Toronto Press, 2021).

6   Childhood studies—sometimes referred to as the "New Sociology of Childhood"—is an interdisciplinary corrective to overly deterministic accounts on children and child development. For more, see: Joseph V. Giunta, "'Why Are You Keeping This Curiosity Door Locked?': Childhood Subjectivities and Play as Conflict Resolution in the Postmodern Web Series Stranger Things," in *Child and Youth Agency in Science Fiction: Travel, Technology, Time*, eds. Ingrid E. Castro and Jessica Clark (Lexington Books, 2019), 24–54.

PART ONE

Storytelling

1

Noble Lady's Beauty Parlor 贵妇美容院: Ba Sing Se Fashion and Coding

Shuyin Yu

In "City of Walls and Secrets" (S2E14), Aang, Katara, Sokka, and Toph are looking for an opportunity to get into the palace and speak to the Earth King. Katara comes up with an idea when she receives notice in the mail that "The king is having a party at the palace tonight for his pet bear!" The ensuing confusion amongst the main cast of characters lead them to ask if she meant platypus bear, skunk bear, armadillo bear, or gopher bear, only for Katara to repeat that she meant "just … bear." Toph draws the conclusion that "This place [Ba Sing Se] … is weird." But to the audience, the idea of a bear is not strange at all. A bear is a creature that exists in the real world, though usually in a far less anthropomorphized and far more untamed state. The obviousness of this reference to the real world does not happen with any other animal in any other city in *Avatar: The Last Airbender* (Nickelodeon, 2005–8). The "just a bear" has been lifted from our world and adapted to fit with the fantasy diegesis while remaining recognizable to audiences. The creative decision to keep Bosco as just a bear, to not hybridize him with another animal, parallels how much of the aesthetics of Ba Sing Se are lifted directly from its real-life counterparts and inspirations. Whereas the world of *Avatar* draws broad and specific inspirations from across Asian and Indigenous cultures, those for Ba Sing Se and its people parallel a particular period of Chinese history, the Qing dynasty (1639–1912), and a particular Chinese ethnic minority, the Manchus. Whereas much of *Avatar* depends on transculturation and hybridization, Ba Sing Se is unique because of how often it directly transposes and imports its real-world influences.

After being referenced in in multiple episodes, Ba Sing Se is actively featured in the second half of Book Two, starting with "The Library" (S2E10), wherein audiences meet a character from Ba Sing Se in the form of Professor Zei, until the season finale, "The Crossroads of Destiny" (S2E20). This chapter builds on information about the Earth Kingdom scattered throughout the second season, with special focus on "The Blind Bandit" (S2E06), but focuses on a few particular episodes that show the day-to-day lives of the citizens of Ba Sing Se, as well as the fashions and cultures of Ba Sing Se in minor characters, such as "City of Walls and Secrets" and "The Tales of Ba Sing Se" (S2E15).

Because not everyone is able to recognize the specifics of the references, the second season of *Avatar* rely on two different layers of coding to convey information. The first is generalized coding, building on familiar tropes in order provide information; even if the audience is not familiar with the specifics of Asian and Indigenous cultures, histories, or aesthetics, they are able to extrapolate information from how Asian and Indigenous cultures are generally depicted, such as in martial arts movies, *xianxia* (仙侠)[1] and *wuxia* (武侠)[2] series, and anime. The second is direct allusions and references, picking up on specific subtle details that are comparable to their historical counterparts. These aesthetic choices are important because these distinctions help both to differentiate between the diegetic fantasy cultures and to showcase the lived distinctions of various Asian and Indigenous cultures, such as Imperial Japanese with the Fire Nation and Inuit culture with the Water Tribe. By preserving culture specificities when transposing, the practice of hybridization in *Avatar* is able to add nuance to the distortions that happen when cultures are generalized into monolithic stereotypes.

By being more careful in their choices of referents, creators are able to encourage viewer engagements in both affirmational and transformative fan spaces in a positive feedback loop. Affirmational fandom spaces that focus on expanding the "canonical" materials—such as analyzing buildings, hairstyles, and clothing—could inspire transformative fandom spaces' outputs, thus creating layers of new information that draws and builds upon the established materials, and thus creating more ways for information on the canonical inspirations and antecedents to be disseminated. In essence, *Avatar* is doing what some critics call "critical reappropriations," in which the text "self-referentially engage[s] with Asian images" and with the nuances of the cultural specificities of aesthetics.[3] While this chapter focuses on the specific Chinese/Qing-dynasty/Manchu influences, the practice could be applied to many of the inspirations in *Avatar*. By focusing on the specificities and layering the different kinds of coding, *Avatar* encourages interested and invested viewers to self-educate, while remaining accessible to more generalized fans.

Allegory, Allusion, Reference, and Coding

There is a fine line between the intentionality of producers and writers and the unintentional inclusions of real-life inspirations; this chapter does not claim any authoritative insight into the production of *Avatar* or the minds of the creators. Instead, this chapter takes a more descriptive approach, making assertions on allegories, allusions, references, and coding through close textual analysis. Allegories, allusions, references, and coding all function in different ways in media as well as in the subsequent consumption of that media. These engagements with intertextuality are not confined to rigid boxes so much as they take place on a spectrum, one dependent on both authorial intent and reader response. Allegory is usually considered the most didactic and tends to be indisputable. These extended metaphors are often done with authorial intent, wherein the parallels are carefully laid out. While there are plenty of examples of children's media that do this kind of allegorical work, *Avatar* is not one of them. This world resists one-to-one allegories, mainly due to the extent of hybridization. The Water Tribes, while drawing inspirations from Inuit clothing and hair, also have crossed collars found in many East Asian outfits. While some readers might recognize the ways the armor of Fire Nation resembles Japanese Samurai, the aesthetics of the Fire Nation also draws upon Southeast Asia, Mesoamerica, and Imperial China. This kind of recognition is closer to allusion, which is "a passing reference, without explicit identification."[4] Allusions are usually not explicitly identified and thus "imply a fund of knowledge that is shared by an author and the audience," unlike references, which do explicitly identify what they are referencing.[5] In the case of visual media, such as animation, most "allusions" fall on a spectrum from allusion to reference, because recognition that depends on knowledge shared by the creators and audiences will vary greatly. For example, this chapter asserts the Earth Kingdom in *Avatar* directly "references" Chinese fashion trends, but a general audience might have considered the fashion to be "allusions" to Chinese clothing because they are not familiar with the specifics. Finally, there is coding, which is a kind of semiotics that is the process of creating information, usually in the form of shorthand that might engage with intertextuality but might also engage with the readership's previous knowledge and assumptions. Even if the general audience is not familiar with the specifics of certain historical fashion trends, they will likely recognize when something is bigger and thus more important because of how most culture places an emphasis on size. This fluidity between allegory, allusions, references, and coding is particularly pertinent to visual mediums, such as animation, wherein explicit references might be missed and implicit allusions might be extrapolated upon. These concepts are all interconnected, and their links may be strengthened or weakened depending on the creators, the audience, their familiarity with the materials, and their base assumptions.

Take, for example, the very first scene of "City of Walls and Secrets" where two earthbenders are pushing a monorail on the tracks. Audiences can tell they are two earthbenders because of their green clothes, which is a reference to the clothing conventions established in previous episodes to be associated with earthbenders, but also because green is generally coded to be associated with trees and earth in broader culture. Similarly, the monorail is clearly an allusion to modern conception of a train, with its many interconnected cars, but the way the paper windows and sloping roofs are drawn was inspired by Asian architectural references. Most strikingly, perhaps, is how both earthbenders pushing the monorail have their hair tied up in long queues behind them. Audiences familiar with Chinese history would recognize the queue as the hairstyle worn by men during the Qing dynasty, when China was ruled by Manchus; Western audiences unfamiliar with the specifics of this aspects of Chinese history might still recognize the queue, but from the images relating to "Fu Manchu" or "Yellow Peril" iconography that dominated the Western imaginary. Indeed, for most of modern history, some of the most prevalent stereotypes still associated with Chinese culture and people are the "Chinese worker's queue and the supposed eating of domesticated animals […] as devices to symbolize Chinese foreignness."[6] The queue is thus functioning as an allusion, which draws upon a fund of knowledge from both the creator and the audience.

Visual cues like the queue become a way to communicate varying levels of information to various audiences: the more familiar audiences are, the deeper the meaning they will gauge from the text, but even those less familiar are gently guided by universals and pattern recognition. For audiences who are familiar with the queue, the hairstyle is a direct reference to the Qing-dynasty tradition, tying together the character design with the other Qing-dynasty influences in Ba Sing Se; for audiences who only recognize the queue as an allusion, the hairstyle adds to the hybridization expected of the *Avatar* franchise. Those who are unfamiliar will still recognize that the queue has a diegetic function. After all, if the audience had been watching *Avatar* in order, the queues would be a reminder of Zei, and audiences are able to connect the dots of how a professor from Ba Sing Se University might style his hair in the fashion of Ba Sing Se.

This scaffolded and multilayered approach makes *Avatar* both approachable and richly detailed. The animation uses semiotic coding to allow for unfamiliar audiences, many of whom are children, to engage with the materials, while the allusions/references become points of entry for more familiar audiences to explore deeper meaning. *Avatar* models its own ethos; like how Aang has to travel the world and encounter things that are strange and new before coming to reckon how all of those ideas and identities and people can be in harmony, the show is interested in exploring various cultures, whether they are familiar or different. To borrow a term from Eve Kosofsky Sedgwick, exploring the world of *Avatar* encourages a kind of "reparative reading," wherein audiences are encouraged to move toward the generative practices that come from affirming the recognizable and transforming the hybridized as well as move away from "paranoid imperatives" that are reflexive, mimetic, and negative in ways that strike a balance between "paranoid and reparative critical practice, not as theoretical ideologies (and certainly not as stable personality types of critics), but as changing heterogeneous rational stances."[7]

Historical Fashion Inspirations and Visual Shorthand

The world of *Avatar* is geopolitically complicated, but numerous crewmembers in the art department put great care to make sure that each of the nations is aesthetically and culturally consistent internally as well as different externally. The Water Tribes were depicted as two distinct but connected parts of a whole; while they do share kinship with the Foggy Swamp Tribe, the Northern and Southern Water Tribes are interconnected because of their culture and, by extension, their aesthetics. The Air Temples, from the decipherable details, are also fragmented parts of a whole; each temple had its own building structure, but the temples most likely ascribe to similar philosophies, going all the way to how they are dressed in yellow and orange robes. The Fire Nation is most like what most audiences would understand as a nation-state, wherein the social organization of the nation (specifically its people and firebenders) are contained in geography of the State (the Fire Nation Islands); the nation's culture and aesthetics are exported alongside its colonial practices, with the Fire Nationals recognizable because of how they are dressed. The Earth Nation, similarly, has a national aesthetic and culture tied specifically their connection to their ability to bend earth. However, the vast geographies mean that the Kingdom is also fragmented. The existence of regional kings, like Bumi from "The King of Omashu" (S1E05), and of bending specializations, such as sandbending in "The Library," suggests that the vastness of this nation has resulted in social and cultural fragmentation, with specializations developing because of the geographical and social climate differences.

These differences throughout the Earth Kingdom are often visually conveyed through the show's aesthetic choices, moving away from the blue tones of the Water Tribes toward the green-yellow-browns of the Earth Kingdom. *Avatar*, being an animated show, is working within a different set of constraints and freedoms than a live-action show would. For live-action productions, the costume designer must consider the practicality and functionality of an outfit, that it must be made out of real material and worn by a real person. Here, though, the designs must be congruent to the animation process. They are simplified and streamlined enough so that they can be reproduced not only by the character designer but also by storyboard artists, keyframe animators, and in-between animators. The chosen aesthetics were also part of the model sheets and were thus an intrinsic part of how these characters were designed. This balance between constraint and freedom is particularly evident with Ba Sing Se hair and costumes. Earth Kingdom designs in general lift much of its inspirations from Chinese aesthetics, pulling from a range of historical eras and ethnicities, increasing in their specificity over the course of the show.[8] As the story progresses in Book Two, the character designs reference a number of Chinese dynasties and aesthetics before finally arriving at the Qing dynasty during the final arc in Ba Sing Se.

For example, when Toph Beifong was first introduced in "The Blind Bandit," she is shown in three distinct outfits, all referencing Tang- and Sui-dynasty clothing. In Bryan Konietzko's character concept sheet, he writes that Toph's fancy dress was modeled after Tang-dynasty clothing, with a design note specifically pointing out how the "scarf draped between arms, hangs in back."[9] The technical term for the scarf/shawl Toph wears is *Pibo* (披帛) which is a kind of traditional shawl, usually made from light silk, that is used to decorate various styles of *Hanfu* (漢服) or classical Chinese clothing, such as the *Ruqun* (襦裙) that Toph is wearing. Indeed, the style that Toph's fancy dress is modeled after is called the *Qixiong Ruqun* (齐胸襦裙/齊胸襦裙) style, whose very name references the chest-high waistline of her white *Qun* (裙) skirt. The shape of Toph's *Qixiong Ruqun*, like many of the other cultural markers in *Avatar*, also plays on familiar Western fashion trends, leading to many possible hybridization interpretations despite the cultural specificity of the character design references. The lacing just below the armpits on Toph's *Qixiong Ruqun* create the image of a high waist, much like the Empire waist silhouette dresses, which often has a bodice that ends just below the bust. This silhouette remains popular for little girls at formal events, such as weddings or gatherings, because the high waist on these dresses tends to cinch them somewhere on their ribcage before a natural waistline exists. This familiar dress pattern helps to ground the image of Toph in her identity as a twelve-year-old girl, encoding the generalities of being dressed in formal clothing that restricts movement and comfort. Much like how she would sit with her hands primly placed on her lap in front of her parents, Toph being dressed in a formal outfit is a part of her performance. The very first thing Toph does after a disastrous dinner with her parents and the rest of Team Avatar is shed the external layers of the *Qixiong Ruqun*—the feminine and the fragile—and put on pants before confronting Aang. Whereas the *Ruqun* was an explicit reference to the nondiegetic historical fashion inspirations, the design choice to put Toph in pale green pajama-style pants also serves a narrative purpose. As Toph opens to Aang about who she is and how she came to learn earthbending, she is also dressed in clothing that allows her freedom of movement. However, unlike the bold green of her Blind Bandit outfit, her main outfit for the rest of the series, this transitional outfit is in the same pastels as her *Ruqun*. Through this tiny color choice, audiences can decode how Toph was straddling the two parts of her identity. When Toph leaves her home to join Aang, she wears her Blind Bandit outfit, with its bold colors, sharp lines, and wide belt tied at her natural waist. In his notes, Konietzko specifically writes that "Toph's arms and legs are not scrawny like Aang's," and thus encodes the character's narrative into the character's design.[10]

Like the rest of the main cast, the Blind Bandit outfit borrows elements from historical inspirations, but the design does not lift from a specific era. However, certain aesthetic choices reveal interesting worldbuilding details. Unlike the wide folded collar of her *Ruqun*, Toph's Blind Bandit outfit includes a mandarin collar, which is usually associated with clothing from the Qing dynasty and, diegetically, with Ba Sing Se. This concurrence suggests the clothing inspired by a wide chronology of Chinese fashions throughout the Earth Kingdom diegetically coexist, which means that these fashion spheres are not separated by time but by geography. Like other kinds of hybridization in *Avatar*, the ways fashion is localized demonstrates how the chronological hybridity could result in interesting regional specificities. This aesthetic detail was likely created to smoothly transition Toph from the outer areas of the Earth Kingdom into Ba Sing Se, but it also expands upon the information encoded in Earth Rumble VI and the ways Ba Sing Se expands outside the boundaries of its walls.

Like much of the series, the Earth Rumble VI scenes work with various levels of audience understanding through allusions, references, and coding. Earth Rumble VI is an unsubtle reference to professional wrestling shows; from the design of the ring to the Russian accept adopted by the heel Fire Nation Man. Between combat, female assistants dressed in closefitting *qipaos* (旗袍) are shown in passing. The closefitting *qipao* the female assistants are wearing is encoded with "multiple ideological investments" the significance of which depends upon audience familiarity and interpretation.[11] For audiences who are reading the scenes through this lens, the female assistants who appear between the rounds of combat are emulations of "ring girls" whose outfits reflect the sexual objectification these women often go through. But, for audiences with more familiarity with the costuming, the *qipaos*—or *cheongsams* (长衫/長衫)—allude to the complex historical changes to Qing-dynasty fashion and implies how Ba Sing Se fashion might have been adapted and adjusted as it moves away from Ba Sing Se and into the various parts of the Earth Kingdom. This closefitting version of the *qipao* comes from late Qing dynasty and Early Republican China, when it was "promoted as an enrichment of reinforcement of tradition, and other times a symbol of modernity."[12] Unlike the looser and "baggier" traditional *qipaos* that often had pants underneath, the modern *qipao* was reimagined with a slim sheath silhouette that was meant to be sexually liberating.[13] The inclusion of this sexy version of the *qipao* thus brings into context the quiet tension between the various levels of interpretation and how hybridization create nuances in how characters are understood.

The design of these female assistants in the closefitting modern *qipao* also raises questions about how the diegetic Ba Sing Se fashion change as it leaves Ba Sing Se, since the clothing inside Ba Sing Se much more closely resemble the traditional, looser Qing-dynasty *qipaos*. Several characters were (re)designed with Ba Sing Se fashion. Hye Jung Kim colored Angela Mueller's designs for "Uncle Iroh and Zuko [in] Earth Kingdom attire in order to blend in" in muted dark greens and browns.[14] Most audiences can recognize what the characters are doing simply from the color; but audiences more familiar with the designs would recognize that Iroh's and Zuko's clothes are not just vaguely Chinese-inspired Earth Kingdom outfits but also draws specific inspirations from the long robes and cuts from *changshan* (長衫) or *dagua* (大褂), which are long tunics often considered the male equivalent to the *qipao*. Even though much of the aesthetic designs were "decontextualized, remixed, remade, appropriated, and otherwise transformed," the inspiration still emerges because of the specificity of the references.[15] Much like with Toph's Blind Bandit designs and the female assistants' outfits, the high mandarin collar is a distinct and explicit connection to Qing-dynasty fashion.

While the *Avatar* artbook describes the "upper ring" clothing of Ba Sing Se as "fancy Tang-dynasty influenced dress," a quick comparison with Toph's "fancy dress [which] was modeled after Tang-dynasty clothing" reveals how different the clothing designs are.[16] Instead, from the mandarin collar to the social commentary, it seems that Ba Sing Se was explicitly referencing the Qing-dynasty fashion and the styles that would eventually become the basis of Chinese Republican fashion; a likely intentional choice considering how the Qing dynasty was a times of great social and political anxieties, reminiscent of the social unrest in the Earth Kingdom during season two of *Avatar*. Many female characters are designed with towering headdresses, with elaborate hairstyles such as the *liangbatou* (兩把頭) in either *yizitou* (一字頭) or *dalachi* (大拉翅) style. Even audiences unfamiliar with the terminology would have likely encountered depictions of it. The popular conception of the "towering geometric headdress colloquially referred to as *liangbatou*" comes from the first decade of the twentieth century at the same time as when Empress Dowager Cixi and the Qing rulers were trying to "re-consolidate its power in the face of mounting criticism of its ability to rule."[17] Thus, the *liangbatou* is as much "an accessory fashioned to impress" as it is an "affective power" that reflects political anxieties, with the "most exaggerated form [having] materialized through Manchu self-fashioning" as a response to "crisis of identity and sovereignty."[18]

Ba Sing Se is unique in *Avatar* because of how much the art department lifts from the real world and thus imports the external influences that are part of the histories and stories of their references. This historical connection seems to be made explicit when Aang's disguise includes Momo's tail peeking out from under his hat in mimicry of the Manchu queue hairstyle, and it is further confirmed when the 52nd Earth King Kuei is revealed with uncanny resemblance to the last Chinese Emperor Puyi. Indeed, the fashion inside Ba Sing Se is carefully branded so that most characters inside Ba Sing Se's walls are wearing some variation of the mandarin collar and/or clothing inspired by the Qing dynasty. Part of this cultural consistency might be the diegetic explanation: Ba Sing Se's authoritarianism extends to the curation, cultivation, and careful management of every aspect of the society including culture—with so much emphasis placed on the cultural elements that Long Feng, the Grand Secretariat, leader of the Dai Li, and actual power behind the throne of Ba Sing Se, introduces himself as a "cultural advisor to the king" in "City of Walls and Secrets." When explaining the role of the Earth King, Long Feng describes how "what's most important to his royal majesty is maintaining the cultural heritage of Ba Sing Se. All his duties relate to issuing decrees on such matters," which diegetically explains why the clothes in Ba Sing Se seem to remain at a point of chronological singularity and actively resists changes.

Just a Bear: Close Reading the Cultural Specificity of Ba Sing Se Fashion

After Toph agreed with Katara's plan to sneak into the party the Earth King was hosting for his pet bear, the episode cuts to a scene wherein Katara and Toph enter the room where Aang and Sokka were playing a game; the shot pans upwards to reveal the details of their dresses and makeup (see Figure 1.1). Even if audiences are not familiar with the specifics of Qing-dynasty *qipao* or hairstyles, they likely recognize the coded presentation of young women, dressing up in fancy dresses, piling their hair up into giant, unwieldy structures, and putting on dramatic makeup (as well as the trope of the big reveal).

The *qipao* that Katara and Toph are wearing in this scene closely resemble the more traditional Qing-dynasty *qipao*, complete with high mandarin collars and large flowers pinned on the *liangbatou*. Like the case with Toph's *Qixiong Ruqun*, Katara's and Toph's high-society outfits are doing double duty, both helping them blend into a new social environment and communicating to the audiences how different the upper ring world is compared to the rest of Ba Sing Se and the Earth Kingdom. To audiences unfamiliar with the various social rankings or significance of *liangbatou* decorations in Qing-dynasty courts, the *liangbatou* is an easy indicator of class and social significance. Bigger is better. Contrast the hemline of

FIGURE 1.1 *Toph and Katara dress up. Still from "City of Walls and Secrets" (S2E14). Blu-ray release of* Avatar: The Last Airbender—The Complete Series *(2018).*

Katara's collar, swirling clouds that matches with the *liangbatou* frame, with Joo Dee's much smaller *bianfang* and simple robes and scarf with the Earth Kingdom logo. The various Joo Dee's are only ever show in one kind of green dress, which means that the *qipao* is both a uniform and a symbol of her status; the simplicity and ease of reproducing the dress are also indicators of Joo Dee's position as a servant that could be easily replaced or cheaply substituted. Both diegetically and nondiegetically, the details in the fancy hair and robes are representative of social roles. Thus, when Toph and Katara enter the party, they are surrounded by Ba Sing Se women with similarly huge and extravagant outfits and hair. Along with huge *liangbatou* frames paired with exquisite details and decorations, the majority of Ba Sing Se characters are coded in a variety of ways to demonstrate their class and the roles they play. When Aang accidentally spills water on a guest at the Earth King's party, her amazed exclamation "The Avatar! I didn't know the Avatar would be here" falls somewhere between a British and Transatlantic dialect. The dialect is usually associated with old money in the United States and is thus as much a coded indicator of wealth and status as the flowing robes and fancy jewelry all the upper ring members are wearing.

This hybridity of historical specificity and modern American sensibilities is further compounded upon in "Tales of Ba Sing Se." Composed of short vignettes written by different members of the staff, this episode particularly relies on these two levels of communication. The designs both make sense diegetically as well as reflect the sensibilities of the real-world audiences, both exploring different angles of life in Ba Sing se and different scopes of knowledge on the part of the writers and audiences.

The vignette "The Tale of Toph and Katara" features Katara and Toph visiting the Fancy Lady Day Spa and exiting with bright blue eyeshadow, prominent pink blush, and frosty pink lipstick.[19] As they pass a group of "mean girls," one of them comments, "Wow, great makeup ... for a clown!" While contemporary audiences might agree with this assessment, Toph's and Katara's makeup was simply a more exaggerated version of what was in style at the time the episode was produced, which audiences of the mid-2000s may have recognized. However, compared to the specificity of the Qing-dynasty clothing and Manchu aesthetic inspirations of the rest of Ba Sing Se, the makeup may seem asynchronous.

This type of dual coding reappears in the vignette "The Tale of Sokka" is also one of the most obvious uses of the Qing-dynasty style to encode information for the audiences. The *liangbatou* hairstyle intuitively have hairpieces called *bianfang* (扁方) get bigger as characters become more powerful, wealthier, or higher class; while almost all the young ladies of the Five-Seven-Five Society are wearing their hair in the *liangbatou* hairstyle, their status and importance are coded in the size of their headpieces (see Figure 1.2). Even before the woman on the right wearing a large white *dalachi* stands up to compete with Sokka in a haiku competition, her significance is encoded in the size and prominence of her headdress. Her headdress is a symbol of her position and importance both diegetically in the society and narratively, "highlight[ing] the performative role of the headdress."[20]

The size of the headdress, the propriety with which the woman performs, and the connotative associations of poetry with class and privilege asserts in how the woman presents herself while creating haikus. However, audiences likely recognized how Sokka's engagement with haiku battles with the Five-Seven-Five Society is more evocative of rap battles, which often challenge assumptions about the very class and privilege the woman displays. As Sokka gets closer to the rhyme and rhythm expected of contemporary rap battles, he simultaneously drifts away from the five-seven-five format. The humor of the episode comes partially from this tension and the subversion of expectations.

The world of *Avatar* is created to have meaning, be meaningful, and generate additional meaning through both specific references and subtle subversions. It feels so rich because it pays respectful homage to a variety of Asian and Indigenous cultures, layering them in ways that create interesting dynamics and parallel significance. This is particularly true of the character designs and style, as the clothing and historical references help to reflect the context of the diegesis as well as the historical references.

FIGURE 1.2 *Sokka regales the ladies of the Five-Seven-Five Society. Still from "Tales of Ba Sing Se" (S2E15). Blu-ray release of* Avatar: The Last Airbender—The Complete Series *(2018).*

The clothing and character designs are intimately linked because they both reflect internal identity and are shaped by external influences. The parallels and intersections of internal identity and external influences also apply to coding. While intentional references and allusions may play a role in the creation process, the audience must also be able to recognize, process, and understand the creative choices, which rely on both their own biases and assumptions. The world of *Avatar* is thus an invitation to explore the variety of ways meaning could be generated collaboratively between the show and audiences. By layering both direct references and general tropes, *Avatar* encourages audiences to engage with the coded information they can pick up and remain curious about ones they are not able to fully comprehend. However, the show is also careful to avoid becoming allegorical. Ba Sing Se was created to be an evocation of reference points different audience members bring to the viewing, revealing how individual understandings, histories, biases, and assumptions could create different layers of meaning and significance in the audiences' interactions with a piece of media.

After all, *Avatar* is an animated children's show, and it wants to create a generative and space. These hints embedded inside the show help guide audiences to take a reparative stance in their engagement, wherein revisiting the medium allowed to greater exploration and engagement, thus participating in the process of hybridity and synthesizing meaning, even if it is exploring already existing historical specificities. Though Bosco the Bear was not hybridized with another animal, he was still reimagined for the animation and made to be friendlier and more accessible for audiences. He was Earth King Kuei's best friend, and demonstrates a certain amount of anthropomorphic affection for Kuei. And even though he eventually rips the clothes off when he starts to travel the world with Kuei in "The Awakening" (S3E01), the majority of Bosco's appearances feature him in a *changshan*, complete with a mandarin collar. Bosco, like the rest of Ba Sing Se, remains on brand to his inspirations.

Notes

1 Literally "immortal hero," referencing a genre of "cultivation" high-fantasy influenced by Chinese epistemologies.
2 Literally "martial hero," referencing a genre of "martial arts" low-fantasy relating to martial arts and martial artists.
3 David S. Roh, Betsy Huang and Greta A. Niu, *Techno-Orientalism: Imagining Asia in Speculative Fiction, History, and Media* (Rutgers University Press, 2015), 7.
4 M. H. Abrams, *A Glossary of Literary Terms* (Heinle & Heinle, 1999), 9.
5 Ibid., 9.
6 Krystyn R. Moon, *Yellowface: Creating the Chinese in American Popular Music and Performance, 1850s–1920* (Rutgers University Press, 2014), 36. For more information about the queue, see: Gary Wang, "Affecting Grandiosity: Manchuness and the *Liangbatou* Hairdo-Turned-Headpiece Circa 1870s–1930s," in *Fashion, Identity, and Power in Modern Asia*, eds. Kyunghee Pyun and Aida Yuen Wong (Palgrave Macmillan, 2018), 167–92; Wu Hung, *Zooming In: Histories of Photography in China* (Reaktion Books, 2016); Michael R. Godley, "The End of the Queue: Hair as Symbol in Chinese History," *East Asian History* 8 (1994): 52–72; and Eva Shan Chou, *Memory, Violence, Queues: Lu Xun Interprets China* (Association for Asian Studies Publications, 2012).
7 Eve Kosofsky Sedgwick, "Paranoid Reading and Reparative Reading; or, You're So Paranoid, You Probably Think This Introduction Is about You," in *Novel Gazing: Queer Readings in Fiction*, ed. Eve Kosofsky Sedgwick (Duke University Press, 1997), 8.
8 Michael Dante DiMartino and Bryan Konietzko, *Avatar: The Last Airbender—The Art of the Animated Series* (Dark Horse Books, 2010), 86.
9 Ibid., 97.

10　Ibid.
11　Sandy Ng, "Clothes Make the Woman: *Cheongsam* and Chinese Identity in Hong Kong," in *Fashion, Identity, and Power in Modern Asia*, eds. Kyunghee Pyun and Aida Yuen Wong (Palgrave Macmillan, 2018), 274.
12　Ng, 360. "Modernity" in this context references Westernization in Early Republican China.
13　Ng, 360, 274.
14　DiMartino and Konietzko, 111.
15　Roger Whitson, *Steampunk and Nineteenth-Century Digital Humanities: Literary Retrofuturism, Media Archeologies, Alternate Histories* (Routledge, 2017), 7.
16　DiMartino and Konietzko, 97, 110. It is likely that the art book made a minor mistake with their reference notes.
17　Wang, 168.
18　Ibid., 168, 170.
19　This paper draws its title from the name of this establishment, 貴婦美容院—literally, Noble Lady's Beauty Parlor.
20　Wang, 173.

2

Zuko Rides into the Sunset: *Avatar* and the Western Film Genre

Francis M. Agnoli

Avatar: The Last Airbender (Nickelodeon, 2005–8) is not a western. If this animated television series emulates any film genres, styles, or modes, they would be *wuxia* or fantasy martial arts from mainland China or anime from Japan. Sometimes, the series alludes to such works through specific intertextual references. The image of Jin and Mei constrained by bamboo spears in the film *House of Flying Daggers* (2004) was adapted into the storyboards of Katara trapped by icicles in "The Waterbending Master" (S1E18). The design of the Night Walker from *Princess Mononoke* (1997) influenced that of "Koizilla" from "The Siege of the North, Part 2" (S1E20). Alternatively, these references are more general. Writing about anime, Stevie Suan identifies "conventionalized facial and bodily expressions" that cite not specific instances from particular texts but instead animated performances from all of anime.[1] When Aang's head balloons in size, turns beet red, and shoots steam out of his ears in "Lake Laogai" (S2E17), the visual not only conveys the character's emotional state but also evokes an entire national animation industry. Through such scenes, *Avatar* creates meaning not only through referencing specific historical and cultural contexts, as discussed by Shuyin Yu in the preceding chapter, but also by gesturing toward other texts and bodies of texts.

In addition to *wuxia* and anime, certain episodes of *Avatar* evoke supplementary genres, from action-adventure films to teen comedies. This chapter, however, focuses on a particular string of installments—composed of "Zuko Alone" (S2E07), "The Chase" (S2E08), "Bitter Work" (S2E09), "The Library" (S2E10), and "The Desert" (S2E11)—that emulate the structural elements and conventions of the western. Co-creator Michael Dante DiMartino and episode writer Joshua Hamilton have discussed how they "were in a big 'western mode'" while writing "Zuko Alone" and "The Chase" as well as how they researched and watched classic western films in order to convey certain feelings.[2] By positioning *Avatar* within this corpus and by reading these episodes as westerns, we can decipher the additional meanings that have been encoded into this show's characters, settings, and storylines. Furthermore, we can explore how these episodes employ visual and narrative shorthand that exploit a viewer's presumed familiarity with other genres. To do so, this chapter defines the western film genre and *Avatar*'s place within it as well as reads one particular episode—"Zuko Alone"—as a western.

Defining the Western Film Genre

By placing a piece of art within a larger corpus, we seek to put one text in conversation with others and thus to develop a deeper understanding of that work. While we also formulate categories based on nationalities, authorships, and studios, genres offer much more amorphous designations. Any film genre, even one as seemingly solid as the western, is fluid and often difficult to define. Generally speaking, for a work to be considered part of a genre, it must fulfill four criteria: it must possess the repeated structural elements of that genre; its producers must recognize that they are producing a work within that genre; its distributors and exhibitors must recognize that they are advertising a work within that genre; and, finally, its audience must recognize that they are watching a work within that genre.[3] Therefore, not only must a western exhibit certain characteristics, both the industry and mass audience must recognize that the text is indeed a western. Of course, what a western is and how the above parties define it change over time and in response to a variety of external factors. After all, genres are defined not only by repetition but also by variation.[4] Each generic corpus can be made to fit a recognizable cycle of growth, flowering, and decay, informed by surrounding technological, industrial, and cultural shifts.[5] In order to properly read *Avatar* as a western, we must first understand the history of the corpus into which we have placed this series.

Adopting the above schema, the western began as other film genres do, by borrowing from existing genres, modes, and mediums. Precursors for the western film did not yet form their own recognizable and recognized cinematic corpus. Instead, they had more in common with the action, crime, melodrama, ethnography, or social issue films, literature, and plays of the

1890s and 1900s. While some texts have been retroactively claimed as westerns, most famously *The Great Train Robbery* (1903), the "western" as a generic designation for films did not emerge until around 1910.[6] Film genres begin to congeal once a work is successful enough for others to imitate it and then once those copies are successful enough for still others to imitate them. This pattern compounds until the industry is no longer emulating a specific film but instead a set of structural elements and conventions, which producers, distributors, exhibitors, and audiences all recognize as belonging to their own distinct genre.[7] After some spurts throughout the early decades of Hollywood, the western really hit its stride after the Second World War and through the 1950s, due to the technological, industrial, and cultural trends of that era. During these years, the US film industry produced its most iconic and classic westerns, the ones that most clearly illustrate the core conventions of the genre. However, oversaturation ultimately preceded audience disinterest and then decline. By the 1970s, the western film genre had grown increasingly self-referential and self-reflexive, with films seeking to justify their existence not only within the era they were produced but also within a larger corpus. These films explored themes of obsolescence, self-mythologization, and old age. They spotlighted racial and ethnic out-groups, whose perspectives were typically whitewashed by earlier westerns. They hybridized with other cinematic genres, modes, and trends. By the end of the twentieth century, the western had become a dormant film genre within the United States. This is where *Avatar*, an animated fantasy series that emulates Chinese *wuxia* and Japanese anime, comes in. By the time that this show was produced, it had been decades since the golden age of the western. Nevertheless, the conventions of that cinematic corpus had so penetrated public consciousness that this children's cartoon still sought to evoke the genre, encoding meanings into characters, settings, and storylines, confident that audiences would be able to successfully decode their shorthand.

Reading *Avatar* as a Western

The central conflict of *Avatar* is between the industrialized Fire Nation, that is seeking to conquer and colonize the world, and the pre-industrial Earth Kingdom and Water Tribe. Despite one side being more technologically advanced, this 100-year war is depicted as one between military equivalents rather than as the incremental encroachment of settlers.[8] There is still, however, something of a frontier as depicted in western films. During the second season of *Avatar*, both Team Avatar and Prince Zuko seek to elude Princess Azula and the Fire Nation by journeying deeper into the Earth Kingdom. Eventually they near the Si Wong Desert at the center of the continent. During their travels, these characters visit struggling and abandoned towns and outposts, the edges of Earth Kingdom civilization, held at bay not by the Fire Nation but instead by the hostile environment. These settings echo the defining characteristic of the western film genre.

Westerns are, first and foremost, frontier myths. They are films about nation-building that whitewash, justify, or critique colonialism. They frame their narratives as conflicts between "civilization"—usually, a Euro-American, white, capitalist, neoliberal civilization—and a wild and untamed "wilderness."[9] Which archetypes represent which side of this conflict as well as which ones elicit an audience's sympathies shift over time and between films. One constant, though, is the need for violence in order to reach a resolution. While this oppositional binary and thus this film genre have long been viewed as quintessentially American, the western has always been transnational. Since the 1890s, filmmakers from around the world have participated in American mythmaking, further divorcing the genre from its historical referents.[10] In addition, such artists have grafted the structures and conventions of the western onto their own national histories. There is no shortage of films about periods of nation-building, marked by colonial expansion, the subjugation of Indigenous populations, and rapid technological advancement, when violent men with guns gathered at the edges of "civilization." The western film genre supplies useful shorthand for palpably conveying this history to an international audience.[11] The same applies to narratives set in wholly fantastical worlds, such as that of *Avatar*.

Across the five "western" episodes, *Avatar* evokes the film genre through its background designs and paintings. They emphasize the vastness of the natural landscape, from towering mountains and deep ravines to a seemingly endless desert. The human structures that persist are overshadowed by these environments, struggling to survive against the wilderness (see Figure 2.1). These locations are truly at the edges of human civilization. The climactic battle in "The Chase," initially between Aang, Zuko, and Azula, takes place in such a ghost town, recalling the ending of the self-reflexive *Man of the West* (1958). The storyboards depicting the leadup to this battle intentionally echo the editing and cinematography of the iconic final showdown in the Spaghetti western *The Good, the Bad and the Ugly* (1966).[12] A wide shot establishes the geography of the scene, followed by a series of increasingly tight close-ups of the three participants. Each shot focuses on the characters looking back and forth between their two opponents as they wait to see who will make the first move. Unlike its live-action equivalent, though, this sequence precedes an extended fight scene rather than a quickdraw resolution. The series' indebtedness to *wuxia* and anime ultimately shines through. In addition to how the show renders these settings, *Avatar* also evokes the western and its central conflict between civilization and the wilderness through its depiction of certain characters and fictional cultures.

Ever since Carl Linneus defined the "American race" as red and choleric, the dominant image of Native Americans within popular culture has been

FIGURE 2.1 *Zuko comes across an unnamed town. Still from "Zuko Alone" (S2E07). Blu-ray release of* Avatar: The Last Airbender—The Complete Series *(2018).*

some variation of the "noble savage" archetype. Indeed, the earliest film westerns were extensions of wild west shows, which spotlighted Native performers and perpetuated the myth of the "vanishing American."[13] These depictions erased and collapsed various and diverse peoples in order to catalogue them under a single and easily identifiable label, reinforced with specific costuming, makeup, and behavior that were divorced from the clothing, appearance, and habits of any real-world tribes. These "white man's Indians" are such quintessential parts of the western that films featuring Native characters but otherwise without the trappings of the genre are often still catalogued within that corpus.[14] If we are to read *Avatar* or any text as a western, as illustrative of a conflict between civilization and the wilderness, then we should consider how this text evokes Native archetypes.

I am hesitant to label any fictional culture as "Indigenous" or "Native," even within the confines of the western film genre, as that term refers to a specific historical and cultural context. Nevertheless, the artists behind *Avatar* frequently referenced real-world Indigenous cultures in their production of fantasy ones. The Air Nomads certainly evoke the image of a vanishing race. Aang is, after all, the last airbender not unlike how Uncas is the last of the Mohicans. However, visual and narrative cues position those fictional people closer to the Tibetans, signifying a whole different set of connotations, as Caleb Horowitz explores in a later chapter. The Water Tribe provides closer parallels. Their designs are emulative of the Inuit and the Māori people, suggesting a transnational Indigeneity; the Southern Water Tribe, in particular, can be viewed as "vanishing" in the face of an industrialized and imperialist civilization; and, as Aang is the last airbender, Katara is the last waterbender at the South Pole. However, here, such similarities end. Within the western film genre, American Indians tend to passively accept their imminent extinction with dignity or futilely fight against it, either way reinforcing the myth that they are a vanishing race. The Water Tribe, in contrast, is an active participant in the war against the Fire Nation, and they are equals with the Earth Kingdom in that fight. Next, the Sun Warriors, precursors to the Fire Nation featured in "The Firebending Masters" (S3E11), visually recall Mesoamerican tribes and, in terms of their narrative function, evoke a different genre entirely. Featuring ancient ruins, booby traps, and a conspicuous golden artifact on a pedestal, this episode emulates the action-adventure genre, in particular the opening of *Raiders of the Lost Ark* (1981). The Sun Warriors, then, function as a "lost civilization," as also seen in films such as *Medicine Man* (1992) and *The Lost City of Z* (2016). While distinct from the western and its version of the "white man's Indian," this genre and these archetypes still contribute to colonial mythmaking.

Out of all of the fictional cultures and subcultures of *Avatar*, only one functions as "Native" as defined by US popular culture and the western film genre in particular. Introduced in "The Library" and appearing in "The Desert" and "Appa's Lost Days" (S2E16), a loose collection of unnamed tribes resides in the Si Wong Desert. In terms of character design, these people, with their protective clothing, are visually evocative of the Tusken Raiders from *Star Wars* (1977), who were, in turn, visually modeled after nomadic tribes in North Africa. More significant, for the purposes of this analysis, is how the Si Wong tribes function within this series. Even though they are earthbenders, they are not part of the Earth Kingdom, existing outside of that civilization. Even though they are made up of many individual tribes, that diversity is flattened and erased. Thus, outsiders label them all "sandbenders." This othering and dehumanization are clearly demonstrated in their first appearance. While Aang and his friends are visiting the Misty Palms Oasis in "The Library," a group of Si Wong tribesmen begin to gather around Appa, Aang's flying bison. Professor Zei, an anthropologist defined by his curiosity, shoos them away as though they were just stray dogs, literally seeing them as less than human. This behavior is seemingly justified when these bandits later kidnap Appa.

Aang's increasingly violent pursuit for these "sandbenders" in the following episode—"The Desert"—is portrayed as excessive but also as understandable and sympathetic. By building on the introduction of the Si Wong tribes in the previous episode, this storyline recalls the narratives of many cinematic westerns that have depicted white men rescuing and avenging women and children kidnapped by American Indians.[15] As with those narratives, the focus is on the main, non-Native character's grief and anger rather than on the damage he inflicts upon these enigmatic and inscrutable others. For their brief appearances in *Avatar*, the Si Wong tribes are held at arm's length, with very limited glimpses into their culture. Viewers learn that banditry is not tolerated and that those who captured Appa are exceptions but little else. We never see any women or children, for example. These people are shown only through their interactions with outsiders. These encounters are apparently tense, since they are emblematic of contact between civilization, as represented by the Earth Kingdom traders and settlers, and the wilderness, as represented by the Si Wong tribesmen and bandits. Thus, through their relationship with other groups, if not necessarily through their character designs, the Si Wong tribes illustrate how *Avatar* evokes the western film genre to flesh out these characters and this fictional culture despite their limited time on screen. In addition, this reading demonstrates how knowledge of the western film genre can enhance and deepen one's understanding of such characters and cultures.

As a television show, *Avatar* tells a serialized narrative across multiple installments. Guest characters, settings, and storylines introduced and contained within one or a few episodes exist only in support of the main characters and of the main story arc. Given this focus, *Avatar* regularly exploits an audience's knowledge of the real world as well as of other pieces of media in order to further develop those elements with limited screen time. For the purposes of this chapter, there was a clear and stated attempt to emulate the western film genre across certain episodes in the second season. We can see how meanings were created and encoded in the text by reading these installments in relation to the western cinematic corpus. By setting these episodes at the Earth Kingdom frontier, this series clearly conveys the extremes to which these characters have gone to evade Azula and the Fire Nation. By having the Si Wong tribes emulate the portrayal of Native Americans in westerns, this series provides an easily recognizable and understandable conflict for an episode as well as progresses Aang's character arc. Thus far, this analysis has focused on evocations of the western within isolated scenes or moments, again in support of larger narratives. However, one episode stands out as particularly emulative of this genre, and it calls for deeper unpacking.

Reading "Zuko Alone" as a Western

Most episodes of *Avatar* follow a familiar structure. There is typically an a-story focusing on Aang and his companions along with a thematically complementary b-story featuring Zuko and Uncle Iroh.[16] "Zuko Alone" is an exception. Banished from the Fire Nation and actively pursued by Azula, Zuko and Iroh have fled into unconquered Earth Kingdom land, where they travel incognito, before the young prince separates from his uncle. In "Zuko Alone," the eponymous solitary character arrives at a small town and is drawn into a local conflict. There is still a thematically complementary b-story, which depicts events from Zuko's childhood leading up to his mother's disappearance and father's coronation. In both storylines, Zuko undergoes a crisis of identity, a struggle that defines his character arc during the second season.[17] Excluding its opening and closing material, this roughly twenty-two-minute episode devotes about two-thirds of its runtime to the main plot and just over one-third to flashbacks. In addition to emulating the western genre as a whole, this episode explicitly evokes a specific text: *Shane* (1953).[18] In both narratives, a stranger rides into town, befriends a settler family, especially their young son, and clashes with local bad guys. Since its release, *Shane* has gained the reputation of being an archetypical western, avoiding the auteurist or star studies readings that have attached themselves to productions by John Ford or with John Wayne.[19] A comparison of these two texts helps guide our reading of "Zuko Alone" as a western, informing how characters, settings, and storylines are encoded with additional meaning through the evocation of certain archetypes.

In both *Shane* and "Zuko Alone," the title characters emulate the western hero. Within traditional westerns, the protagonist is an exceptional man—often played by John Wayne, Gary Cooper, or Henry Fonda—who safeguards civilization from the wilderness. Alternatively, he opposes the destructive and inevitable expansion of civilization. Either way, he is only able to do so because he exists within a liminal space between the two opposing sides.[20] He belongs fully to neither civilization nor the wilderness, yet he is able to traverse both spheres. Consider, for example, the sheer number of western heroes who are raised by, married to, or can converse fluently with Natives. Due to these qualities, the western hero possesses the knowledge and skills—expressed primarily through a capacity and willingness for violence—to defeat whichever side the narrative has deemed the "bad guys." During the opening credits for *Shane*, the protagonist rides in from the wooded mountains onto the plains and toward the homesteaders. After getting a steady job in the community, he trades in his buckskin outfit for a set of store-bought clothes. Despite being the title character of a nearly two-hour movie, Shane remains an enigma. He knows about guns and gunfighting, but there is no elaboration about his past. This immediately contrasts with the depiction of Zuko.

While "Zuko Alone" also begins with an extended, dialogue-free sequence of the protagonist riding in from the wilderness, regular viewers would already be familiar with this character. In fact, childhood flashbacks throughout this episode flesh him out even further. Instead, the episode exploits characteristics of the western hero, such as Shane, to further progress Zuko's character arc. Both Shane and Zuko are originally just passing through, but they are offered work and a place to stay. Soon, they are drawn into a conflict within these communities, one that audiences can understand as being between civilization and the wilderness. By retelling the common western narrative of the stranger who rides into and cleans up the town, *Avatar* highlights and progresses Zuko's character arc. He too exists within a liminal or transitional space for the majority of this season. His growing awareness of the impact of Fire Nation imperialism and empathy for Earth Kingdom civilians challenges the banished prince's self-image. As with Shane, these seemingly conflicting identities are reflected in the character's clothing. The coloring for Zuko's outfit is closer to a mossy brown than the trademark green of the Earth Kingdom, suggesting the red-and-black motif of the Fire Nation. He does not belong fully to either nation. Ultimately, this crisis of identity resolves with Zuko denouncing the Fire Nation's role in the hundred-year war and joining Team Avatar in the second half of the third season. For now, episodes such as "Zuko Alone" chip at the edges.

When placed within a western narrative, these Earth Kingdom citizens are representatives of civilization. Just as Shane befriends the Starretts, Zuko encounters Lee's family. Again, with just under fourteen minutes for the main plot, this episode relies on shorthand in place of and perhaps as a form of characterization. In *Shane*, the Starretts and other homesteaders are the latest wave of settlers in the Wyoming Territory. Instead of trapping or herding cattle, they are bringing whole families to the valley and dividing the land into plots of private property. Shot on location near Jackson, Wyoming, the natural landscape—from the high plains to the Grand Teton massif—overwhelms and overshadows their meager, man-made structures. Even without additional threats, "taming" this wilderness would be a hard-fought struggle. To depict this conflict, the film devotes a significant portion of its runtime to developing the Starretts and their neighbors. These supporting characters appear in scenes that do not feature Shane, and they also have private moments with the title character.

By contrast, "Zuko Alone" is unable to define the three members of Lee's family—let alone the entire community—to the same degree. The episode instead focuses on these guest characters' interactions with Zuko, on how these moments impact him and his serialized character arc. Lee is the only one with considerable screen time, filling the same narrative function as Joey from Shane. Lee is the first one to see Zuko and starts to idolize him as a big brother surrogate. Both texts even feature a scene where the stranger teaches the young boy how to use his weapon—a gun for Shane and swords for Zuko. Across their brief encounters, the character design, writing, and vocal performances quickly convey a "traditional" family at the edges of civilization, weathered but not hardened. The character designs put Lee's family in faded and worn clothing; their hair, while tied back in the Earth Kingdom style, is loose and unkempt. Those familiar with *Shane* or other western films interpret these visuals, recognize these characteristics, and fill in the gaps.[21] Viewers thus understand why Zuko would fight to defend them, especially once Lee is threatened.

Just as "civilization" can mean many things within western films, so too can "the wilderness." In *Shane*, the primary conflict is between the homesteaders, who are settling in the Wyoming Territory, and cattle baron Rufus Ryker, who seeks to retake control of the valley. Ryker and his henchmen threaten not just the homesteaders but also the very institutions of family and private property, which the text treats as quintessential to the American way of life. The film consciously and even sympathetically positions Ryker as a precursor to the homesteaders. He too once "tamed" the wilderness and expanded civilization, killing the Native inhabitants and bringing cattle to the valley. However, because of his baser and violent instincts, there is no place for his kind in a more civilized world. By lingering, Ryker has become the new representative of the wilderness, standing in opposition to the spread of civilization. The Starretts and their neighbors organize against these men, but they are unable to resist them. Here, Shane, with his mysterious past and knowledge of gunplay, offers a solution.

In "Zuko Alone," Gow and three other unnamed Earth Kingdom soldiers are garrisoned in this small town. They leverage what little authority they have to bully, harass, and rob the Earth Kingdom citizens. By viewing these characters through the lens of the western film genre, we can also understand them as threats to the tenets of civilization. Like Ryker, they are betraying civilization by going against their supposed role in the community. As soldiers, they are meant to safeguard the town from external threats, but instead they are exploiting the very people they were assigned to protect. Appearing in only three scenes, there is not sufficient time to develop these characters beyond that. In response, the townsfolk can only mutter their resentment, calling them "thugs" and "bullying soldiers." They are both unwilling and unable to actively resist Gow and his men's implicit threats of violence. Here, Zuko, with his mysterious past and knowledge of swordplay, offers a solution.

In both *Shane* and "Zuko Alone," the only resolution is through violence. The representatives of civilization cannot exercise that option. They need the western hero to enter that liminal space in the pursuit of peace. For the final showdown, the hero can only win by embracing their true selves. As Shane tells Joey, "A man has to be what he is … Can't break the mold." As Zuko's mother tells him in a flashback, "No matter how things may seem to change, never forget who you are." For Shane, he displays his true nature through gunfighting and his original buckskin outfit. For Zuko, he does so through firebending and reclaiming his name. When Gow and his cronies kidnap Lee and threaten to draft him into the Earth Kingdom army, Zuko confronts them in the town center. After denouncing the soldiers as "freeloaders" and "sick cowards," Zuko quickly dispatches three of the men without having to fully unsheathe his swords. The fight with Gow goes less smoothly, as the senior soldier's earthbending keeps Zuko from getting close. After being knocked down and revisiting a memory of the last time he saw his mother, Zuko fights back with a combination of swordplay and firebending. This technique easily overpowers Gow. Now, after episodes of traveling disguised as an Earth Kingdom citizen, Zuko proudly identifies himself in front of the whole town. Such decisions come at a price.

After ridding the valley of its tormentors, the western hero cannot stay. In more optimistic narratives, they would ride out toward the next battle between civilization and the wilderness or perhaps settle down and be "tamed" by a good woman. In both *Shane* and "Zuko Alone," the denouement is more bitter. For civilization to truly prosper, there must be no more guns in the valley. As Shane tells Ryker before their shootout, the only difference between the two of them is that Shane knows that his days are over. So, wounded, he must ride off into the dark night, toward those wooded mountains from the opening of the film. After defeating Gow and his men, Zuko must also leave town. However, unlike Shane, he does not depart voluntarily. Whereas Joey famously cries, "Shane, come back!" Lee tells Zuko, "I hate you!" A banished prince of the Fire Nation is far more threatening and dangerous to this town than a few freeloading Earth Kingdom soldiers. If nothing else, his presence serves as a reminder of all they have lost in the past hundred years of war. Just as Shane realizes that he could never live peacefully among the homesteaders, the fantasy where Zuko could play the hero is shattered. In the episode's closing moments, Zuko rides off into the sunset, an iconic symbol of the western genre, a promise of new adventures and of an ever-expanding frontier. Here, it represents the prince's continued exile, as he is pushed away from civilization and back into the wilderness (see Figure 2.2).

FIGURE 2.2 *Zuko rides into the sunset. Still from "Zuko Alone" (S2E07). Blu-ray release of* Avatar: The Last Airbender—The Complete Series *(2018).*

Conclusion

Avatar is not a western. However, by reading it through the lens of the western film genre, we can uncover how the show exploited presumed audience knowledge when introducing certain characters, settings, and storylines. In "Zuko Alone," by copying the narrative elements of many western films, such as *Shane*, this television series propelled Zuko's character arc, retooling the western hero's liminality in order to convey the banished prince's ongoing crisis of identity. Through generic shorthand, it fleshes out the guest characters and settings for this episode, inviting viewers to apply their knowledge of other texts to fill in the gaps left by the twenty-two-minute runtime. Furthermore, by reading the subsequent episodes as westerns, we can see how this series can succinctly convey information to audiences when establishing new fictional cultures and locales. Thus, Aang's and Zuko's flights from Azula take on greater urgency. Thus, the Si Wong tribes become more defined.

This series has approached other episodes in a similar manner, emulating specific films and genres. Chinese *wuxia* and Japanese anime are omnipresent influences throughout the series. In addition, both the aforementioned "The Library" and "The Firebending Masters" evoke action-adventure films, most notably *Raiders of the Lost Ark*. In season three both "The Headband" (S3E02) and "The Beach" (S3E05) evoked 1980s teen comedies, most notably and inexplicably *Footloose* (1984). By utilizing these intertextual references, these episodes were able to quickly introduce and execute an episodic narrative with guest characters as well as progress serialized storylines and character arcs. In short, by referencing other texts or bodies of texts, even ones otherwise outside of a work's genre, pieces of media are able to create additional layers of meaning. By placing them within certain cinematic corpuses for analysis, we can decode those meanings.

Notes

1. Stevie Suan, "Anime's Performativity: Diversity through Conventionality in Global Media-Form," *Animation: An Interdisciplinary Journal* 12.1 (2017): 64.
2. "Audio Commentary—Chapter 8: The Chase" (supplementary material on DVD release of *Avatar: The Last Airbender—The Complete Book 2 Collection*), Viacom International Inc. (2007). Because their discussion emphasizes western films over western television shows, this chapter seeks to situate these episodes within the western film genre, which is distinct from its television equivalent.
3. Rick Altman, *Film/Genre* (British Film Institute, 1999), 14, 17.

4   Steve Neale, "Questions of Genre," in *Film and Theory: An Anthology*, eds. Robert Stam and Toby Miller (Wiley-Blackwell, 2000), 165.

5   This is actually a matter of some debate. Steve Neale identifies three main conceptions of genre history, Hans Robert Jauss' "evolutionary schema," which Neale criticizes as "teleological" and "mechanistic"; Thomas Schatz's progression toward "self-conscious formalism," to which Neale levies similar objections; and, Neale's preference, the historical model of the Russian formalists who foreground "wider cultural formations." Neale, "Questions," 167–8. For this chapter's account of the western film genre, I have attempted to find a happy medium between these three approaches.

6   Steve Neale, *Genre and Hollywood* (London: Routledge, 2000), 43–4.

7   Altman, 60–1.

8   For a more detailed overview of this fictional conflict as well as its relationship with real-world colonialism and imperialism, please see the chapters by Ryanne Kap and Caleb Horowitz from later in this collection.

9   Jim Kitses, *Horizons West: Anthony Mann, Budd Boetticher, Sam Peckinpah: Studies of Authorship within the Western* (Indiana University Press, 1969), 10–2; Jacquelyn Kilpatrick, *Celluloid Indians: Native Americans and Film* (University of Nebraska Press, 1999), 39–40; Neale, *Genre*, 135–6; Jim Kitses, *Horizons West: Directing the Western from John Ford to Clint Eastwood* (British Film Institute, 2004), 13–14. Of course, as these sources note, the western film genre does not hold a monopoly on renderings of this oppositional binary.

10 Euro-westerns, especially the spaghetti westerns of Italy, are prime examples of this trend.

11 Australian cinema, in particular, has long portrayed its colonial history in a form comparable to the western, with major texts including *The Story of the Kelly Gang* (1906), *Mad Dog Morgan* (1976), *The Chant of Jimmie Blacksmith* (1978), *The Proposition* (2005), *The Nightingale* (2018), and *True History of the Kelly Gang* (2019). For additional examples, the South Korean film *The Good, the Bad, the Weird* (2008) adapts the conventions of the western genre to fit into 1930s Manchuria, the Chinese film *Let the Bullets Fly* (2010) takes place in Sichuan during the Warlord era of the 1920s, and the Japanese remake *Unforgiven* (2013) transposes the originally American story to Hokkaido in the early Meiji period.

12 "Audio." Episode writer Joshua Hamilton and director Giancarlo Volpe cite this Italian film by name when discussing this sequence.

13 It is beyond the scope of this chapter to fully summarize the history of Native representation within American popular culture, particularly within the western film genre. For those interested in this subject, I highly recommend Jacquelyn Kilpatrick's *Celluloid Indians: Native Americans and Film* (1999), which chronicles the history of such depictions in US film, as well as Michelle H. Raheja's *Reservation Reelism: Redfacing, Visual Sovereignty, and Representations of Native Americans in Film* (2010) and Liza Black's *Picturing Indians: Native Americans in Film, 1941–1960* (2020), both of

which highlight the involvement of Native artists in the production of these texts as well as the role of Native viewers in watching them. All three works greatly influenced how this chapter views the "white man's Indian" within the western film genre and its influence on the construction of "Native-ness" within western-influenced texts.

14   These include films set before or during the American Revolutionary War, such as the numerous adaptations of the book *The Last of the Mohicans* (1826) as well as *Drums along the Mohawk* (1939) and *Unconquered* (1947). At the time of this writing, this pattern has repeated in regard to the upcoming *Killers of the Flower Moon*, which has been promoted as director Martin Scorsese's "first western" despite being a true-crime murder-mystery set in the 1920s.

15   Originating within literature, this narrative trope has persisted into film, from the British proto-western *Kidnapped by Indians* (1899), to the genre's postwar golden age with *The Searchers* (1956) and *Comanche Station* (1960), as well as continuing into the twenty-first century with *The Missing* (2003), *Alone Yet Not Alone* (2013), and *Bone Tomahawk* (2015). For a more thorough account of the history of these stories, see: Edward Buscombe, *"Injun!" Native Americans in the Movies* (Reaktion Books LTD, 2006), 40–2.

16   Chapters by Gia Coturri Sorenson and Ryanne Kap demonstrate how this structure is used to reinforce the core themes of specific *Avatar* episodes, "The Swamp" (S2E04) and "The Southern Air Temple" (S1E03), respectively.

17   For more context see the chapter by Joseph V. Giunta, which covers Zuko's character arc across *Avatar*.

18   "Audio." *The Good, the Bad and the Ugly* and *Shane* are the only western films named as inspirations for these episodes, although writer Joshua Hamilton mislabels *Shane* as a "show" rather than as a "film" or "movie."

19   This dubious honor is due more so to the fading reputations of director George Stevens and actor Alan Ladd in comparison to their contemporaries. Their abilities to adapt to various genres have actually impeded later attempts to develop coherent corpuses around their cinematic works. For more on this film and its status within the western canon, see Stephen McVeigh, *American Western* (Edinburgh University Press, 2007), 122–7.

20   This particular quality is especially prominent within William S. Hart and Harry Carey star vehicles of the 1910s and 1920s, such as *Hell's Hinges* (1916); "western noirs" of the 1940s and 1950s, such as *Man with the Gun* (1955); as well as various "going native" westerns, such as *Run of the Arrow* (1957).

21   In their respective chapters, both Max Dosser and Ashley Hendricks address how aspects of *Avatar* can inspire or provoke fans to create works that fill in these gaps. However, here, I am describing a more passive and casual process whereby viewers are prompted through visual, aural, and narrative cues to contribute to the characterization, worldbuilding, and storytelling by incorporating their own preexisting cultural knowledge.

3

Environmental Bending: How *Avatar: The Last Airbender* Introduces Viewers to Environmentalism

Gia Coturri Sorenson

Beginning with the first Earth Day in 1970 and continuing through the 1990s, scholars worked to create a new area of research: environmental studies. Interdisciplinary from the very start, environmental studies gathered scientists, historians, psychologists, and literary scholars under the same umbrella to study how humans interact with the natural world and start mending that relationship. A subfield called ecocriticism arose as scholars studied how the environment was depicted in literature and film and how authors, directors, and animators use their medium to encourage readers and viewers to forge a new connection to the natural world. Ecocritics ask a variety of questions, from "How is nature depicted in this sonnet?" and "How do our metaphors of the land influence the way we treat it?" to "Should place become a new critical category alongside race, class, and gender?" and "In what ways and to what effect is the environmental crisis seeping into contemporary literature and popular culture?"[1] Scholars question how texts depict the environment to better understand how various cultures interact with the natural world but also to help others forge environmental connections. While most ecocritics focus on books and occasionally films directed toward adults, recent scholarship has begun to study how children's media, like Disney films and *Avatar: The Last Airbender* (Nickelodeon, 2005–8), influence how children understand and approach the natural world.[2]

Combining literary analysis and scientific understanding enables scholars and viewers alike to better understand how environmental ideas are communicated. Lawrence Buell argues that the border between science and culture is indefinite because the latter inevitably influences the former, which means that "science and literature must be read both with and against each other."[3] Similarly, ecologist Neil Evernden shows that environmental scientists frequently lack the language needed to convince people to change their relationship to the natural world but that the humanities often provide strong tools for convincing people to embrace environmentalism.[4] Indeed, he suggests that the arts help emphasize "relatedness, and the intimate and vital involvement of self with place."[5] While ecocriticism combines many perspectives and approaches, scientists like Evernden and literary scholars like Buell help us understand why it is worthwhile and, indeed, vital to utilize environmental studies to analyze how a popular animated show like *Avatar* fosters environmental consciousness.

When *Avatar* started showing, ecocritics did not hail it as an environmental masterpiece, but several key episodes help demonstrate that the showrunners had a keen interest in helping viewers, particularly young people, develop environmental awareness. Many pieces of media aimed at children, especially ones that explore dystopic or apocalyptic scenarios, often function as "proto-political instruction, even ... propaganda," and environmental texts often establish a situation that implies that children "will naturally work to preserve [nature] on behalf of the(ir own) future, but only if we tell them they have to, and even then only if we trick them into it."[6] While the show's role as propaganda is beyond the scope of this chapter, it does help young viewers better understand why they ought to protect the natural world. For instance, *Avatar*'s opening narration helps convey the problems that arise when one of the four elements is out of balance, which makes it easy for viewers to apply elemental balance to real-world issues such as unsustainable living.

Nevertheless, *Avatar* tries to offer its viewers hope and approaching the text through an environmental studies lens reveals how the show's writers and artists manage to offer an optimistic environmental message. Scholars have long studied how environmental media ostensibly aimed at young people devolves into "a bizarrely prospective, highly cynical and brutally effective exercise in victim-blaming," but *Avatar* offers a more supportive take, mingling various environmental themes to help viewers evolve their environmental understanding.[7] One episode that brings environmentalism to the forefront is "The Swamp" (S2E04), which follows Aang, Katara, and Sokka after they land in an eerie swamp. During their time in this setting, they encounter "plantbenders," specialized waterbenders who can manipulate the water within plants, and Aang learns more about how environmental factors connect the world and the people in it. Asking ecocritical questions about "The Swamp" episode helps illuminate the episode's ecofeminism, nuanced inclusion of anthropocentrism and ecocentrism, and complicated relationship to pastoralism.

Heeding the Call: Ecofeminism and Defending the Environment

If ecocriticism studies how texts depict the relationship between the natural world and humans, ecofeminism focuses on power structures and how they influence a person's environmental interactions. In brief, ecofeminists argue that "the injustices directed at marginal social groups share similar ideologies with those that legitimate the exploitation and degradation of the environment."[8] When the field first emerged, ecofeminists primarily studied the connections between the white male treatment of women, animals, and the environment and how the experience of women mirrors the treatment of the natural world.[9] However, the approach of early, predominately white, middle-class ecofeminists elided the experience of scholars of color, so environmental justice activists have expanded ecofeminism's borders to incorporate how women, people of color, disabled people, people of low socioeconomic levels, and LGBTQ+ people are subject to varying degrees of oppression that impacts their relationship to the natural world.[10] Ecocriticism's various evolutions help display the wide range of ways to understand and interact with the natural world, and a show like *Avatar*, which combines political, social, and environmental arguments, demonstrates why it is important to combine approaches.

Ecofeminists address an array of issues but remain committed to studying how women approach, understand, and experience environmental issues. Thus, ecofeminists seek to restructure and challenge economic, political, and institutional structures that foster "unequal power relationships" because they value "culture and biological diversity"; they ultimately see their work as "reconnecting and grounding humans in place" by "focusing on the body as a moral agent."[11] These goals share the desire to develop "forms of attention that enhance awareness of the living environment … as a separate, different but knowable entity."[12] Finally, many ecofeminists are staunchly anti-capitalist and argue that capitalism and patriarchal power work in tandem to destroy the environment and communities alike.[13] Even the most recent ecofeminist scholarship acknowledges that many scholars "have yet to fully tap [ecofeminism's] analytic potential to deepen our understanding of gender violence."[14] *Avatar* showcases various non-Western approaches to the natural world and depicts how clashes between different philosophical and economic systems profoundly scar people and their surroundings.

Even as ecofeminism helps illuminate how "The Swamp" depicts the relationship between power, women, and the natural world, eco-justice displays how other factors like race, ability, and relative economic level influence how characters interact with the natural world. Environmental justice scholars examine how "colonization, war, white supremacy, and other forms of dispossession had robbed generations of their connection to the land."[15] Melissa Tuckey argues that eco-justice writers and scholars recognize that "the fate of the land is connected to the fate of people" and that we can use texts to understand and analyze the natural world because "culture is how we negotiate with and survive in our environments."[16] Environmental justice activists have helped prove the "link between race, class, and pollution" as well as continue to study how climate change and other environmental catastrophes "do not affect us all equally, or in the same ways" and that we do not "have equal power to decide solutions to these problems, or to take the necessary action to solve them."[17] Environmental justice has expanded over the past few decades until it encompasses not just "environmental hazards and pollution" but "almost everything that is unsustainable about the world."[18] While the concerns of ecofeminists and environmental justice critics overlap, using both of their approaches help us better understand *Avatar* and how "The Swamp" depicts various traumas and environmental relationships.

Using intersectional environmentalism to better understand the visions that Katara, Aang, and Sokka have in the swamp helps viewers understand how women and people of color are impacted by environmental violence as well as how forging an environmental connection can help people better understand and begin coping with their trauma. Combining ecofeminism and environmental justice helps emphasize their shared goals while also acknowledging that "ecofeminist values oppose all forms of hierarchy and domination, [while] environmental justice is a movement challenging the continued colonization of nature and marginalized humans."[19] However, doing so minimizes the racial and economic disparities between the two groups. Therefore, it is important to remember that, even as ecofeminism strives to become more intersectional, it is a field dominated by mostly white, middle-class women whereas environmental justice is dominated by working-class women of color.[20] Combining the two approaches thus helps better describe the experiences of women from the Water Tribe, which is partly based on Inuit culture, as well as how they differ from those who have faced trauma through a male lens.[21] After becoming separated from each other, Katara, Sokka, and Aang all have visions, each of which reminds them of who they have lost and encapsulates their basic approach to the natural environment.

Katara experiences a vision of her mother, which reopens the emotional and environmental wounds caused by Fire Nation imperialism.[22] When Katara gets separated from her companions, the animators create a strong contrast between Katara—whose blue clothing appears bright in the swamp—against the background painting—which is composed of muddy greens. Katara catches sight of a figure likewise dressed in blue and instantly recognizes the shape as her mother. She races toward her mother, tears of joy streaming from her eyes, but when she arrives at the figure, a beam of light highlights the figure, forcing Katara to realize that her vision was merely a distortion of a tree stump. Katara's response to seeing her mother showcases her trauma and reveals just how thoroughly her mother's death colors her daily life. She is willing to believe that her mother is alive, despite knowing her mother was killed by Fire Nation imperialism years ago; that her trauma-response involves a dead tree also encourages an ecofeminist and environmental justice reading.

To help viewers connect to the natural world and to consider the costs of imperialism, the animators encourage them to grieve alongside Katara. The episode's background painters juxtapose a murky, out-of-focus background with a highly detailed tree stump, which highlights the tree and implicitly asks viewers to mourn Katara's mother as well as the dead tree (see Figure 3.1). The scene further helps viewers associate the death of natural objects with the death of people. Katara's mourning at the foot of

FIGURE 3.1 *Katara mourns the loss of her mother next to a dead tree stump. Still from "The Swamp" (S2E04). Blu-ray release of* Avatar: The Last Airbender—The Complete Series *(2018).*

a dead tree becomes a metaphor for the violence of imperialism and seeing the stump acts like a trigger, inspiring her to reexperience her mother's loss and relive the environmental costs of imperialism. Katara is not alone in linking precious loved ones and the environment; her brother has a parallel experience.

Sokka's vision forces him to relive the trauma of his girlfriend Yue's death in a way that helps him reconsider his relationship to the natural world, which in turn asks viewers to contemplate how their actions impact the natural world. After hacking through vines as he tries to find the others, Sokka catches sight of Yue in a beam of light. Much like with Katara's vision, Sokka's blue clothing contrast sharply with the swampy background and his vision is revealed by a beam of light. However, Sokka's vision is much more aggressive than Katara's; Yue appears and disappears, frequently startling him and forcing him back into the mud. Even as he tries to rationalize the vision, Yue says to him, "You didn't protect me." She disappears and reappears, and Sokka menaces the vision with his machete. Sokka manages to understand he is experiencing a vision and does not directly conflate the vision-Yue with the Yue he lost, but the vision's words still clearly impact him. Indeed, the manner in which he threatens violence against the vision echoes the way he has hacked through in the swamp. He does not try to adapt to the swamp but instead tries to physically "bend" the swamp to his will through violence.

Unlike Katara's passive vision, Sokka's violence seemingly forces the swamp to literally tell him that he is harming it. The differences between Katara and Sokka's visions encapsulate their gendered experiences and thus highlight the way gender influences how an individual relates to the natural world. The expectations placed on Sokka frequently cause him to be opposed to the natural world for his survival and the survival of those dependent on him. In the swamp, he experiences a vision that conflates his guilt over Yue's death with his antipathy toward the natural world and finally begins reconsidering his environmental relationships.[23] Katara and Sokka experience visions that prime them to reconsider their relationship to their surroundings, but Aang's vision leads him in a slightly different direction.

While both Katara and Sokka have visions that benefit from ecofeminist and environmental activist perspectives, the episode's final vision helps illustrate a more general point about environmentalism. Aang's vision of an elusive young girl is not something from his past but rather a premonition, one which helps him improve his environmental connections. A young girl—later revealed to be the earthbender Toph Beifong—and a winged boar lead Aang on a merry chase, eventually reuniting him with his companions and helping him find the swamp's heart. While the animators contrast his clothing with the backgrounds to ensure that Aang's vision is reminiscent of Katara and Sokka's visions, it is markedly more playful; rather than preying on his traumas and guilt, his vision guides him further along his spiritual journey. Indeed, while both Katara and Sokka have environmental reasons for their visions, Aang does not; his is the only vision that does not spring from trauma and remains unexplained by natural phenomena like dead tree stumps or swamp gas. Indeed, Sokka, acting as the audience surrogate, dismisses Aang's experiences as "Avatar stuff." The animators have the vision appear and disappear much like Yue—indeed, Toph's white clothing serves as an additional parallel to Sokka's vision—but, like Katara's mother, she says nothing; she only laughs. The vision's mixture of active and passive helps viewers visualize the difficult, winding path toward environmental thinking. The vision does not follow a clear pathway and does not offer any vocal guidance; throughout, Aang must form his own conclusions, just as viewers must make their own environmental decisions. In Aang's case, his vision literally leads him to ecocentrism: Toph leads the group to the center of the swamp and a wise man who will radically change Aang's environmental perspective.

Branching Out: Ecocentrism and the Banyan Tree

Ecocritics frequently utilize ecological and literary approaches to better understand environmental texts, but many also use philosophy, law, and even religion to understand how people approach the natural world. Environmental philosophers have helped scholars think about how "anthropocentrism," a term that describes the tendency to put humans at the center of everything, rules almost everything that humans do but particularly their legal and ethical systems.[24] Most who analyze how a text displays anthropocentrism ask questions about how "the human [is] defined through or against animal and objectified Others, abstract environments and ecologies, and constructed cosmologies."[25] Importantly, anthropocentrism does not necessarily imply worthiness. Instead, it simply provides "order and structure to humans' understanding of the world, while unavoidably expressing the limits of that understanding."[26] Unsurprisingly, there are alternatives to anthropocentrism, and scholars often contrast anthropocentrism with ecocentrism, which refers to "a nature-centered approach … where the Earth is valued not merely instrumentally as a commodity belonging to us but also intrinsically as a community to which we belong."[27] It is hard to imagine anything outside of human experience, but ecocentrism "simply enlarges the boundaries of the community to include soils, waters, plants, and animals, or collectively: the land."[28] "The Swamp" illustrates people moving from anthropocentrism to ecocentrism, which helps viewers begin thinking about the world and their environmental relationships in new ways.

Avatar helps viewers conceptualize the differences between anthropocentrism and ecocentrism through a banyan tree, a type of tree famous for appearing "as a small forest," and the wise man that Aang, Katara, and Sokka encounter beneath it.[29] The episode personifies the banyan tree in several ways and in so doing, helps viewers better understand ecocentrism. Personification, the act of applying human characteristics to nonhumans and objects, encourages readers to see the similarities between themselves and the natural world and trees are personified with great regularity.[30] Films, television shows, and even video games often take personification to an extreme and depict sentient trees, like the one that guards the master sword in *The Legend of Zelda* series or Grandmother Willow in Disney's *Pocahontas* (1995). These trees help viewers extend sympathy and understanding to the natural world. Trees are a particularly useful environmental object to use in these instances, and "there are many, many examples in poetry, literature, and art that merge" humans and trees.[31] Why trees? There are no definitive answers, and the answer varies greatly from culture to culture, but in general humans see trees as unusually humanlike. Gabriel Popkin, in an article about a town's response to "their" tree's death, writes that "To mourn a tree as if it were human is understandable, even natural. There are ways, after all, that trees really are like us."[32] How are trees "really like us"? Popkin cites the fact trees and humans have similar bodies and that we both communicate with neighbors and families. So, while *Avatar* helps viewers imagine ecocentrism throughout the show's run, "The Swamp" articulates this position explicitly by using a tree metaphor.

When the group arrives at the banyan tree near the swamp's middle, Aang and Sokka explicitly debate personification. Aang claims that the tree is "the heart of the swamp" and that it has "been calling us here." Sokka refutes Aang, pointing out that "It's just a tree ... It can't call anyone." The heated interaction between Sokka and Aang helps viewers begin considering the point the two are arguing. Can a tree call to a person? Can a tree be the heart, spiritually or physically, of anything? Is personification simply a matter of perspective? Before the two boys can resolve their dispute, violence interrupts them, which functions as a reminder that environmental violence and lack of compromise influence how characters and viewers alike understand the natural world. It is only when Aang and Katara finally speak out that the violence can end, and compromise can be found. Their experience overcoming violence through communication and compromise enables them to accept ecocentric advice.

"The Swamp" next employs allusion to relate humans and trees and thus illustrate ecocentrism. The trio meets Huu, a "plantbender" who can bend the water within plants, and he tells them that he also heard the tree calling and achieved "enlightenment right here under the banyan-grove tree." Huu's experience closely parallels the Buddha's enlightenment beneath a bodhi tree, which further blurs the line between humans and trees by situating trees as spiritual guides.³³ Huu rebuts the anthropocentric perspective viewers typically encounter by demonstrating ecocentrism to Aang and directly refuting Sokka's anthropocentric rationality.

The episode defines and illustrates ecocentrism, which helps the Avatar consider the balance between humans and nonhumans, benders and non-benders. Huu says that "this whole swamp is actually just one tree spread out over miles. Branches spread and sink, take root, and spread some more. One big, living organism. Just like the entire world." In part, Huu's perspective echoes aspects of modern ecology.³⁴ Recently, scientists have begun studying the rhizomatic connections between trees and the way these connections enable trees to communicate.³⁵ Furthermore, there are trees that expand to cover hundreds of acres; the most famous American example is Pando, but banyan trees similarly expand to cover acres.³⁶ Thus, trees serve as a metaphor for global connection even as they literally connect with other trees and with clones across hundreds of miles.³⁷ Explicitly defining ecocentrism and emphasizing connections between humans and nonhumans helps viewers understand how to move beyond pure anthropocentrism and add the natural world into their purview. The way the episode animates the banyan tree reinforces Huu's ecocentrism.

The animators emphasize Huu's message through the visuals and a second allusion. As he speaks, an immense static image of the whole swamp is slowly revealed; the detail eventually diminishes until no individual tree can be picked out (see Figure 3.2). The animators illustrate the forest in a way that minimizes humanity and instead showcases the connections between natural elements. Furthermore, throughout the episode, the swamp functions as a visual allusion to the Toxic Jungle from *Nausicaä of the Valley of the Wind* (1984). Referring to Miyazaki Hayao's environmental film enables the animators to make a doubled environmental argument. Nausicaä's world was destroyed by humans and can only be rebuilt when people start forging connections rather than resorting to violence. In a way, having the swamp echo *Nausicaä*'s Toxic Jungle helps viewers understand the possible consequences. If the Fire Nation continues to consume the world and if people like Sokka continue to destroy the natural world for their own comfort, only a poisonous wasteland will remain. Huu's ecocentrism becomes an antidote to anthropocentrism and he carefully guides the trio, and the audience, away from their traditional mindset.

As Huu explains the trio's visions, he helps use anthropocentrism to better understand ecocentrism. He claims that the swamp shows visions of "people we've lost, people we loved, folks we think are gone" but in so doing, "the swamp tells us they're not. We're still connected to them." Huu mingles ecocentrism with mysticism, but his overall point revolves around connection and acceptance. He uses an ecocentric model to help Aang, Katara, and Sokka overcome their blind spots and begin moving toward the resolution of their traumas. While all three will continue to struggle

FIGURE 3.2 *The swamp's heart—an immense banyan tree—connects an array of smaller, indistinguishable trees. Still from "The Swamp" (S2E04). Blu-ray release of* Avatar: The Last Airbender—The Complete Series *(2018).*

with their trauma for many episodes to come, without this moment in the swamp, all three would have remained trapped within a mindset that encourages division and separation. Huu uses the natural world to illustrate the connections between people and the connections between humans and nature. He lays the groundwork for a rhizomatic network that connects all people in addition to all of nature.

After providing an ecocentric model for Aang, Huu enables him to draw on the natural world to find the answers he needs. Aang touches the tree and uses Huu's lesson that everything is connected to find the group's animal companions, Appa and Momo. By animating Aang using ecocentrism, the show helps viewers see ecocentrism in action. It is only when Aang is willing to connect to his surroundings that he can overcome the distance that divides his group. Arguably, Aang keeps honing his ability to compromise and connect until it reaches its pinnacle in the lead-up to the series finale when Aang connects with the Ancient One, a giant lion turtle, and seeks a way to resolve his fight with the Fire Nation that avoids killing. But Aang has a long way to go before he can forge any sort of connection between himself and the Ancient One. While Katara and Sokka struggle to connect to nature as readily as Aang, this episode shows their budding awareness of the connection between themselves and other people. Learning about ecocentrism has enabled the siblings—though Katara seems to internalize the message more readily—to expand their understanding of who they can connect with, and models for viewers the way they should seek to build connections with others rather than considering themselves separate. While the trio learns to utilize ecocentrism, their approach contrasts sharply with the experiences of Zuko and Iroh, who face repeated acts of violence during their time as refugees.

Singing to Survive: Pastoralism and Imperial Violence

Even as ecocriticism expands to accommodate scholarship on how people experience environmental oppression differently as well as on how we can encourage people to see the natural world as worth defending, people continue to debate how we contrast natural and urban spaces, or what ecocritics call "pastoralism." Broadly speaking, pastoralism refers to the idea that life in the countryside is better than life in the city, which is often expressed through a "yearning for a simpler, more harmonious style of life, an existence 'closer to nature.'"[38] Many environmentalists have expanded this idea to include the idea that life in nature is better than life in urban spaces. The debate over pastoralism is important because environmentalists sometimes use it to argue that anyone who lives in the city is utterly separate from nature and more inclined towards "corrupt" actions that negatively impact humans and the environment alike.[39] However, pastoralism can also help readers and viewers think about what happens in cities and what happens outside of cities as well as help us think about who is harmed by living in the city.

Pastoralism is present in everything from poetry and fiction to advertisements and political speeches and has several recurring features. In general, pastoralism draws on themes initially seen in ancient Roman poems that describe a withdrawal "from the great world and … a new life in a fresh, green landscape" and those who draw on the pastoral tradition tend to "idealize a simple, rural environment" rather than "an intricately organized, urban, industrial, nuclear-armed society."[40] Life outside the city is perceived to be simpler and more authentic, though what various pastoralists mean by "authentic" varies widely and rarely takes into account how gender, class, race, and ability dramatically impact how a person experiences the natural world. Pastoral texts frequently trace "motion away from centers of civilization toward simplicity, or … away from the city toward the country."[41] Obviously, pastoralism has issues, even as it remains an incredibly attractive theme for environmentalists and ecocritics, but very few scholars have studied how animated media employs pastoral themes or how animation—even more so than live-action film and television—can help viewers question pastoral tendencies.

Pastoral texts frequently downplay the reality of rural life and typically forefront anthropocentricism. Even as pastoralism has "activated green consciousness," it has also disguised and justified land appropriation, particularly from Indigenous people.[42] Pastoral texts can direct people toward nature, but they often offer an abstract version of the natural world and can make it hard for them to understand nature or accept the realities of life outside cities.[43] Even as some use pastoral themes to argue for environmental protections or social change, many have used it to propel colonial and fascist projects.[44] This is not to say that pastoralism is bad or that it should be avoided; instead, pastoral tendencies need to be questioned. Why does a particular text use a pastoral contrast? Why do animators and background artists lovingly illustrate natural scenes but emphasize the bad aspects of urban spaces? When *Avatar* emphasizes the Fire Kingdom's war machines and connects machines to destruction and imperialism, how does that change how viewers consider about urban centers and technological advancement? Pastoral scholarship primes us to question contrasts between natural spaces and human ones as well as helps viewers better understand their own relationship to technology.

Many animated shows rely on pastoralism for aesthetic reasons, but *Avatar* uses the trope to help emphasize the radically different experiences of various characters. For instance, while most of "The Swamp" follows the ecocentric awakening of Aang, Sokka, and Katara, the episode begins and ends in an Earth Kingdom town and follows Zuko and Iroh as they travel incognito. Bookending the episode with human-centric scenes sharply contrasts with "wild" environments like the banyan grove and emphasizes the environmental messages Aang and his companions hear in the swamp. However, even as the episode draws on pastoral tropes, it also questions what should happen to those who reside in cities. In the end, "The Swamp" uses pastoralism to showcase various ways to respond to violence.

The background designs of the Earth Kingdom village along a river provide a sharp contrast to the swamp and the avatar's experiences there. "The Swamp" begins by emphasizing the agricultural setting, with the background painting including idyllic rice paddies and a seemingly harmonious relationship between farmers and the surrounding forest. The harmony is shattered when viewers see Prince Zuko and his uncle, dressed in their Earth Kingdom garb, begging for coin. Iroh actively begs for money, highlighting his apparent feebleness and flirting with passersby who offer him their spare change, while Zuko glowers. Iroh strives for the sort of acceptance that Aang and his companions learn about in the swamp, but he must attempt such a position in the middle of a human-centric area and as an economically disadvantaged refugee. In contrast,

Zuko continues to think of himself as better than others and consciously separates himself from those who surround him.[45] Overall, Iroh's upbeat attitude is rewarded; Earth Kingdom citizens are generous with the refugees and do not treat the pair badly, despite Zuko grumpily talking about his humiliation. Violence eventually proves Zuko's point and places Iroh in danger.

Pastoral criticism helps explain why the harmonious, bucolic scene does not last. Eventually a man approaches, promises a gold coin, and tortures the coin's worth out of Iroh by using a sword to make him dance while he sings. The scene is extremely tense; Iroh's song is comedic, but the possibility of fatal violence remains constant. For instance, viewers have no idea how Zuko will react to the man demeaning Iroh for his physical attributes and economic position. Iroh's humiliation and the man's cruelty are typical of pastoral depictions of city life. Leo Marx writes that in a developed or mechanized environment, people seem "forlorn and powerless," which happens because urban, settled areas are depicted as places "where natural objects are of no value in themselves."[46] Iroh and Zuko's experiences as refugees help viewers consider the way humans are "natural objects" and what happens when those "objects" are not seen as intrinsically valuable. Iroh is subjected to humiliating abuse in the city; in contrast, Aang and his friends realize their own intrinsic worth and the worth of the natural world during their time in the swamp. The pastoral contrast between the opening scene and the rest of the episode encourages viewers to ponder what is possible in cities and what is possible outside of cities—and ask them to consider whether life outside cities is inherently better.

The fashion in which the background artists situate the city scenes fosters the episode's pastoralism. The episode's opening scenes are a combination of rich agricultural areas and dull, dusty city streets. When viewers see the area surrounding the city, the world is fertile and rich, with blues and greens dominating; when we see Iroh and Zuko begging, the color palette becomes muted and dusty greens and browns predominate. The scenes in the swamp are illustrated with a limited palette as well, but the colors are richer: mysterious dark browns and grays with some bright greens that signal new growth. The contrast between the city and the swamp emphasizes the differences between the two areas. Life flourishes outside the city, but in the city, living is difficult and stale. Applying a pastoral lens to the episode draws attention to the way the animators and background artists contrast city and wild environments, as well as helping us understand why violence seemingly becomes unavoidable in the city. As the opening scene draws to a close, Iroh seemingly forgives the man who menaced him, saying without any apparent irony, "Such a nice man." Zuko clearly does not share in his uncle's assessment, looking thunderously in the direction the man has gone. His anger comes to fruition at the episode's end, marking the episode's pastoral zenith.

Pastoralism enables viewers to understand why the city's violence escalates and why the episode offers such a strong contrast between the swamp and the city. The final scene of the episode is extremely quick and shows Zuko, masked as the Blue Spirit, mugging the man who tortured his uncle. The episode suggests that Zuko cannot see an alternative to violence or make any compromises; trapped in the city, he cannot forge connections like Katara could with the Foggy Swamp Tribe. Indeed, Zuko sees violence as justified and even rational, and the final scene reiterates the fact that "the aspirations once represented by the symbol of an ideal landscape have not, and probably cannot, be embodied in our traditional institutions."[47] Pastorals divide city and countryside, thus implicitly arguing that the lessons learned in wild areas like swamps and forests cannot be translated to urban settings; this model does not offer any hope for those who cannot live outside of cities. In "The Swamp," viewers see Aang and his companions achieving "an inspiring vision of a humane community," while Zuko's actions are a mere "token of individual survival."[48] As happens so often, the pastoral ends with a hero that is "totally alienated from society, alone and powerless."[49] Unsurprisingly, the American western-inspired episode "Zuko Alone" (S2E07) aired soon afterward and showcases how pastoralism fails characters like Zuko.[50] While Aang and his companions can achieve a higher state of consciousness outside the city, such a future seems impossible for Zuko, who continues to endure hardship and isolation for two dozen more episodes.

Conclusion

Ecocritics, by and large, pay very little attention to animated media directed toward children. For those rare exceptions, environmental scholars typically address either Disney films or overtly ecologically minded texts like *Nausicaä of the Valley of the Wind* (1984) and *FernGully: The Last Rainforest* (1992), which leaves a large gap in the literature.[51] The trend of ignoring vast swathes of contemporary culture is troubling, because content like *Avatar* has a deep impact on viewers and therefore helps channel how people understand issues like humanitarian crises, war, and, as this chapter shows, the environment. In the end, "Representations, images, metaphors, and cultural narratives have social and political consequences for both humans and nonhumans. Such rhetoric sets us up for the risk of lived experiences being shaped or even replaced by stereotypical cultural narratives."[52] Ignoring popular narratives has a steep cost, as it makes it more difficult to understand how young people will interact with the natural world and how viewers are persuaded to support environmental causes. Examining how a show like *Avatar* builds its environmental argument is vital, especially if we are going to build a more equitable and sustainable future.

Notes

1. Cheryll Glotfelty, "Introduction," in *The Ecocriticism Reader*, eds. Cheryll Glotfelty and Harold Fromm (The University of Georgia Press, 1996), xvii–xix.
2. Cheryll Glotfelty's ecocritical anthology, widely considered the first such collection, contains no mention of film or animation, though several chapters, like William Rueckert's "Literature and Ecology" and Scott Russell Sanders' "Speaking a Word for Nature," address how fiction influences popular understandings of environmentalism. Paula Willoquet-Maricondi's anthology *Framing the World* establishes a strong argument for environmental readings of "all forms of cinematic productions, not just those that overtly focus on environmental issues" (xi), and contains a wide array of analyses, including Lynne Dickson Bruckner's "*Bambi* and *Finding Nemo*: A Sense of Wonder in the Wonderful World of Disney?," which explores how children's media can begin an environmental conversation even as the companies that produce content for children want to sell environmentally unfriendly products. Other important contributions to the ecocritical study of children's media include Sidney I. Dobrin and Kenneth B. Kidd's anthology *Wild Things: Children's Culture and Ecocriticism*, which includes essays on children's fiction, magazines, and film, and David Whitley's *The Idea of Nature in Disney Animation*, which discusses how Disney films provide a strong environmental foundation for children. The academic journal *Animation* includes occasional ecocritical analyses like William J. Brown and Terry R. Lindvall's "Green Cartoons: Toward a Pedagogy of the Animated Parable," in *The Ecocriticism Reader: Landmarks in Literary Ecology*, eds. Cheryll Glotfelty and Harold Fromm (University of Georgia Press, 1996); *Framing the World: Explorations in Ecocriticism and Film*, ed. Paula Willoquet-Maricondi (University of Virginia Press, 2010); *Wild Things: Children's Culture and Ecocriticism*, eds. Sidney I. Dorbin and Kenneeth B. Kidd (Wayne State University Press, 2004); David Whitney, *The Idea of Nature in Disney Animation* (Ashgate, 2008); William J. Brown and Terry R. Lindvall, "Green Cartoons: Toward a Pedagogy of the Animated Parable," *Animation: An Interdisciplinary Journal* 14.3 (2019): 235–49.
3. Lawrence Buell, *The Future of Environmental Criticism* (Blackwell Publishing, 2005), 19.
4. Neil Evernden, "Beyond Ecology: Self, Place, and the Pathetic Fallacy," in *The Ecocriticism Reader*, eds. Cheryll Glotfelty and Harold Fromm (The University of Georgia Press, 1996), 102.
5. Ibid., 103.
6. Gerry Canavan, "Unless Someone Like You Cares a Whole Awful Lot: Apocalypse as Children's Entertainment," *Science Fiction Film and Television* 10.1 (2017): 83, 84.
7. Ibid., 85.

8   Gwen Hunnicutt, *Gender Violence in Ecofeminist Perspective* (Routledge, 2020), 1.
9   Greta Gaard, "New Directions for Ecofeminism: Toward a More Feminist Ecocriticism," *Interdisciplinary Studies in Literature and Environment* 17.4 (2010): 647; Josephine Donovan, "Ecofeminist Literary Criticism: Reading The Orange," *Hypatia* 11.2 (1996): 161.
10 Gaard, 647; Maria Mies and Vandana Shiva, *Ecofeminism* (Zed Books, 2014), 2.
11 Gaard, 656.
12 Donovan, 18.
13 Mies and Shiva, 2–3.
14 Hunnicutt, 1.
15 Melissa Tuckey, "Introduction," in *Ghost Fishing: An Eco-Justice Poetry Anthology*, ed. Melissa Tuckey (The University of Georgia Press, 2018), 2.
16 Ibid., 2.
17 Tuckey, 3; Ryan Holifield, Jayajit Chakraborty and Gordon Walker, *The Routledge Handbook of Environmental Justice* (Routledge, 2018), 1.
18 Ibid., 2.
19 Gaard, 648.
20 Ibid., 648.
21 Meghan Sullivan, "*Avatar*'s Representation of Inuit," *Indian Country Today*, November 5, 2020, https://indiancountrytoday.com/news/avatars-representation-of-inuit. Ruth Richards' chapter in this volume provides much more context on gender in *Avatar*, helping viewers better understand Katara in particular.
22 To better understand the trauma derived from imperialism, see: Ryanne Kap's chapter in this volume, which examines the episode "The Southern Air Temple" (S1E03), and Caleb Horowitz's chapter, which analyzes the generational trauma that follows the Air Nomad genocide.
23 Sokka's transformation is not wholly successful. Later in the episode, he filters his experience through his gender and suggests that the violence he saw was only "a regular guy defending his home. Nothing mystical about it."
24 Rob Boddice, *Anthropocentrism: Humans, Animals, Environments* (Brill, 2011), 1. Ecocentrism shares many characteristics with posthumanism, in that both philosophical approaches attempt to de-center the human experience, but the former is closely associated with ethics while latter primarily studies agency. For instance, posthumanists like Başak Ağın and Şafak Horzum ask, "If we are … imbued with nonhuman bodies around and within us, then how are we supposed to disentangle ourselves and understand their agency?" Başak Ağın and Şafak Horzum, "Diseased Bodies Entangled: Literary and Cultural Crossroads of Posthuman Narrative Agents," *SFRA Review* 51.2 (2021): 150. Since Aang is deeply concerned with how to treat others, I apply ecocentrism

to his interaction with Huu. A posthumanist reading would further illuminate how *Avatar* situates the natural world and agency.

25 Boddice, 1.
26 Ibid., 1.
27 Brian J. Preston, "Internalizing Ecocentrism in Environmental Law," in *Exploring Wild Law: The Philosophy of Earth Jurisprudence*, ed. Peter Burdon (Wakefield Press, 2011), 75.
28 Aldo Leopold, *A Sand County Almanac* (Ballantine Books, 1970), 239.
29 Kevin Hobbs and David West, *The Story of Trees* (Laurence King Publishing, 2020), 87.
30 Michael Ziser, *Environmental Practice and Early American Literature* (Cambridge University Press, 2013), 2.
31 Joan Maloof, *Teaching the Trees* (The University of Georgia Press, 2005), 124.
32 Gabriel Popkin, "What the Death of an Oak Tree Can Teach Us about Mortality," *Aeon*, December 6, 2016, https://aeon.co/ideas/what-the-death-of-an-oak-tree-can-teach-us-about-mortality.
33 Hobbs and West, 91.
34 See, for instance: Robin Wall Kimmerer, *Braiding Sweetgrass: Indigenous Wisdom, Scientific Knowledge and the Teachings of Plants* (Milkweed Editions, 2013), which combines Indigenous knowledge and ecology to develop a more sustainable environmental ethic.
35 Peter Wohlleben, *The Hidden Life of Trees* (Greystone Books, 2016), 10.
36 Ibid., 183–4; Hobbs and West, 87.
37 Intriguingly, Hobbs and West highlight that the banyan's root system "inspired the name for [a] computer network operating system" (87), a fact that provides a useful model for the blurry lines between "natural" objects and "unnatural" objects.
38 Leo Marx, *The Machine in the Garden* (Oxford University Press, 1964), 6.
39 Ibid., 5.
40 Ibid., 3, 5.
41 Ibid., 9–10.
42 Lawrence Buell, *The Environmental Imagination* (The Belknap Press of Harvard University Press, 1995), 31.
43 Ibid., 31.
44 Ibid., 32.
45 For a more detailed examination of Zuko's character arc across the series, see: Joseph V. Giunta's chapter in this volume.
46 Marx, 356, 358.
47 Ibid., 364.
48 Ibid.

49 Ibid.
50 For more about this episode and its relationship to the western, see Francis M. Agnoli's chapter in this volume.
51 See, for instance, Gwendolyn Morgan, "Creatures in Crisis: Apocalyptic Environmental Visions in Miyazaki's *Nausicaä of the Valley of the Wind* and *Princess Mononoke*," *Resilience: A Journal of the Environmental Humanities* 2.3 (2015): 172–83; Michelle J. Smith and Elizabeth Parsons, "Animating Child Activism: Environmentalism and Class Politics in Ghibli's *Princess Mononoke* (1997) and Fox's *Fern Gully* (1992)," *Continuum* 26.1 (2012): 25–37.
52 Hunnicutt, 38.

PART TWO

Identity

4

Social Identity in *Avatar: The Last Airbender*

Douglas Schulz

Identity and notions revolving around identity permeate the world of *Avatar: The Last Airbender* (Nickelodeon, 2005–8) and are prominent features in the conversations Aang and his friends have with others throughout their journey of restoring peace to the world after a century of Fire Nation terror and tyranny. Over the course of the series, viewers are confronted with instances of characters differentiating between "good" and "bad," "us" and "them," and the Fire Nation and non-Fire Nation, as well as the importance of Aang and his role in restoring peace and unity in a world ravaged and terrorized by the Fire Nation.

This chapter aims to explore and conceptualize identity in the world of *Avatar*, utilizing Social Identity Theory and the "looking-glass self"—sociological concepts—in order to highlight how popular culture animated series like *Avatar: The Last Airbender* are able to communicate social phenomena such as social interactions, ideas, attitudes, and behaviors. Furthermore, this chapter will aim to explore how the world of *Avatar* and its inhabitants has been designed to showcase group memberships such as the Four Nations.

Richard Jenkins noted that the word "identity" has two basic meanings: First, the notion of absolute sameness, when two things are identical; second, a sense of distinctiveness and continuity over a certain period of time.[1] Identities are features human beings have and rely on in order to communicate who they are in relation to others. According to Kath Woodward, identity involves the establishment of boundaries, which can locate someone or something as being similar or different to us. Those with whom we have an identity are marked as the same, featured through the use of pronouns such as "us," "we," and "our," while those excluded, the ones who we do not share an identity with, are characterized as "them" or "other." Woodward also noted that identity provides people with a way to think about the connections between the personal and the social.[2] Identity is the meeting place of society and the psyche. Without the ability to identify ourselves, we are not able to relate to other human beings in a consistent and meaningful manner. It would not be possible to live our lives if we did not have any means of identifying one another and knowing who others are.[3]

Identity is a prominent notion in *Avatar* as characters' identities are oftentimes scrutinized and their identity is established, questioned, and reinforced. In *Avatar*, notions of identity revolve around nationhood, group memberships, beliefs, attitudes, and values—all factors in the establishment of "social identity," which will be explored in the upcoming part.

Social Identity Theory Explained

Throughout the course of everyday life, we encounter a large and varied social world. In order to make sense of this social world, we oftentimes view ourselves and the people around us in terms of their group membership.[4] The world we inhabit and the people we encounter can be viewed through the lens of in-groups and out-groups—the groups we are members of and the groups we are not members of. Social Identity Theory is a theoretical framework which creates an understanding of the processes which result in people selecting their social groups, as well as how groups' social norms, behaviors, and attitudes are subsequently represented.[5] Social Identity Theory is situated within sociology and social psychology as a core foundation regarding social cognitive theories that attempt to describe self-concept, group processes, inter-group relations, and identity formation.[6]

According to John C. Turner and Penelope J. Oakes, three principles are at the core of Social Identity Theory. First, people derive a part of their own self-concept from the memberships of their social groups. Second, a conceptual focus is placed on the "collective self"—the self is defined in terms of the social group and in relation to other mutual group members. Lastly, the social identification of mutual features with group members results in the creation of inter- and intra-group behaviors.[7] Henri Tajfel noted that social identity is a part of a person's self-concept which derives from their knowledge of their membership of social groups, together with the emotional significance that is associated with that particular group membership.[8]

People are continually engaged in locating themselves in relation to one another and think about themselves and their own self-images, continually developing their sense of self.[9] Individuals derive part of their self-concept from affiliations with social groups and are thus motivated to create and maintain a sense of distinctiveness of their groups in relation to other relevant out-groups. This motivation, to create and maintain a sense of distinctiveness, is, according to Tajfel and Turner greater amongst people who identify more greatly with the group than members who do not.[10] Consequently, people with high levels of identification toward a certain group are less likely to leave or abandon the group, even after experiencing spells of negative events and decreased social standing.[11]

Social Identity Theory at Work in *Avatar*

With the above explanation of Social Identity Theory, there are countless examples of Social Identity Theory at work in the world of *Avatar*. As mentioned in the previous part, people encounter a large and varied social world. All of the interactions people have throughout the course of their everyday life shape their experience of the world. In this regard, in the context of *Avatar*, members of the in-group may be fellow members a nation such as the Earth Kingdom or on a smaller scale, localities such as Ba Sing Se or Kyoshi Island. Having a social identity means that an individual has mutual attributes with other members of that particular group or community.[12] The Four Nations are perhaps the most prominent example of social identity at work and social identity based on nationhood is perhaps one of the most salient features in the world of *Avatar*.

Social identity researchers have found that individuals who identify with a group have strong attachments to the overall group, regardless of individual attachments within the group.[13] In other words, people may feel attached to the overarching group they are a member of without necessarily knowing any of the members personally. In order to have a feeling of collectivity, people need to have one thing in common, no matter how vague or mundane it is.[14] For example, a group of youths from different parts of the Earth Kingdom may feel a sense of belonging based on the fact they share the same nationality, despite being from different regions. Jenkins noted that there are two types of collectivities. In the first type, members of a group are able to identify themselves as members of a particular group. In the second type, they may not be aware of their membership, or even acknowledge the group's existence. Given this, the first type of collective exists due to it being recognized by its members, whilst the second type of collectivity is based on the recognition of observers. Thus, group identity is the product of a collective internal definition.[15]

In *Avatar*, a prominent and effective means of establishing and showcasing identity is through the clothing styles of the Four Nations, and how members of each nation have been designed to reflect each respective cultural background. One notable feature of the clothing designed in *Avatar* is that each nation "wears" colors symbolizing each respective element. Members of the Earth Kingdom wear predominantly brown, yellow, and green; members of the Water Tribes wear blue, white, and purple; the Air Nomads traditionally wore orange and yellow; and the citizens of the Fire Nation wear different shades of red, brown, pink, black, and gold. Whilst clothing is sometimes overlooked, it is an effective method of communicating identity and groups memberships through it.[16] The way that characters and their clothing styles have been designed in *Avatar* gives the viewer important clues about who they are, which groups they belong to, and potential attitudes they may have—in particular sentiments regarding the *Avatar*, the Fire Nation, or the state of the world.

Constructing "Us" and "Them"—Social Identity at Work in *Avatar*

A key assumption of social identity is that people possess a motivation to evaluate their own social groups more favorably and perceive them in a more positive manner than the groups they are not members of, enhancing and maintaining a positive sense of self. According to the principles of Social Identity Theory, establishing and maintaining a favorable view of one's group in comparison to other groups or rather through a sense of in-group favoritism is helpful in achieving what Maykel Verkuyten and Angela De Wolf call a positive group identity.[17] In-group favoritism is regarded as an integral means of securing a positive sense of identity and research on adolescents has demonstrated that in-group favoritism does positively and causally affect self-feelings.[18] It is, however, important to note that in terms of Social Identity Theory, in-group favoritism is not an automatic result of group differences but rather, an emphasis on the fact that psychological processes should be observed and explored in a social setting.[19]

Jet, the leader of a gang of freedom fighters, is a prime example of social identity's construction of "us" and "them"—a reoccurring theme in his interactions with Aang and other characters throughout the show. A part of Social Identity Theory and the establishment of a sense of "us" and "them" is self-categorization, which describes the ways in which cognitive processes facilitate how people construct their social identities. Tajfel noted that this involves an individual knowing that they belong to a specific group, mixed with an emotional involvement with that group.[20] In the case for Jet, he is aware of his group membership of being a freedom fighter, but he also holds the group and its values and beliefs close to this heart. In "The Serpent's Pass" (S2E12), this is exemplified that Jet cares about his group, how his group is perceived, and the relationship between his group and other social groups:

> Jet: Here's the deal. I hear the captain's eating like a king while the refugees have to feed off his scraps. Doesn't seem fair, does it?
> Iroh: What kind of king is he eating like?
> Jet: The fat, happy kind. You want to help us "liberate" some food?

Jet and his crew portray themselves as freedom fighters, who engage in combat or other forms of activity, where the primary goal is to acquire something which is highly desirable or holds great meaning and value to them. This something can be land, liberty, or more sociopolitical things such as equality or the end to existing oppression. Freedom fighters often originate from groups which are marginalized within a society and have been deprived of something they value highly.[21] In "Jet" (S1E10), Jet and his crew want to bring an end to Fire Nation oppression by sabotaging Fire Nation troops in the Earth Kingdom village of Gaipan, with the aim to rescue the town from its oppressors. Furthermore, there is an element of greed and envy in Jet and his gang of freedom fighters. In many circumstances, greed and envy are clustered together in order to portray a person or group as having a desire to possess something that someone else owns. At the same time, however, there are a number of differences between greed and envy. Greed is about the desire to acquire something that someone else already possesses. Envy however, is not directed at the group of people—the out-group. The aim of envy is to destroy the happiness of the other group, not the desire to acquire something of material basis or value. It merely seeks to destroy and rejoice in the misfortune and suffering of the other group.[22] This is particularly the case when Jet and his gang try to flood and destroy Gaipan.

In regard to in- and out-groups, there is an explicit potential for intergroup conflict, as can be seen in the views Jet holds regarding the captain of the ferry and the Fire Nation, respectively.[23] As previously mentioned, members of the in-group will demonstrate a sense of in-group favoritism and will exhibit negative attitudes toward members of the out-group.[24] Alongside the favoritism and bias, the out-group is oftentimes regarded as a homogeneous group, whereas differences within the in-group are appreciated. As out-groups are regarded as homogeneous, the notion of "they are all the same" is another prime example of social identity at work in the world of *Avatar*—as can be seen in the following exchange of "The Great Divide" (S1E11):

> Zhang Leader: You're not seriously gonna cave into these spoiled Gan Jins? I mean we're refugees too! And we've got sick people that need shelter.
> Gan Jin Tribesman: We've got old people who are weary of traveling.

Zhang Leader: Sick people get priority over old people.
Gan Jin Leader: Maybe you Zhangs wouldn't have so many sick people if you weren't such slobs.
Zhang Leader: If you Gan Jins weren't so *clean*, you wouldn't live to be so *old*.
[...]
Aang: Uh, you could *share* the earthbender and travel together?
Gan Jin Leader: Absolutely not! We'd rather be taken by the Fire Nation than travel with those stinking thieves!
Zhang Leader: We wouldn't want to travel with those pompous fools anyway!

In the above example, while the Gan Jin and Zhang tribe feud with each other, tribesmen involved in the exchange make use of their social identity. Their views of the respective out-group influence their attitude toward each other. Self-categorization explains how people make use of their own personal frames of reference in order to label and describe groups of people based on shared attributes.[25] Furthermore, the way that people behave within their social groups can communicate group norms, and the group itself is influenced and configured through the norms.[26] In some groups, prejudiced and discriminatory norms and behaviors are used by in-group members as grounds to deprive out-group members of resources which may aid in the improvement of their social standing and well-being. At the same time, it is important to note that discriminatory behavior of in-group members toward out-group members may jeopardize the in-group's image and social standing.[27]

The Looking-Glass Self

The "looking-glass self" is a frequently and widely accepted theory in contemporary psychology and sociology. The notion was conceptualized by Charles Cooley in 1902 as he observed and examined the processes in which a person's experience of the self are created and altered through social interactions.[28] The main idea of the looking-glass self contains two rudimentary principles. First, self-consciousness involves the continual monitoring and observation of self from the point of view of others. As Cooley suggested, we live in the minds of others. Second, "living" in the minds of others, in an imaginative sense, results in the experience of genuine and intense emotions: pride or shame.[29]

Victor Gecas and Michael L. Schwalbe referred to the looking-glass self as the idea that people perceive themselves through the eyes of others, much like our physical characteristics are reflected back toward us when we stand in front of a mirror and observe our reflections.[30] David C. Lundgren notes that the looking-glass self is made up of three elements: (1) the imagination and idea of our own experience to other people, (2) the thought and imagination of their judgment regarding our appearance, and (3) our own individual experience of judgment based on the reaction we receive from others, which is followed by the experience of pride or shame.[31] Cooley argued that the reactions and responses we receive from other people provide us with a viewpoint from which we are able to define our attributes in a more meaningful and consistent manner, as well as alter them if necessary.[32]

As the Avatar, Aang is perhaps the most vulnerable character of the series in terms of the looking-glass self. Throughout the seasons, there are countless references to his century-long disappearance and how he feels directly responsible for letting people down. Throughout the first season, there are a number of instances in which Aang feels a sense of pride and shame, paired with the worry of disappointing people, as well as many instances in which Aang feels shame for letting the world down, allowing the Fire Nation to take control when it was his duty to ensure that the four nations lived together in harmony.

Sokka provides another prominent example of the looking-glass self at work. Too young to join the other Southern Water Tribe warriors in battle, he had to remain at the South Pole, "training up" young soldiers, who are just little children, and protecting his little sister, Katara. He does still, however, feel a responsibility for providing some form of basic training in the case of a Fire Nation attack. Whilst Sokka wants to be seen as a brave soldier, or at least becoming one, he is oftentimes left embarrassed when things do not go according to his plans or when he overestimates his own strengths and abilities. An example of this is in "The Warriors of Kyoshi" (S1E04), when he and the others first encounter the Kyoshi Warriors:

> Katara: He's just upset because a bunch of girls kicked his butt yesterday.
> Sokka: They snuck up on me!
> Katara: Right. And *then* kicked your butt.
> Sokka: Sneak attacks don't count!

Later on in the episode, Sokka visits the Kyoshi Warrior training school, and acts overconfident, saying he did not mean to "interrupt your dance lesson" and is generally obnoxious in his behavior. During the practice fight with their leader, Suki, the looking-glass self becomes apparent again, as Sokka not only loses the fight—much to his dismay—but is also embarrassed by losing to a girl. Sokka's looking-glass self is his own belief that others see him as a brave warrior and competent fighter and is often visibly upset or ashamed when this image of him is not fulfilled. Throughout the series, Sokka develops in terms of the looking-glass self. Sokka is talented in engineering and combat tactics, which he is able to use to his advantage on multiple occasions throughout the series—for instance, using rotten eggs as a sign for gas leaks or making use of the gas to fend off attacking fire nation soldiers in "The Northern Air Temple" (S1E17). Sokka has a talent for thinking outside the box. In "Sokka's Master" (S3E04), he alters the landscape of Master Piandao's yard in order to create an environment that he can use to his advantage. In the same episode, he proves his skills by using a meteorite to forge his own sword. Oftentimes, Sokka finds his happiness when he is able to take control in his own way—through the use of his ingenuity in terms of combat tactics and strategies. Sokka is most fulfilled when he is able to influence things through his sharp mind and senses and rather than being a leader purely in a brave warrior sense, he is a leader through his ideas paired with his bravery in combat.

The looking-glass self suggests that a sense of self derives from the ongoing social interactions people have with each other during the course of their daily lives. The view of "ourselves" originates from the contemplation of our own individual qualities and impressions of how others perceive us. In this sense, the way we perceive ourselves does not originate from who we *really* are, but rather, from how we *believe* other people perceive us. Thus, we create our own self-image in accordance to the responses and evaluations of others who are part of the same environment we inhabit with them.[33] This also suggests that reference groups are crucial in regard to understanding the looking-glass self. Individuals do not internalize *all* of the perceptions and opinions that others have of them, but rather, carefully select which people's perceptions of them are the most influential, important, meaningful, and relevant.[34] With this in mind, Joachim Vogt Isaksen noted that as long as people participate in social interactions with others, they are inevitably vulnerable to the judgments of other people about them, which means they are constantly engaged in thinking about and altering our self-image throughout the course of our everyday lives.[35]

Socialization and the Role of Others in Social Identity

When people are born into the world, they learn behaviors, attitudes, values, and beliefs from the culture they live and grow up in—in the social sciences known as socialization. In *Avatar*, the four nations have distinctive features of how their inhabitants grow up and see the world. Each of the corresponding elements has its own attributes, as Iroh explained to Zuko in "Bitter Work" (S2E09):

> Fire is the element of power. The people of the Fire Nation have desire and will and the energy and drive to achieve what they want. Earth is the element of substance. The people of the Earth Kingdom are diverse and strong. They are persistent and enduring. Air is the element of freedom.

The Air Nomads detached themselves from worldly concern and found peace and freedom. Water is the element of change. The people of the Water Tribe are capable of adapting to many things. They have a deep sense of community and love that holds them together through anything.

Each of these attributes is noticeable in the traits of the people and benders Aang and his friends encounter throughout their adventure. The notion of fire as the element of power is commonly shown in *Avatar*. In "The Deserter" (S1E16), Aang is taught firebending by Jeong Jeong, who advises him that "fire will destroy everything in its path." With the power of firebending comes the knowledge and discipline to control it, much like Iroh forces Zuko to repeat firebending drills repeatedly. Toph is a great example of earthbenders being diverse and strong. Despite her blindness, Toph overcomes obstacles by sensing vibrations in the ground when someone is approaching or talking as well as by being able to bend metal. The Air Nomads were highly spiritual, allowing them to focus their training to master the art of soaring the heavens and making the skies their territory. The sense of community is present in the interactions between Water Tribe people. In "The Waterbending Master" (S1E18), when Aang and his friends reach the North Pole, Chief Arnook notes that they are "celebrat[ing] the arrival of our brother and sister from the Southern Tribe." Furthermore, in "Bato of the Water Tribe" (S1E15), Bato facilitates a coming-of-age ice dodging ceremony for Sokka, and he invites Aang and Katara to participate. Aang, despite being non-Water Tribe, is seen almost as an equal on the basis of his friendship with Katara and Sokka.

Jeffrey J. Arnett identified three central features of socialization: (1) impulse control—including the development of a conscience; (2) role preparation and performance—including occupational roles, gender roles, and roles in institutions such as marriage and parenthood; and (3) the cultivation of sources of meaning—what is important and what is to be valued.[36] All three of these central features are prevalent in the *Avatar* series. In terms of impulse control, Zuko is often seen to be short-tempered, using the destructive power of his firebending in order to combat others. Gender roles and role institutions are prevalent in the traditions of the Water Tribes, where girls and women are not allowed to be waterbenders. Returning to "The Waterbending Master," Katara is angered by the way she is treated by Master:

Aang: Uhh … This is my friend, Katara. The one I told you about?
Pakku: I'm sorry, I think there's been a misunderstanding. You didn't tell me your friend was a girl. In our tribe, it is forbidden for women to learn waterbending.
Katara: What do you mean you won't teach me? I didn't travel across the entire world so you could tell me no!

> **Pakku:** No.
> **Katara:** But there must be other female waterbenders in your tribe!
> **Pakku:** Here, the women learn from Yagoda to use their waterbending to heal. I'm sure she would be happy to take you as her student, despite your bad attitude.
> **Katara:** I don't want to heal; I want to fight!
> **Pakku:** I can see that. But our tribe has customs, rules.

Lastly, in regard to the cultivation of meaning and what is to be valued and deemed important is a prevailing feature in "The Headband" (S3E02), when Aang goes to the Fire Nation school under the alias of Kuzon and later invites his classmates back to his hideout for a secret dance party. Throughout the episode, there are instances in which Aang's behavior is regarded as a nuisance by the teachers—his answers to the Fire Nation history pop quiz or moving his feet in time to the music. It is clear from this episode, that the Fire Nation places an emphasis and importance on order, decorum, and discipline.

It is evident in Zuko's behavior and narratives of his upbringing that he was also raised in a strict environment where emphasis is placed on customs, respect, obedience, and discipline. In "The Boy in the Iceberg" (S1E01), Zuko is seen repeatedly practicing the same firebending drills much to his dismay, yet Iroh insists that the key to successful bending lies in repetition and perfection.

> **Iroh:** (*sighs*) No! Power in firebending comes from the breath, not the muscles. The breath becomes energy. The energy extends past your limbs and becomes: Fire! Get it right this time.
> **Zuko:** Enough! I've been drilling this sequence all day. Teach me the next set. I'm *more* than ready!
> **Iroh:** No, you are impatient. You have yet to master the basics. Drill it again!

Similarly, Zuko's role in the world and the hierarchy of the Fire Nation is shown in "The Storm" (S1E12), in the memory of him speaking up against the war tactics, subsequently leading to the Agni Kai or firebending duel with his father, Fire Lord Ozai.

> **Iroh** (*narrating*): When Prince Zuko saw that it was his father who had come to duel him, he begged for mercy.
> **Zuko:** Please Father. I only had the Fire Nation's best interests at heart. I'm sorry I spoke out of turn!
> **Ozai:** You will fight for your honor.
> **Zuko:** I meant you no disrespect. I am your loyal son.
> **Ozai:** Rise and fight, Prince Zuko!

Zuko: I *won't* fight you.
Ozai: You *will* learn respect, and *suffering* will be your teacher.
[...]
Jee (*in present*): I always thought that Prince Zuko was in a training accident.
Iroh: It was no accident. After the duel, the Fire Lord said by refusing to fight, Zuko had shown shameful weakness. As punishment, he was banished and sent to capture the Avatar. Only then could he return with his honor.

Adolescence is a time in people's lives with continuous, and at times drastic, changes in which individuals are required to reorient themselves in regard to who they are, how they came to be that person, and who they aspire to become. Developing identity and a sense of self is an important task during the course of adolescence and identities become more salient after the occurrence of important life events.[37] Dramatic and traumatic life events have been found to be a strong predictor of various developmental outcomes, such as mental health aspects.[38] In Zuko's case, speaking out at the war meeting was a crucial event in his life and influenced his attitudes and group memberships. As a result of the Agni Kai and his consequent banishment, there were only a limited number of people who stood by his side, such as Iroh and the crew, on his quest to capture Aang. Zuko's experience and punishment illustrate how life events that occur during important transitional phases of one's life have long-lasting effects.

Mats Alvesson and Hugh Willmott noted that the social processes in identity work and identity regulation function together in the process of shaping self-identities. "Identity work" refers to the continual process of forming and maintaining, strengthening and revising of one's own identity constructions as people's sense of self becomes more distinctive and coherent. One's identity work is influenced and shaped through social interactions with other people, with identity regulators.[39] Zuko repeatedly reminds himself that capturing Aang will restore his honor and right to the throne, which influences his attitudes and viewpoints regarding people who are "on his side" and who are not. Similarly, Aang is frequently reminded of his duty as Avatar, to restore peace and unity to the world, even when he is unsure of himself.

When people experience positive self-evaluations, positive self-worth is achieved through a desire for communion and interpersonal connectedness with other people. When the feeling of belonging is threatened, this may result emotional distress which serves as a motivation for people to behave in ways which gain and maintain a feeling of acceptance from others.[40] Aang is perhaps the most vulnerable, particularly in the first season, when his reemergence is noticed by an increasing number of people, and when he is continuously reminded by people regarding his job as the Avatar. Similarly, other characters experience this sense of connectedness and belonging through their respective actions. Bato, a warrior from the Southern Water Tribe who knows Katara's and Sokka's father, facilitates a traditional coming-of-age ritual for Sokka. Ice dodging is an important rite of passage for young boys in the Southern Water Tribes. After passing, he receives the mark of wisdom, further deepening his connection to his tribe and his aspirations of becoming a brave warrior.

Conclusions

Throughout the *Avatar* series, viewers are continually confronted and inundated with notions of self, identity, and inter-group dynamics and relations. In a world ravaged and dominated century-long Fire Nation oppression and tyranny, social identity is one of the most prominent and salient boundaries as well as is one of the main ways to establish relations between "good" and "bad" and between "us" and "them." Social identity researchers recognize that there is a core sense of self which remains stable over the course of time; however, there are elements of change.

Zuko, for example, begins as the main villain in the first season of *Avatar*. As the series progresses in seasons two and three however, his circumstances change and his aspirations and outlook on life change. Whilst he still maintains an obsession of capturing Aang and restoring his honor, this slowly fades and is replaced by a willingness to help Aang and his friends instead, stopping Azula's and Fire Lord Ozai's plans for complete world domination. Similarly, Aang becomes increasingly aware of his role in the world as becomes increasingly skilled in mastering the elements, and through his friends grows as a person. In the final episode of Season Three, Zuko pledges to restore the honor of the Fire Nation, as he promised Iroh, and notes that through working *together*, a new era of love and peace is able to begin. Another character who undergoes noteworthy development is Sokka. Initially too young to join the other warriors of the Southern Water Tribe in battle, he is left at the South Pole and "trains" up young children. Throughout the series, Sokka matures and hones in on his intelligence, tactical combat skills, and outside-the-box thinking.

These examples illustrate how identities are located across places, times, and through people.[41] Identity develops through and from the ongoing interactions with others and when shared with them—in particular members of the in-group, through which a shared sense of community can develop. Through the expression of identity, people develop social networks which enhance, support, and reaffirm their group memberships. This is particularly relevant and noteworthy in *Avatar*. In a number of episodes, in particularly in Season One, when it is discovered that Aang has returned and endeavors to fulfill his duty as the Avatar, the general feeling seems to be support—Aang is on the side of the people, "our side," in his quest to restore peace and unity in the world. The looking-glass self is of particular importance in *Avatar* and in the general context of social interactions. Isaaksen noted that for as long as people participate in social interactions with others, they are inevitably vulnerable to the judgments of other people around them, meaning they are constantly engaged in thinking and altering their self-image throughout the course of their everyday life.[42]

Lastly, *Avatar* combines elements of sociological theories in its scripts, allowing viewers to experience and thinking about dynamics, intergroup relations, and identity processes. Dialogue is not the only way that identity can be expressed, but also artifacts such as clothing or the way that characters have been designed or animated can provide useful clues about characters and the group memberships they possess. Popular culture channels such as television shows like *Avatar* are able to convey to viewers notions of understanding differences in cultures and attitudes, working together to achieve change, in the case of *Avatar*, peace and unity. One person may begin a story as a "bad guy" but be able to change his ways and become a crucial factor in bringing said change. *Avatar* is a series which may inspire viewers to think about their own identities and attitudes toward in- and out-group members, as every person is a social being, with attitudes and prejudice toward out-groups. Lastly, series like *Avatar* are a means to communicate conflicts which occur in everyone's lives at some point and the lesson of collaborating with others in order to overcome challenges, highlighting that working together for a common cause results in not what is best for *one* individual, but rather, what is best for *many* people.

Notes

1 Richard Jenkins, *Social Identity* (Routledge, 2004), 4.
2 Kath Woodward, *Understanding Identity* (Arnold, 2002), 1.
3 Jenkins, 4.
4 John B. Nezlek and Veronica C. Smith, "Social Identity in Daily Social Interaction," *Self and Identity* 4.3 (2005): 243.
5 Michael A. Hogg and Scott A. Reid, "Social Identity, Self-Categorization, and the Communication of Group Norms," *Communication Theory* 16.1 (March 2006): 8; Manya C. Whitaker, "Us and Them: Using Social Identity Theory to Explain and Re-envision Teacher-Student Relationships in Urban Schools," *The Urban Review* 52.4 (2020): 692.
6 Hogg and Reid, 9.
7 John C. Turner and Penelope J. Oakes, "The Significance of the Social Identity Concept for Social Psychology with Reference to Individualism, Interactionism and Social Influence," *British Journal of Social Psychology* 25 (September 1986): 239.

8   Henri Tajfel, "La Categorization Sociale [Social categorization]," in *Introduction à la psychologie sociale [Introduction to social psychology]*, ed. Serge Moscovici (Larousse, 1972), 292.
9   John P. Hewitt, *Self and Society: A Symbolic Interactionist Social Psychology* (Allyn and Bacon, 2007), 88.
10 Henri Tajfel and John C. Turner, "An Integrative Theory of Social Conflict," in *The Social Psychology of Intergroup Relations*, eds. William G. Austin and Stephen Worchel (Brooks/Cole, 1979), 35.
11 Naomi Ellemers, Russell Spears and Bertjan Doosie, "Self and Social Identity," *Annual Review of Psychology* 51.1 (1999): 1964.
12 Jan E. Stets and Peter J. Burke, "Identity Theory and Social Identity Theory," *Social Psychology Quarterly* 63.3 (2000): 226.
13 Michael A. Hogg and Elizabeth A. Hardie, "Prototypicality, Conformity and Depersonalised Attraction: A Self-Categorisation Analysis of Group Cohesiveness," *British Journal of Social Psychology* 31.1 (March 1992): 42.
14 Jenkins, 4.
15 Ibid., 84.
16 Andrew Garner, "Living History: Trees and Metaphors of Identity in an English Forest," *Journal of Material Culture* 9.1 (March 2004): 88.
17 Maykel Verkuyten and Angela DeWolf, "The Development of In-Group Favoritism: Between Social Reality and Group Identity," *Developmental Psychology* 43.4 (June 2007): 902.
18 Maykel Verkuyten, "National Identification and Intergroup Evaluation in Dutch Children," *British Journal of Developmental Psychology* 19 (December 2001): 561; Maykel Verkuyten, "Ethnic In-group Favoritism among Minority and Majority Groups: Testing the Self-Esteem Hypothesis among Preadolescents," *Journal of Applied Social Psychology* 37 (March 2007): 488.
19 Verkuyten and De Wolf, 902.
20 Tajfel, 292.
21 John Bolt, "Terrorists or Freedom Fighters: What's the Difference?," *Action Institute*, November 14, 2001.
22 Ibid.
23 Bryan Burford, "Group Processes in Medical Education: Learning from Social Identity Theory," *Medical Education* 46.2 (February 2012): 144.
24 Verkuyten and De Wolf, 909.
25 Whitaker, 693.
26 Hogg and Reid, 8.
27 Whitaker, 693.
28 Charles Cooley, *Human Nature and Social Order* (Scribner's, 1902).
29 Thomas J. Scheff, "Looking-Glass Self: Goffman as Symbolic Interactionist," *Symbolic Interactionism* 28.2 (December 2005): 147.

30 Victor Gecas and Michael L. Schwalbe, "Beyond the Looking-Glass Self: Social Structure and Efficacy-Based Self-Esteem," *Social Psychology Quarterly* 46.2 (1983): 77.

31 David C. Lundgren, "Social Feedback and Self-Appraisals: Current Status of the Mead-Cooley Hypothesis," *Symbolic Interactionism* 27.2 (December 2004): 268.

32 Cooley, 108.

33 Joachim Vogt Isaksen, "The Looking Glass Self: How Our Self-Image Is Shaped by Society," *Popular Political Science*, May 27, 2013.

34 Donald Reitzes, "Beyond the Looking Glass Self: Cooley's Social Self and Its Treatment in Introductory Testbooks," *Contemporary Sociology* 9.5 (1980): 634.

35 Isaksen.

36 Jeffrey J. Arnett, "Adolescents' Use of Media for Self-Socialization," *Journal of Youth and Adolescence* 24.5 (October 1995): 520.

37 Elisabeth De Moor, et al., "Stressful Life Events and Identity Development in Early and Mid-adolescence," *Journal of Adolescence* 76 (August 2019): 75.

38 Odilia M. Laceulle, et al., "Stressful Events and Psychological Difficulties: Testing Alternative Candidates for Sensitivity," *European Child & Adolescent Psychiatry* 23.2 (June 2014): 103.

39 Mats Alvesson and Hugh Willmott, "Identity Regulation as Organization Control: Producing the Appropriate Individual," *Organization Science* 18 (2002): 626.

40 Jan E. Stets and Peter J. Burke, "Self-Esteem and Identities," *Sociological Perspectives* 57.4 (July 2014): 410.

41 Rachel Hurdley, "Dismantling Mantelpieces: Narrating Identities and Materializing Culture in the Home," *Sociology* 40.4 (August 2006): 729.

42 Isaaksen.

5

"What Does Me Being a Girl Have to Do with Sewing?" Representations of Gender in *Avatar: The Last Airbender*

Ruth Richards

Although the hero of *Avatar: The Last Airbender* (Nickelodeon, 2005–8) is Aang, the titular airbender who sets out to master the four elements and unite the warring nations, he would not have succeeded without Katara. A young waterbender from the Southern Water Tribe, Katara, along with her brother Sokka, discovers and helps revive Aang from his 100-year entrapment in an iceberg, and aids him throughout his journey to master the elements. However, Katara's role in *Avatar* is more than just to support Aang. Throughout the series, she develops her own talents and abilities as a waterbender, and from being largely self-taught is soon acknowledged as a Waterbending Master. Her skills are demonstrably equal to many of the benders from the four nations the group encounters throughout their journey. She not only trains Aang in his own waterbending, she also plays pivotal roles in key battles throughout the series.

Over a decade since the show first aired on Nickelodeon, *Avatar* continues to receive praise for its positive representations of female characters. Critics have argued that one of "the greatest qualities of this show is how it approaches the treatment of its male and female characters," and that its "reliance [on] and development of strong female characters" is one of "biggest draws" for the series.[1] *Avatar* features a number of female characters in key and supporting roles throughout its three seasons. Although Katara is the only primary female protagonist in Book One, she is joined by earthbender Toph and the villainous Princess Azula of the Fire Nation in Book Two. Women and girls are also featured in a variety of roles throughout the series as either one-off or recurring characters, including, but not limited to, Suki, Mai, Ty Lee, and Princess Yue. Despite the overall praise the series has received critically, there has been less scholarly attention given to the series' representation of gender. The following chapter examines the ways *Avatar* positions and treats its female characters through a feminist framework. The textual analysis will largely limit itself to the depiction of Katara in Book One of *Avatar*, where I have identified key moments and episodes that are demonstrative of the ways the series approaches representations of gender.

For my approach, I take inspiration from the scholarly analysis by Emma A. Jane of the depiction of gender in *Adventure Time* (Cartoon Network, 2010–18). Jane proposes that this series responds to the question proposed by Dafna Lemish regarding the critique of gender portrayals in popular media: "we know what we do NOT want to see, but DO we know what we WANT to see?"[2] *Adventure Time* and *Avatar* are, of course, two very different series. However, just as Jane argues in her analysis that *Adventure Time* offers progressive and fluid depictions of gender, providing a response to this question of "What's next?" for academics interested in the representation of gender in various media, I also argue that *Avatar* offers positive and progressive representations of female characters. Although Katara's narrative trajectory as the nurturing, feminine support in some ways relies on certain stereotypical tropes associated with female supporting characters, I argue that Katara's depiction overall, taken alongside other girl characters in *Avatar*, offers a nuanced and complex approach to the representation of gender.[3] Rather than being considered a weakness, Katara's empathetic nature is one aspect of a character who develops in nuanced ways throughout the series; Katara's personality is not fixed, and she adapts to new situations, grows and matures alongside Aang and her friends throughout their journey. In order to show this, the following chapter examines Katara's characterization to demonstrate how she, and the series overall, offers viewers a progressive and positive representation of girls in animated children's media. The chapter begins by situating *Avatar* within the history of US television animation, before examining key questions around gender and representation in children's media. I then undertake a close textual analysis of three episodes in Book One of *Avatar*: "The Boy in the Iceberg" (S1E01), "The Warriors of Kyoshi" (S1E04), and "The Waterbending Master" (S1E18).

Like Jane, it is not within my scope here to consider the "possible ramifications" of the "media effects" debate of gender representations on the audience.[4] However, it is my intent to situate *Avatar* within the history and body of literature examining the depiction of gender in children's media—specifically, animated media—more broadly. It is also necessary to contextualize *Avatar* within its time of production. At a basic level, this means we must first acknowledge that *Avatar* is a series created by two men, Michael Dante DiMartino and Bryan Konietzko, which aired on Nickelodeon, a major network primarily known for producing children's media, from 2005 to 2008. Its production was preceded and is framed by a movement in children's media toward empowered girl characters. The term "empowered" in this sense refers to the depiction of female characters who are shown to be confident, assertive, or powerful in either physical, emotional or intellectual capacity. To be "empowered" is a somewhat abstract yet aspirational quality. This kind of language has often been taken up by "girl power" discourses within children's media, discussed in more detail below. It is therefore not only important to contextualize *Avatar's* representation of its female characters within the broader scholarship surrounding girl characters in cartoons during this period but also *Avatar's* position *as* children's media.

Cartoons, Girls, and Representation

Avatar is an animated series whose target audience is primarily children. This is significant as gender representation and the depiction of so-called feminine and masculine characteristics in children's media has been a topic of critical debate and analysis for some time.[5] It has also been suggested that animation as a form of children's entertainment has itself been a neglected topic within animation studies. In his formative text, *Understanding Animation*, Paul Wells argues that "The idea that animation is an *innocent* medium, ostensibly for children, and largely dismissed in film histories, has done much to inhibit the proper discussion of issues concerning *representation*."[6] While scholars in the field of animation studies were seeking to validate the study of animation as "more than" a form of children's entertainment, this has meant that the significance of animated children's media as a *specific form* has been under-acknowledged. Animation scholar Amy Ratelle notes that due to the popular perception that animation is "only" for children, "animation studies has, paradoxically, continued to marginalise the study of animation for children."[7] In seeking to "legitimise" the study of animation as a serious artistic and cultural medium, the study of animation for children has been pushed to the side, even though it is a multi-million-dollar industry. This does not mean that animation intended for younger audiences has gone completely unstudied, but that its role as entertainment *for children* has been under-theorized. Ratelle thus contextualizes children's animation within "the larger historical, cultural and theoretical framework of children's media."[8] Importantly, she points out that the association of cartoons and childhood, and the reputation of cartoons as inherent to the experience of childhood, is a "particularly Western and middle-class concept."[9] The following textual analysis of *Avatar* is situated against this very same historical and cultural context.

Ratelle describes the emergence of the child audience as separate to adult audiences and how, in the mid-eighteenth century, an emphasis on the pedagogical function of children's literature began to form. Literature aimed specifically at children was seen as "a vehicle for cultural values," while also serving as a means of entertainment.[10] Ratelle writes, "Moral instruction adhering to these ideals was made palatable to the child audience with entertaining storylines, popular characters and anthropomorphized animals" and that this balance or tension between "entertainment" and "education" is something that has continued to underpin debates surrounding children's media to this day.[11] Narrowing her focus to a US context, Ratelle goes on to describe the specific development of cartoons as a medium for children, from Walt Disney's *Snow White and the Seven Dwarfs* (1937) to the "Saturday morning cartoon." With the decline of the cinematic short, the primary means of distributing cartoon animation in the United States from the 1920s to 1940s, and the rise of television in the 1950s, cartoon animation quickly emerged as a mainstay of children's programming.[12] Streaming services now cater to child audiences with curated offerings that heavily feature animated programming, such as Netflix Kids. We can see this balance of education and entertainment taking place in *Avatar*, which delivers compelling storylines and characters, while also presenting these characters with problems to solve as well as moral and ethical dilemmas that emphasize particular cultural values that resonate within its production context. Some of these values pertain to the ways women and girl characters are represented.

Although child audiences are often demarcated from adult audiences, the question of how to define "children's media"—and, more specifically, "children's television"—becomes problematized when we consider the difficulties of having to define this child audience. Ewan Kirkland examines this question in his book, *Children's Media and Modernity*, where he reminds us that not only does the idea of "children's television" resist easy definition but that "Adults also consume culture considered 'for children', and broadcast media is no exception."[13] This is, of course, true of *Avatar*. The child audience who consumed this series when it was originally broadcast are now adults themselves, while new generations of children and adult audiences alike are being introduced to the series either through syndicated re-runs, physical media such as DVDs and Blu-rays, or through access to subscription video-on-demand (SVOD) services. Following Marsha Kinder, Kirkland also notes that the distinction between child and adult audiences is further complicated when considering the ways networks like Nickelodeon are marketed: "the early days of Nickelodeon [was] emblematic of a 'transgenerational address' within the 1990s American culture."[14] While

Nickelodeon is a channel that has primarily been associated with children's and youth media, their programming was designed to appeal to audiences across different age groups and demographics. Programs like *Avatar*, while first intended for children, may also appeal to adult audiences due to factors such as complex worldbuilding, sophisticated storytelling, characterization, and animation aesthetics.

With the rise of television animation as a popular form of children's media, questions and debates around its representation of gender have followed. In their study of gender representation in children's television in a global context, Maya Götz and Dafna Lemish write that it can "supply important messages and perspectives that can make a strong impression and influence on children's imagination, particularly in regard to gender-oriented learning."[15] As stated above, it is beyond the scope of this analysis to consider the potential influence that depictions of gender in *Avatar* may have on its young audience. However, critique of the ways children's cartoons are supposedly demarcated based on the targeted genders of the audience is ongoing. Sociologist and popular culture scholar Katia Perea discusses the emergence of what she terms the "girl cartoon" in the United States during the 1980s. According to her definition, these cartoons feature a young girl, usually under twelve years old, as the main character, whose gender "is marked as a girl in a standardized feminine way with eyelashes, higher-pitched voiced actors, and girl-gendered hairstyle and clothing."[16] The emergence of these cartoons was closely tied to the US toy industry, which was also strongly demarcated along a gender binary ("boys toys" and "girls toys"). Perea cites cartoons like *He-Man and the Masters of the Universe* (syndication, 1983–5), *G.I. Joe: A Real American Hero* (syndication, 1983–6), and *Transformers* (syndication, 1984–7) as key examples of "boy cartoons" and *My Little Pony* (syndication, 1986–7), *Rainbow Brite* (syndication, 1984–6), and *The World of Strawberry Shortcake* (1980) as examples of "girl cartoons." Perea goes on to describe the emergence of a "second wave" of girl cartoons in the 1990s, coinciding with new regulations restricting advertising in toy-based cartoons. She writes:

> While this second wave of girl cartoons had many similarities to the first wave, US toy-based girl cartoons of the 1980s in that the characters were resourceful, capable leaders, these new girl cartoons were no longer bound to rainbow friendship communities resolving conflict through verbal communication, and though some of the new girl cartoons still revolved around personal drama, self-doubt and didactic teachings, most of these second-wave girl cartoon characters were cunning, witty, logical and brave, and often used physical fighting skills to resolve conflicts.[17]

Perea cites *The Powerpuff Girls* (Cartoon Network, 1998–2005) as a key example of this second wave of girl cartoons. There are some exceptions that complicate Perea's analysis of the girl cartoon genre. *She-Ra: Princess of Power* (syndication, 1985–7) is also a toy-based cartoon and a "sister" series to *He-Man*, marketed toward girls, that does not quite fit the definition of a girl cartoon as Perea describes, given that She-Ra/Adora is over twelve years old and often uses her physical fighting skills as well as her wits to defeat her enemies. However, Perea's description of these first and second wave of girl cartoons is a useful way to understand how children's television animation has in the past been demarcated along a somewhat inflexible gender binary. Building upon Perea's analysis, I suggest that we can identify a "third wave" of cartoons that feature girls as either the main character or part of an ensemble cast. These cartoons do not fall into either category of "girl cartoons" or "boy cartoons," with the characters themselves complicating and challenging such strict, "traditional" gender binaries. This "third wave" of children's cartoons not only dissolves such arbitrary boundaries but reminds us that cartoons have never been strictly for "boys" or "girls" to begin with.

First broadcast from 2005 to 2008 on Nickelodeon, *Avatar* would fall under this "third wave," which happens to coincide with a significant period in the "girl power" movement in mainstream media. The term "girl power" came to be both a cultural movement and media product: "Rooted in a neoliberal language of choice, girl power offers girls and women a sense that they can choose when to be girly and when to be powerful."[18] Sarah Banet-Weiser describes Nickelodeon as a "key producer of girl power culture" during this time.[19] In her exploration of gender, feminism, and Nickelodeon, she describes the "tension between Nickelodeon's embrace of the girl power consumer market and its role as a producer of girl power ideology."[20] Writing before the release of *Avatar*, Banet-Weiser naturally does not take into account its position within this body of programming, however several of the series she references in her analysis—including *The Wild Thornberrys* (1998–2004) and *As Told By Ginger* (2000–6)—were broadcast either at or around the same time as *Avatar*.

According to Banet-Weiser, girl power programming, as part of the broader girl power movement of the 1990s and early 2000s, despite its sometimes contradictory representations, does function "as a kind of feminist politics" emerging out of Third Wave feminism.[21] Unpacking the tension between girl power ideology and commercial culture, she argues, "[G]irl power is not just a fad, although it is that; it is not just about empowerment, although it is that as well."[22] Issues emerging out of Third Wave feminism included a focus on visibility, representation and the concept of empowerment within popular culture. Ewan Kirkland summarizes:

> "Girl Power" constitutes an articulation of popular feminism that emerged in the mid 1990s, celebrating autonomy and self-determination, the exploitation of traditional signifiers of femininity, and a playfully confrontational attitude towards traditions considered sexist or repressive.[23]

This "playfully confrontational" attitude can be observed in *Avatar* and is something I will return to below. While girl power ideology celebrates representation and holds up the visibility of strong girls and women in the media as a sign of empowerment, a criticism of this movement is how it has played out through consumer culture. As Banet-Weiser asks, "Once feminism (as represented through girl power), becomes part of the mainstream it has traditionally challenged, can we still talk about it as political?"[24] Despite these contradictions between feminist politics, girl power ideology and consumer culture, Banet-Weiser argues that ultimately, this kind of programming on Nickelodeon represents "a kind of feminism, one that is fundamentally about tension and contradiction."[25] While Nickelodeon was an important girl power producer, the commercial interests of the company remained a key factor in the legitimizing and mainstreaming of these feminist ideologies. However:

> This does not mean that girl power television is not feminism; but it does mean that a significant component of Third Wave and girl power feminism is about media visibility ... Thus, the network itself speaks to its child audience in a mix of conflicting feminist voices.[26]

It is important to keep in mind these "conflicting feminist voices" in any textual analysis of gendered representations in animated children's media. I am not arguing that *Avatar* is wholly representative of girl power culture or that it was deliberately commissioned by Nickelodeon as girl power programming. I am arguing that the positive critical reactions to *Avatar*'s depiction of girl characters and its treatment of gender are in part due to the positive and progressive representations of its female characters, which are very much tied into the popular ideas about empowerment, self-determination, and media visibility outlined above. *Avatar* features several female characters who are depicted as both powerful and empowered and who are active participants in the events of the series. At the same time, the series maintains nuanced depictions of femininities and masculinities.

Gender in *Avatar*

Although there has been a general lack of scholarly works addressing gender in *Avatar*, there have been some useful analyses. In her study of the depiction of gender-stereotypical behaviors in *Avatar*, Megan E. Jackson finds that there is "no apparent relationship between the gender of the analyzed characters and gender-stereotypical behavioral traits."[27] This study was conducted via sampling forty-five characters across the first two seasons and performing a content analysis in order to measure gender-stereotypical behaviors ("feminine" and "masculine" traits) displayed by these characters, whether or not these characters were coded "male" or "female." Jackson's study is a productive overview of the ways the series rejects strict binaries when it comes to stereotypically "feminine" or "masculine" behaviors; for example, Jackson finds that the male characters display what may been considered stereotypically gendered feminine behaviors such as "tenderness" or "emotionality" on a similar level to female characters, while female characters are just as likely to display stereotypically masculine behaviors such as "assertiveness" and "leadership abilities."[28] To develop this kind of analysis further, I will perform a close reading of the character of Katara, highlighting key moments throughout her narrative and character development in order to demonstrate how she breaks down these kinds of binary understandings of gendered behaviors. First, I will discuss more broadly the ways the series establishes its attitudes toward gender through the representation offered by its female characters.

One of the most important ways the series establishes its positive treatment of women and girls is in the story of the Avatar themself. In the mythology of the series, the Avatar is reincarnated into the next nation in the cycle whenever they pass on. It is established early in Book One that who may become the Avatar is not restricted by gender. Although we get glimpses of Aang's past lives in "The Southern Air Temple" (S1E03), which suggests as much, this is confirmed in "The Warriors of Kyoshi," when Aang, Katara and Sokka visit Kyoshi Island in the Earth Kingdom, named for the former female Avatar. Aang even gestures to a statue of Avatar Kyoshi and tells a group of children, "Me in a past life!" prompting one of the children to respond, "You were pretty." This is a particularly significant episode as it not only confirms that the Avatar may be of any gender when reincarnated, but it establishes expectations and behaviors in the *Avatar* story world around gender. In doing so, it directly challenges what are considered, by girl power and feminist ideologies, sexist and regressive behaviors. This episode will be discussed in more detail in the next part.

Until the introduction of Toph and Azula in Book Two, Katara is the only primary female character in *Avatar*. By "primary character," I refer to a character who appears regularly across a majority of episodes and whose actions help drive the narrative forward. This is not to say that Katara is the only female character to appear in Book One. As noted in the introduction to this chapter, there are a number of women and girl characters who appear in either one-off or supporting roles throughout the series. Largely, the representation of female characters in *Avatar* is diverse; in the world of *Avatar*, women are benders, healers, leaders, mothers, and warriors. Women and girls in *Avatar* are not limited to being only "good" characters either, as is demonstrated through Azula, daughter of Fire Lord Ozai and one of the series primary antagonists. Azula is a firebending prodigy who also has the ability to manipulate lightning. Undeniably powerful, she is also shown to be cruel, ruthless, and cunning—in many ways, the opposite of Katara—and shows no kindness toward her outcast brother and uncle. Azula's closest allies, for a time, are Mai, a sullen yet skilled knife-thrower and daughter of a high-ranking Fire Nation lord, and Ty Lee, a cheerful circus performer and martial artist. Katara and Azula directly confront each other on multiple occasions.

As noted above, Perea writes that in first and second wave girl cartoons, characters are marked as girls in "a standardized feminine way."[29] In *Avatar*, Katara's gender is marked through dialogue—Sokka introduces her as his sister, and other characters use she/her pronouns—as well as through other visual signifiers such as her dress and hairstyling. It is important to remember that in animation, these signifiers are an inherent element of character design, rather than simply a costume that an actor puts on.[30] She wears her hair typically long and tied back in a ponytail, characteristic of the other women in her tribe. Her clothing is also typical of the other members of her tribe and is designed more for practicality and warmth than fashion. The clothes allow her to move easily and freely, which is particularly important given how crucial form and movement are to her waterbending.

Many of Katara's behaviors and actions throughout the series can be considered typical of teenager. She argues with her brother, she is sometimes stubborn, and occasionally makes rash decisions. For example, in "The Waterbending Scroll" (S1E09), Katara steals a scroll from a group of pirates when the three friends cannot afford to pay for it, leading to a dangerous pursuit. She also displays romantic interest in other characters. In "Jet" (S1E10) it is strongly implied that she has a crush on the titular leader of a group of rebel teenagers who use guerrilla tactics against the Fire Nation. In "The Fortune Teller" (S1E10), she is interested in finding out about her future love life and is told she will marry a "powerful bender." This episode also serves to establish Aang's crush on Katara, a recurring plot point throughout the series as we see their relationship develop, although Katara only sees him as a good friend in this episode. Indeed, throughout most of Book One, Katara's relationship with Aang quite nurturing; she is generally the most responsible of the group—less hot-headed than Sokka and not as easily distracted as Aang.

While all the female characters in *Avatar* are treated differently in terms of characterization, dress, and appearance, the contrast between Katara and Toph is the most obvious demonstration of the ways the series does not demarcate characters by specifically gendered traits. Their differences are also the most easily observable because they travel together in the same group with the Avatar, and as such are the two female characters who interact with each other most often. While both are Aang's teachers and his friend, Katara and Toph do not always agree and are often argumentative. While Toph was raised in a noble household—with "society manners," as she describes it in "City of Walls and Secrets" (S2E14)—she generally rejects "proper" manners and "ladylike" behaviors as a rebellious act. Her attitude sometimes puts her at odds with Katara, whom she even refers to as

"Madam Fussy-Britches" in "The Runaway" (S3E07). Nevertheless, Katara and Toph are good friends, and their arguments are usually quickly resolved. When Toph begins training Aang in earthbending in "Bitter Work" (S2E09), her direct and blunt approach differs to Katara's, who suggests that Aang responds better to positive reinforcement. Toph later uses this approach to help Aang break through his earthbending block. Katara asks, "You tried the positive reinforcement, didn't you?," with Toph responding, "I did. It worked wonders." In "The Tales of Ba Sing Se" (S2E14), Katara declares that she and Toph need a "girls day out" with the two visiting a spa together. They leave feeling "girly" and Katara even reassures Toph she is pretty after when they are made fun of by a group of "mean girls"—after the two have used their bending abilities to dump them in a river. Katara at times displays what may be described as an overt interest in her own appearance. However, although she occasionally demonstrates these "stereotypically feminine" behaviors, this does not lessen the complexity of her character. Characters such as Azula and Ty Lee also demonstrate these kinds of behaviors and interests. Indeed, Katara's male counterparts display an equal, if not more pronounced interest, in "shallow" matters—such as Sokka's interest in his appearance and love of shopping—as well as in matters of romance. Aang's feelings for Katara and their potential consequences, made apparent in "The Crossroads of Destiny" (S2E20), become a prominent plot point as the series progresses. Aang almost loses the ability to enter the Avatar State because he cannot give up his feelings for her. *Avatar* is demonstrative of a series where it is necessary and productive to conceptualize characters outside of strict gender binaries of "feminine" and "masculine" characteristics and stereotypes. In light of this, the following part examines some key moments in Book One that show how Katara's character development is demonstrative of *Avatar*'s attitude toward gender.

"Master Katara"

Katara is introduced alongside her brother Sokka in the series premiere, "The Boy in the Iceberg." As noted above, Katara is the first character we are introduced to in the world of *Avatar*; she narrates the Avatar's story, and it is her voice we hear at the beginning of each episode. In this first episode, Katara's opening narration serves to inform the audience of everything that has happened in her world and why the four nations are at war:

> Water … Earth … Fire … Air. My Grandmother used to tell me stories about the old days—a time of peace. When the Avatar kept balance between the Water Tribes, Earth Kingdom, Fire Nation, and Air Nomads. But that all changed when the Fire Nation attacked.

Through this voice over, we learn that the Avatar vanished from the world 100 years previously and that the Fire Nation is "nearing victory" in the war. We also learn that Katara's father and the men of her tribe have been away fighting in the war for the past two years, leaving Katara and her brother, Sokka, to look after the tribe. Considering that Katara is fourteen years old during this series, with Sokka being one year older at fifteen, this means Katara has been helping to look after her tribe since she was at least twelve. Katara's narration in this episode ends with, "I still believe that somehow the Avatar will return to save the world." In subsequent episodes, Katara's opening narration is a much shorter recap, recounting how she and Sokka discovered Aang trapped in ice. The narration now ends with her saying of Aang, "although his airbending skills are great, he has a lot to learn before he's ready to save anyone. But I believe Aang can save the world."

After Katara's initial opening narration in "The Boy in the Iceberg," we open on a sweeping shot of the waters of the South Pole. We soon focus on Katara and Sokka sitting back-to-back in a small boat, fishing amongst the icebergs. Sokka, who does not have the ability to waterbend, is using a fishing spear, and urges Katara to "watch and learn" while he catches a fish. Katara, noticing a shadow in the water, attempts to somewhat clumsily use her bending ability to lift a bubble of water enveloping a fish out of the ocean toward the boat. She excitedly calls out to Sokka, who is not paying attention, to see. When he raises his spear he bursts the bubble of water, splashing himself and losing Katara's fish in the process. This leads to an argument about Katara's waterbending, with Sokka declaring, "Why is it that every time *you* play with magic water, I get soaked?" When an annoyed Katara corrects him and tells him it is not "magic water" but waterbending, Sokka retorts, "If I had weird powers, I'd keep my weirdness to myself." Initially frustrated, Katara then smirks and implies that Sokka is the weird one for making muscles at his reflection in the water. This scene quickly establishes the kind of banter and rapport we can expect from the two siblings. After this short exchange the two are then suddenly caught in strange rip, which drags their boat out of control along a fast-moving current before it eventually smashes against the ice. Seemingly trapped on a small iceberg, Sokka sarcastically tells Katara she should have "waterbended us out of the ice" before further complaining, "I knew I should've left you at home. Leave it to a girl to screw things up." Furious, Katara starts to yell, "You are the most sexist, immature, nut-brained—Ah! I'm embarrassed to be related to you!" all the while angrily gesticulating, unknowingly bending the water and cracking the larger iceberg behind her. Her facial expressions are animated in such a way as to exaggerate her anger, with her eyebrows furrowed, eyes large, and teeth bared (see Figure 5.1). As the iceberg behind her finally breaks with a loud crash, the ice containing Aang emerges glowing from underwater. Spotting Aang encased within the ice and realizing he is alive, Katara rushes forward to help, ignoring her brother's warnings.

FIGURE 5.1 *Katara yells at Sokka. Still from "The Boy in the Iceberg" (S1E01). Blu-ray release of* Avatar: The Last Airbender—The Complete Series *(2018).*

This scene, and indeed this first episode, establishes several key details about Katara's character. First, it is established here how powerful Katara's bending is. She is amazed that she was able to cause such damage, while Sokka quips that she has gone from "weird to freakish." We also learn while she is yelling at Sokka that Katara has, for all intents and purposes, taken on the role of a mother while Sokka "plays soldier"; she does "all the work around camp," including washing all the clothes. In "The Serpent's Pass" (S2E12) it is even revealed that she helps her grandmother perform matriarchal duties, such as delivering babies. Katara will often fulfill or take up this "caregiver" role at various points throughout the series, something Sokka and Toph discuss in "The Runaway." While chastising Toph for recklessly running a series of money-making scams in a Fire Nation village, Toph accuses Katara of acting like a mother, to which Katara indignantly responds, "I don't act that way!" Later, Sokka tells Toph how after their mother's death, Katara is the one who stepped up and "helped fill the void that was left by our mom." Toph, who has a difficult relationship with her own mother and is a little younger than the others, admits, "The truth is, sometimes Katara does act motherly, but that's not always a bad thing. She's compassionate and kind, and she actually cares about me." Overhearing this, Katara decides to pull a scam with Toph, in an attempt to show her that "I can have fun too." Katara struggles throughout the series with the expectations of fulfilling this responsible, "motherly" role, while wanting to "have fun" the way the others do.

Part of Katara's excitement at finding Aang in "The Boy in the Iceberg" and realizing that he is also a bender—before she learns he is the Avatar—is that she feels she may have found someone who can help her with her own waterbending. When she asks him to do so, Aang asks if there are not any other waterbenders at the South Pole who can teach her, and she replies, "No. You're looking at the only waterbender in the whole South Pole." Aang then offers to take Katara to the North Pole and her sister tribe in order to find a Waterbending Master. After learning Aang is the Avatar, Katara is given her grandmother's blessing and encouragement to travel to the North Pole and help him on his journey in "The Avatar Returns" (S1E02). After rescuing Aang from Zuko's ship, Katara, Aang and Sokka set off for the North Pole together. This marks the first time we witness Katara using her waterbending powers in combat, as she freezes several Fire Nation soldiers to help her, Sokka and Aang escape on Appa, Aang's sky bison.

"The Warriors of Kyoshi" is the next episode in which the question of gender roles and representation comes to the forefront. When we first see Aang, Katara and Sokka in this episode, they are riding on Appa as they continue their journey to the North Pole in search of a Waterbending Master. Katara is sewing—mending a pair of her brother's pants—while Aang attempts to impress her with some airbending tricks. She absentmindedly tells him, "That's great, Aang," without looking up from her task. This prompts Sokka to say, "Stop bugging her airhead, you need to give girls space when they do their sewing." Looking up now, annoyed, Katara asks, "What does me being a girl have to do with sewing?" Sokka's dismissive reply is, "Simple. Girls are better at fixing pants than guys, and guys are better at hunting and fighting and stuff like that. It's just the natural order of things." Katara throws the unfinished pants at him, sarcastically proclaiming "Look what a great job I did." This scene establishes the primary conflict of the episode. Sokka is shown to be out of touch through his vocalization of a kind of ignorant, "everyday sexism" and the misguided belief that women and girls are better suited to stereotypical, "homely" tasks like sewing.

The three friends soon land on the island of Kyoshi, where they are promptly ambushed and captured. Sokka is surprised to learn that here the village warriors are all women and once again reacts in a rude and dismissive manner. Upon being faced with his captors, his first response is, "Who are you? Where are the men who ambushed us?," followed by, "There's no way a bunch of girls took us down." When Suki, the leader of the warriors, threatens to throw Sokka back in the ocean to be eaten by the monstrous Unagi, Katara speaks up, saying, "My brother didn't mean it, he's just an idiot sometimes." Upon realizing that they have arrived at Kyoshi, Aang is soon able to secure their release by proving his status as the Avatar. The warriors of Kyoshi model their dress and fighting style after the island's namesake, and the inhabitants lovingly care for the statue of her that stands in the center of their village.

Sokka spends much of the initial part of this episode sulking. When Aang asks him what is wrong and why he is not eating breakfast, Sokka simply says he is not hungry. Katara, however, observes that "He's just upset because a bunch of girls kicked his butt yesterday," prompting Sokka to storm off. Katara speaks here in a dry, teasing manner, reminiscent of previous examples of her banter with her brother. Her tone with Aang in this episode is different. Aang is being treated as a minor celebrity of sorts by the people of Kyoshi, while Katara tries to remain practical, warning him that they cannot stay in one place too long and not to let the attention go to his head. Of course, Aang *does* let the attention go to his head, and Katara's position as the more responsible member of the group is reiterated. For instance, when Aang spends his time playing and showing off for the village children, Katara is buying food and supplies for their journey, leading to an argument between the two. Aang later apologizes, and Katara jokingly calls him a "big jerk." She soon must use her waterbending to save him from the Unagi, which Aang has been attempting to ride as another means of showing off. Katara swims out into the bay to grab Aang and uses her bending to thrust the two out of the water away from the creature. She even uses her bending to pull water out of Aang's lungs, presumably saving him from drowning.

This episode takes on what Kirkland describes above as a "playfully confrontational attitude" toward outdated and sexist gender norms, that women cannot be warriors and are best suited to sewing, directly addressing gender-based prejudices. We can see this most clearly through Katara's sarcastic retorts, and through animated facial expressions. Katara is the first in this episode to immediately call out Sokka's behavior when he makes sexist remarks. Sokka, in turn, gradually learns to respect the skills and customs of the Kyoshi Warriors. The confrontational attitude, typical of girl power media, established for Katara in this episode remains consistent throughout the rest of *Avatar*. While Sokka does occasionally espouse certain outdated ideas around gender and girls throughout the series, he is usually shut down or rebuked by Katara, and later by Toph. For example, in "The Drill" (S2E13), when the group are attempting to stop a Fire Nation drill from breaking through the defenses of Earth Kingdom capital Ba Sing Se, Sokka yells at Katara to "Just bend the slurry, woman!," which prompts Katara to smack him by bending with mud.

"The Waterbending Master" is the last key episode I will turn to in detail, as it is the episode which rounds out Katara's narrative arc in Book One. Katara, Sokka and Aang finally arrive at the North Pole to find the Northern Water Tribe, where Aang and Katara intend to seek out a Waterbending

Master to train them. Master Pakku agrees to take on Aang as a student, with Aang telling him, "My friend and I can't wait to start training with you." However, when Pakku realizes that the friend in question is Katara, he bluntly tells them, "I think there's been a misunderstanding. You didn't tell me your friend was a girl. In our tribe it is forbidden for women to learn waterbending." Furious, Katara confronts him, "I didn't travel across the entire world so you could tell me no!" Katara learns that the women in the Northern Water Tribe are taught to use their waterbending to heal, a talent Katara has previously discovered she possesses in "The Deserter" (S1E16). In support of Katara, Aang declares he will not learn from Pakku either, but Katara convinces Aang that he must, putting the needs of the Avatar and the world ahead of her own. Her unhappiness is made clear, however, when she joins a healing lesson taught by Yagoda and surveys the group of young girls, who smile at her as she enters. It is in the healing lesson that the significance of Katara's relationship with her grandmother is revealed. After the healing lesson, Katara thanks Yagoda, who asks when she is getting married, gesturing to her necklace. Katara tells her that it was her grandmothers' necklace, which was passed down to Katara's mother, and now to her. Yagoda says she recognizes the carving, telling her that she is the spitting image of Kanna, Katara's grandmother. Katara discovers her grandmother was born in the Northern Water Tribe and was engaged to a young waterbender who carved her the necklace before she disappeared without any explanation.

Later, Katara confronts Pakku, who is refusing to instruct Aang any longer because Aang has been giving Katara lessons in secret. While initially willing to apologize for disrespecting the tribes' customs, when Pakku refers to her as "little girl" Katara instead declares she will not apologize. In her anger she throws her arms backwards, cracking the ice underfoot and smashing some jars of water, echoing her first fight with Sokka and the breaking of Aang's iceberg in episode one. She tells Pakku, "I'll be outside if you're man enough to fight me." When Sokka tells her she cannot win, she simply responds, "I know." When Aang tells her she does not have to do this for him, Katara tells him, "I'm not doing it for you." This marks the first time in Book One where Katara fights aggressively, for her own personal motivations, not just to help others or to escape the Fire Nation. It is also a departure from the previous "playfully confrontational" attitude that Katara has shown toward Sokka and others in previous episodes. She is direct with her anger and with her challenge toward what she perceives as an unfair and sexist system.

Katara's demonstration of anger may appear incongruous with her more nurturing qualities. However, it is *how* Katara uses and acts upon these feelings that demonstrates the nuance of her character. Her expression of anger ranges from annoyance—as shown in her interactions with Sokka— to rage—as seen in her encounters with members of the Fire Nation, especially in "The Southern Raiders" (S3E16). In many instances, this anger is portrayed as a natural response to a harm that has been committed against her or her friends, and she learns to better process and express these emotions throughout her journey. Jilly Boyce Kay and Sarah Banet-Weiser have discussed the differing attitudes and discourse surrounding women's (and feminist) anger, particularly regarding whether it can be considered politically productive as well as the role it might play in bringing about effective change.[31] In this particular instance, in her battle with Pakku, it is Katara's anger that drives her to directly challenge what she perceives as an unfair and unjust tradition that is preventing her from achieving her full potential as a waterbender.

Katara and Pakku fight, with Katara holding her ground. Pakku tells Katara he is impressed and that she is an excellent waterbender. The fight takes places in an extended sequence; full body shots of Katara highlight her form, her fluid movements mirroring Pakku's, while close-ups of her face convey her focus and concentration (see Figure 5.2). Similar close-ups of Pakku's face show us first, his condescension and later his surprise and even annoyance as he realizes that Katara is more skilled than he first anticipated. Katara is soon incapacitated, but here Pakku finally notices her necklace, which has fallen to the ground the fight. It is revealed that Pakku was the one who was betrothed Kanna. He tells Katara that Kanna was

FIGURE 5.2 *Katara runs into battle. Still from "The Waterbending Master" (S1E18). Blu-ray release of* Avatar: The Last Airbender—The Complete Series *(2018).*

the love of his life, and Katara realizes that Kanna left because it was an arranged marriage: "Gran-gran wouldn't let your tribe's stupid customs run her life; that's why she left."[32] Kanna, like her granddaughter, refused to be bound by a tradition that she did not agree with. The next time we see Master Pakku, he is teaching Aang once more, and teasingly chastises Katara for being late to the lesson. By the time Aang, Katara, and Sokka leave the Northern Water Tribe in search of an Earthbending Master to continue Aang's training, Pakku is acknowledging her as "Master Katara" and gifts her a unique water amulet with special properties. Aang will continue to learn to master waterbending from Katara throughout their journey.

The above three key episodes demonstrate a clear progression in Katara's narrative from self-taught waterbender, to Waterbending Master, as well as the ways *Avatar*'s attitudes toward gender overall. Alongside Toph, she is one of the two female benders who train Aang on his journey to master the four elements. She is shown multiple times throughout the series confronting outdated and regressive sexist behaviors either directly, or playfully, such as when she teases Sokka in response to his sarcastic quips. This is an example of an empowered girl character typical of the movement toward "girl power programming" prominent in the early 2000s. But Katara is also significant for the nuanced ways "traditional" notions of femininities and masculinities are played out through her actions and interactions with others. Katara is depicted as responsible, as a leader, and as a fighter, but she is also allowed to be emotional and displays traditionally feminine characteristics, such as kindness and emotionality. Overall, Katara's actions and behaviors are emblematic of an empowered girl character.

Conclusion

While *Avatar: The Last Airbender* is not an explicit example of "girl power programming" as described by Banet-Weiser, the series nevertheless demonstrates through characters like Katara examples of "empowered girl characters." In terms of characterization and narrative, it builds upon and extends the concept of the first and second wave "girl cartoons" of the 1980s and 1990s. *Avatar* can neither be classified as cartoon for "girls" or "boys," and through its ensemble cast and the series overall treatment of gender, may in fact be considered part of a "third wave" of cartoons that is not marketed along strict gender binaries. Its characters confront, both directly and indirectly, attitudes and behaviors that are considered sexist and outdated, with the series featuring women and girl characters in a variety of roles and with varying characterizations. Katara and others demonstrate a positive progression in the representation of female characters in children's cartoons; both male and female characters in the series are shown rejecting and complicating notions of binary gendered behaviors. In her opening narration, Katara states that she believes "Aang can save the world," but without characters like Katara—or Toph, or Suki—this is simply something that Aang would not have been able to achieve. While also performing a nurturing and supportive role, Katara's actions and behaviors serve to drive the action and further the narrative of *Avatar,* not just because of her desire to help Aang but because of her own desire to master waterbending and to help save the world. In "The Painted Lady" (S3E03), Katara says it best herself: "I will never, ever turn my back on people who need me."

Notes

1. Erica Bahrenburg, "The Ambitious Equality of *Avatar: The Last Airbender,*" *Film School Rejects*, June 29, 2016, https://www.filmschoolrejects.com/avatar-the-last-airbender-gender-equality-afecf02a8ae4/; Afiya Augustine, "*Avatar: The Last Airbender, The Legend of Korra*, and Their Assortment of Badass Women," *Syfy Wire*, April 9, 2019, https://www.syfy.com/syfywire/avatar-korra-bad-ass-female-characters.
2. Emma A. Jane, "'Gunter's a Woman?!'—Doing and Undoing Gender in Cartoon Network's Adventure Time," *Journal of Children and Media* 9.2 (2015): 232.
3. For more on this, see Ryanne Kap's chapter in this edited collection on the ways *Avatar* negotiates the trauma of imperialism.
4. Jane, 231.
5. Beth Hentges and Kim Case, "Gender Representation on Disney Channel, Cartoon Network, and Nickelodeon Broadcasts in the United States," *Journal of Children and Media* 7.3 (2013): 319–33; Maya Götz and Dafna Lemish, *Sexy Girls, Heroes and Funny Losers: Gender Representations in Children's TV around the World* (Peter Lang, 2012).
6. Paul Wells, *Understanding Animation* (Routledge, 1998), 187.
7. Amy Ratelle, "Animation and/as Children's Entertainment," in *The Animation Studies Reader*, eds. Nichola Dobson, Annabelle Honess Roe, Amy Ratelle and Caroline Ruddell (Bloomsbury Academic, 2019), 191.
8. Ibid., 191.
9. Ibid., 192.
10. Ibid., 192–3.
11. Ibid., 193.
12. Ibid., 194.
13. Ewan Kirkland, *Children's Media and Modernity: Film, Television and Digital Games* (Peter Lang, 2017), 135.
14. Ibid., 135.

15 Götz and Lemish, 9. For more on this subject, see: Douglas Schulz's chapter in this collection on social identity.
16 Katia Perea, "Girl Cartoons Second Wave: Transforming the Genre," *Animation: An Interdisciplinary Journal* 10.3 (2015): 190.
17 Ibid., 193.
18 Emilie Zaslow, *Feminism, Inc.: Coming of Age in Girl Power Media Culture* (Palgrave Macmillan, 2009), 3.
19 Sarah Banet-Weiser, "Girls Rule!: Gender, Feminism, and Nickelodeon," *Critical Studies in Media Communication* 21.2 (2004): 120.
20 Ibid., 121.
21 Ibid., 120.
22 Ibid.
23 Ewan Kirkland, "The Politics of Powerpuff: Putting the 'Girl' into 'Girl Power'," *Animation: An Interdisciplinary Journal* 5.1 (2010): 10.
24 Ibid., 122.
25 Ibid., 136.
26 Ibid..
27 Megan E. Jackson, "(Gender)Bending in the Animated Series *Avatar: The Last Airbender*," *Film Matters* 4.2 (Summer 2013): 15.
28 Ibid., 15.
29 Perea, 190.
30 See: Shuyin Yu's and Douglas Schulz's chapters in this volume for further discussions of the role of clothes and hairstyling in forming social identities in *Avatar*.
31 Jilly Boyce Kay and Sarah Banet-Weiser, "Feminist Anger and Feminist Respair," *Feminist Media Studies* 19.4 (2019): 603–9.
32 This plot line parallels that of Sokka and Princess Yue, who have fallen in love despite Yue's impending arranged marriage to a Northern Water Tribe warrior.

6

A Queer Relationship: Mapping *The Legend of Korra*'s Industrial Journey across Mediums

Emily Baulch and Oliver Eklund

The Legend of Korra (Nickelodeon, 2012–14; nick.com, 2014), the sequel to *Avatar: The Last Airbender* (Nickelodeon, 2005–8), started its life as an animated children's television series. *Korra* initially aired on the global, US-based children's cable television network Nickelodeon and on Nickelodeon's digital platform nick.com. *Korra* returned to the *Avatar* universe under the original showrunners Michael Dante DiMartino and Bryan Konietzko, picking up seventy years after the original series. The titular Korra is the new Avatar, the only individual in who can wield the power of all four elements and communicate with the Spirit World. This confrontational and headstrong young woman succeeds Aang, the previous male Avatar, who was easy-going and spiritual. *Korra*'s final episode, "The Last Stand" (S4E13), ended with a landmark scene. Two female characters, Korra and Asami, hold hands as they prepare for a journey into the Spirit World. The show's queer end was immediately lauded as "one of the most powerful, subversive shows" of 2014.[1] However, the pathway from *Avatar* to the end of *Korra* was far from straightforward, and the end of the television aspect of *Korra* heralded new developments for the franchise.

Korra ran for four seasons, compared to *Avatar*'s three, and comprised fifty-two episodes to *Avatar*'s sixty-one. The sequel series moved from cable television to emerging streaming technologies during its run. The premieres appeared on Nickelodeon and nick.com, with reruns on Nicktoons and eventual on-demand distribution on Netflix. After finishing its onscreen run,

Korra was adapted into comics. The *Turf Wars* comics, written by DiMartino and Konietzko, were published in three parts from 2017 to 2018 as the official continuation of *Korra*, with the trilogy republished as a graphic novel. *Turf Wars* is published by Dark Horse Comics, one of the largest independent comics publishers in the United States. The comics expand one of the landmark queer moments in children's television by focusing on the female-female relationship between Korra and the femme-fatale-turned-romantic-interest Asami. *Korra* spans across television, streaming platforms, comics, and graphic novels. How did such a complex cross-platform history come into being, what does it say about industrial perceptions of screen and print, and how did the mediums involved influence the depiction of the relationship between Korra and Asami?

Korra epitomizes the messy and conglomerated narrative world that stories exist in today. *Korra* and *Avatar* are the intellectual property of Viacom, a large media conglomerate, the parent brand of Nickelodeon. As such, *Korra* offers a rich opportunity to investigate how and why media industries use the increasing variety of distribution platforms at their disposal. In its transition from screen to print, *Korra* reveals that particular media are perceived as having specific attributes and can be used to package content in the most beneficial way to the owning corporation. Often, this benefit is monetary, but *Korra* also points to the importance of a brand maintaining status and identity for a broader audience.

Investigating industry motivations is often challenging, with little explicit information provided. Moreover, the motivations of corporations are nebulous. Konietzko notes this problem, explaining that when it came to depicting Korra and Asami's queer relationship, the creators "operated under this notion, another 'unwritten rule' that we would not be allowed to depict that in our show ... But as we got close to finishing the finale, the thought struck me, How do I know we can't openly depict that? No one ever explicitly said so."[2] Nickelodeon has a history of being different and supporting gender and inclusion across the 1990s and early 2000s through strategies around "girl power" and "gender neutrality."[3] So, why do these pressures coalesce around *Korra*, a property that, in some ways, is the culmination of earlier, progressive iterations of Nickelodeon's brand identity? To address this issue, we use a combination of testimony from the creators, corporation posts on social media, and industrial documents and logics. Various stakeholders are involved in the perceptions of what media can do and what audiences will accept—and what audiences desire to see. Many of these same stakeholders are also interested in creating narratives around what happened to *Korra* during its production.

The "queer relationship" describes both the corporation's approach to *Korra* and the in-universe relationship between Korra and Asami, with the two intertwined. "Queer" is used as an "elastic term that can mean many different things, but its essence is the general upending of normativity. Beyond demarking same-sex behavior, it is sometimes used as an umbrella term for the LGBTQ+ community."[4] Teasing apart some of the competing and conflicting narratives about *Korra*'s production highlights how Nickelodeon's internal policies, emerging distribution technologies, and changing social demands created a TV show that was, on one hand, innovative and progressive and, on the other, seems to have been pejoratively pushed aside. With a defiantly strong female-led and trail-blazing queer representation, is *Korra* a case study of industrial censorship or the product of the ever-expanding transmedial world?

Early *Korra* and Gender

Korra began with an in-built challenge; it was the sequel to a beloved children's franchise, set seventy years later. The new Avatar, Korra, is a reincarnation of Aang, the last airbender. By the nature of the story world's logic, that means that Aang must be killed off. *Korra* did return characters from the original series—some appeared as their older selves in mentor roles across the seasons, like Toph, Katara, and Fire Lord Zuko. Others in dreamlike sequences and flashbacks, like Sokka and Aang. *Korra* also followed the children of the original characters from *Avatar* and, in the process, showed that they and their parents were flawed. Moreover, *Korra*'s characters were slightly older and aimed at a more mature audience. Society, too, had advanced since *Avatar*, largely due to bending-led industrial change. Such an approach, like the one taken by the rebooted *Star Wars* sequel trilogy, risked alienating fans of the original. *Avatar* has an avid, multi-generational fandom that has been developing since 2005. In making brave yet controversial leaps forward in the narrative world of *Avatar*, *Korra* was from the outset the sort of franchise extensions that can threaten the "integrity of a treasured storyworld."[5] It is no surprise that *Korra*'s reception was nowhere near as smooth as the original series.

Korra's initial uphill battle amongst audiences was compounded by industrial difficulties, with distribution complicated by changing time slots and ultimately a move to online streaming. Season one of *Korra* began airing in April 2012 at 11 am on Saturdays—a prime slot for younger viewers of children's television. The premiere attracted 4.5 million viewers, with the first episode coming in as basic cable's top-ranked children's television show, the top animated program for the week, and the most-viewed Nickelodeon animated series premiere in three years. Season one's ratings were not as high as *Avatar*'s, which averaged 5.7 million viewers per episode.[6] Still, the numbers were good enough for Viacom to term *Korra* a "Nickelodeon programming highlight" in their annual report in 2012.[7]

After a positive first season, distribution challenges reared their head in season two. Across the second season, *Korra* aired in a new Friday night-timeslot, a more appropriate time given *Korra*'s increasingly adult themes. Once on Fridays, it moved from 7 pm to 8.30 pm to 8 pm. Moving to Friday nights, when *Avatar* originally aired, should have been a homecoming for *Korra* and the franchise. It was, however, confusing for audiences to track the show across changing timeslots. Viewers scrambled to follow *Korra* across the last-minute schedule changes. A controversial, complex, multipart storyline with a deeper exploration of the Spirit World offered further challenges with the audience.

Season three returned to a more action-oriented storyline, albeit one that dealt with Korra's mental health issues, but the damage to the viewership was done. The premiere attracted only 1.5 million viewers, a mere third of the show's initial first season premiere.[8] Season three only saw eight of the thirteen episodes aired, with episodes after "The Terror Within" (S3E08), the lowest-rated episode of the series, released digitally on Nickelodeon's nick.com portal.[9] With minimal marketing to advertise it, *Korra* was moved to the nick.com portal for episodes 9 to 13. Low ratings and higher audience engagement online were a reason highlighted by both Nickelodeon and the creators for the show's move off the Nickelodeon television channel.[10] Season four was not televised at all, only offered online.

Across this troubled distribution period, corporate documents from Viacom, the parent company of Nickelodeon, revealed little interest in *Korra*. After celebrating *Korra* in the 2012 Viacom annual report, neither the 2013 nor the 2014 report mention the show. However, Viacom continued to discuss the importance of the original *Avatar* series. In 2012, 2013, and 2014, the reports noted the importance of *Avatar* for Nickelodeon's sister channel, Nicktoons, describing Nicktoons as "a leading cartoon destination targeting boys and featuring signature franchises such as *Dragon Ball Z Kai* and *Avatar: The Last Airbender*."[11] Nicktoons was a best-hits channel for children's animation and aired reruns of *Korra*. *Avatar* continued to be celebrated internally and repackaged for audiences well after its initial run had finished and while *Korra* was on-screen for the first time.

"Boys" became a key phrase in the Nicktoons reports. In 2011, while *Korra* would have been in the production pipeline, the reports describe Nicktoons as a "leading cartoon destination targeting boys."[12] Nicktoons' emphasis on appealing to boys was a relatively newfound aspect of the Nickelodeon corporate strategy. Developing a "boy's" channel adhered to the most basic gendered marketing logics. It enabled Nickelodeon to segment children's television into easily understandable markets along gender lines, thereby reinforcing "dominant mythologies and practices of gender in an uncomplicated way."[13] *Avatar* continued to be mentioned in annual reports as part of the Nicktoons' gendered targeting until 2015, despite its final season finishing in 2008.[14]

Yet, it went against Nickelodeon's history of gender neutrality, an approach that treated all kids as kids. Gender neutrality was a different marketing strategy to other networks.[15] In 2002, Nickelodeon began broadcasting the then "Nicktoons Network" channel, which was billed as featuring "a wide variety of programming that have defined kids' and animation lovers' television for more than 10 years."[16] The focus on "kids" highlights Nickelodeon's gender-neutral approach at the time. The reports reverted to non-gendered language in 2016, two years after *Korra* finished airing, marketing Nicktoons for "kids" once again.[17]

Nickelodeon cultivated girl power before their gender neutrality focus in the 2000s. In the 1990s, Nickelodeon harnessed empowerment by creating strong female lead characters, "garnering the channel an industry and public reputation as a vanguard in challenging television stereotypes about girls."[18] More than just a reputation, the Nickelodeon brand was tied to its female protagonists, as "the gesture to be more explicitly inclusive of girls was certainly a visible and powerful way to mark Nickelodeon's difference."[19] *Korra* continued the tradition of assertive and defiant female leads in Nickelodeon shows like *Clarissa Explains It All* (1991–4), *As Told by Ginger* (2000–6), and *The Wild Thornberrys* (1998–2004). These shows had already "actively rejected the conventional industry wisdom that children's shows with girl leads could not be successful."[20] *Korra*'s test screenings further proved this established logic. Konietzko revealed that "Conventional TV wisdom has it that girls will watch shows about boys, but boys won't watch shows about girls. During test screenings, though, boys said they didn't care that Korra was a girl. They just said she was awesome."[21] The gender of *Korra*'s characters did not seem to be a problem with its audiences.

With a strong-willed action-oriented female lead who forcefully rejects patriarchal norms and control, *Korra* should have found a home at Nickelodeon. Korra first appears in "Welcome to Republic City" (S1E01) as a four-year-old smashing through a wall while yelling, "I am the Avatar! You gotta deal with it!" (see Figure 6.1). Korra breaks through the wall of the family home, breaking down the barriers of the domestic—and coded feminine—space. There is nothing subservient about Korra, even as a young child. Her non-conforming behavior and bald announcement, which brooks no debate and becomes part of her trademark stubbornness, challenges gender stereotypes. She is centered in the frame, lit by golden light flowing through the neat hole she just made in the wall. Arm punched into the air, Korra possesses none of Aang's hesitation. Korra quickly demonstrates mastery of three of the four elements, thereby proving herself the Avatar, even though her display is somewhat childish in its force. She shocks and drives back the three dubious old men who are there to check if she is, indeed, the Avatar. Their faces move from cynical to thunderstruck, cloaks ruffles, eyes-bulging, and glasses knocked askew in an animated demonstration of shock.

FIGURE 6.1 *Young Korra makes an entrance. Still from "Welcome to Republic City" (S1E01). Blu-ray release of* The Legend of Korra—Book One: Air *(2012).*

In-world, the men have "gotta deal with" Korra being the Avatar; however, the line takes aim at doubting executives and uncertain fans.

Advances in representation are not always linear. Nickelodeon's prior excursions into girl power in the 1990s should have seen *Korra* lauded at the network. Even the gender neutrality of the 2000s might have worked in *Korra*'s favor. Yet, at the time of *Korra*'s screening, the reports suggest the network was focused on creating a conventional male-orientated brand. *Korra* was, with its female-lead, manifestly out of step with that strategy, perhaps because of a perceived need to rebalance or pivot audiences and reduce risks. Or perhaps because girl power products had "shifted from a somewhat narrow marketing niche to a normalized generalized brand."[22] It is also possible that, at least in terms of gender, *Korra* had the misfortune of being the wrong show in the wrong place and time.[23]

Late *Korra* and Queerness

The final moment of *Korra* pushed the envelope on what was perceived as possible for diverse representations of sexuality in children's animated television. The show concluded its four-season run in 2014 with a deceptively simple moment: Korra and Asami held hands. In front of the portal to the Spirit World, which represents Korra's achievements in the series, Korra and Asami share a glance, join hands, and walk into the portal together (see Figure 6.2). The final shot of *Korra* is a single, continuous moment. It

FIGURE 6.2 *Korra and Asami hold hands as they enter the Spirt World. Still from "The Last Stand" (S4E13). Blu-ray release of* The Legend of Korra—Book Four: Balance *(2015).*

begins with a close-up of Korra and Asami's joined hands before panning out, so their bodies frame the shot and then moves to focus on their faces. Korra and Asami maintain eye contact, their body language concentrated on each other. It was a landmark moment for children's television and sent the show into uncharted territory for queer representation. Not only did it depict a queer relationship on animated children's television, but the show's main character was one of the parties in the relationship; rather than being relegated to a side character, queer identity was centralized. The quietly queer ending saw the show recognized for "breaking racial, sexual, and political ground," leading to show to become "the most badass, subversive show of 2014."[24]

Korra was subversive in numerous ways. Korra and Asami's relationship began to develop after five combined seasons of heteronormativity in the *Avatar* universe. Asami was introduced as a "femme-fatale," a seductive and beautiful young woman with her own agenda, complete with iconic red lips. The brothers, Mako and Bolin, rounded out the new Team Avatar and produced a dizzying number of love triangles across the series. Korra and Asami's relationship was instead built firmly on a sustained and compassionate friendship. "A Breath of Fresh Air" (S3E01) was an important turning point for Korra and Asami, in which they begin to bond over their shared ex boyfriend, Mako. By the end of the third season, "Venom of the Red Lotus" (S3E13), Asami tends to a traumatized and depressed Korra. She promises to be there for Korra if she needs her. The slow progress of the relationship between Korra and Asami retrospectively allows both characters to experiment with their sexuality and their relationship to evolve organically. *Korra* did not label Korra and Asami's sexuality and relationship, leaving their representation open to lesbian, bisexual, or pansexual readings.

While 2014 seems uncomfortably recent to be celebrating the arrival of diverse representations in mainstream Western screen media, it is worth remembering that Korra was one of the first queer main characters on children's television. Contextually, *Korra*'s ending predated same-sex marriage in a number of Western countries, such as the United States in 2015, Australia in 2017, and Northern Ireland in 2020. While queer content in animation already did exist at the time of *Korra*, particularly in anime and adult television, it is less apparent in mainstream animated children's television and rarely involved major characters. Since the end of *Korra*, queer relationships in animated children's television have become more widespread. Shows such as *Steven Universe* (Cartoon Network, 2013–19), *Adventure Time* (Cartoon Network, 2010–18), *Arthur* (PBS, 1996–2022), *She-Ra and the Princesses of Power* (Netflix, 2018–20), and others have followed suit with further representations of queer characters in major roles.

Many of the tensions and challenges which inhibited the depiction of "Korrasami" sadly remain. In March 2019, Alabama Public Television, a state network of the Public Broadcasting Service, banned the broadcast of the episode "Mr. Ratburn and the Someone Special" (S22E01a) of the children's television show *Arthur*. This episode featured a marriage between two male side characters.[25] While Nigel Ratburn was a recurring character, his husband was first introduced in this episode. The director of programming at APT, Mike McKenzie, stated that airing the episode would be a "violation of trust" because parents allow children to watch APT "without their supervision."[26] *Korra*'s queer ending—while less explicit—aired five years before the *Arthur* incident, and *Korra*'s queer relationship featured the main character.

While a milestone for queer representation in mainstream children's television, the full depiction of Korrasami primarily exists in subtext and through intertextuality. Korra and Asami's relationship is curtailed in a manner that never applied to the relationship between the original and much younger heterosexual couple, Katara and Aang, in *Avatar*. Aang and Katara kiss and discuss their feelings, yet such an overt display of affection between Korra and Asami never made it to the screen.

After the series finale, DiMartino wrote in a Tumblr post titled "Korrasami Confirmed" that the creators' "intention with the last scene was to make it as clear as possible that yes, Korra and Asami have romantic feelings for each other."[27] Handholding was, apparently, the clearest possible depiction of a romantic relationship that was possible for Korra and Asami on screen at that time. Likewise, Konietzko also posted "Korrasami is Canon" on Tumblr, explicitly stating that, while the creators had the network's "support … there was a limit to how far we could go."[28] Konietzko apologizes, writing, "I'm only sorry it took us so long to have this kind of representation in one of our stories."[29] His comment begs the question, why was there a limit? And whose limit was it?

The differing impetuses placed upon the people within cultural industries become apparent in the production of *Korra*, especially regarding the depictions of gender and queerness. As previously mentioned, Viacom is the parent corporation that owns the intellectual property of *Avatar* and *Korra*. The *Avatar* franchise is a way for Viacom to generate more capital, whether through further expansion and monetization, increased brand recognition, or stock value. The corporation is also unwilling to risk a loss of capital. To the network, protecting the trusted Nickelodeon brand was the most important activity. These gambles are often preconceived and sometimes self-fulfilling notions of what sells.

The cautious approach to risk and backlash is grounded in history. In 2005, Nickelodeon drew ire from conservative and homophobic groups after flagship Nick character SpongeBob SquarePants appearance in an educational video that encouraged diversity and inclusion and featured gay parents.[30] SpongeBob has continued to attract criticism from homophobic stakeholders given his diverse sexuality. The parents of children watching and the lobby groups claiming to represent parents are large, somewhat invisible stakeholders who control the purse strings.

Korrasami was a curtailed milestone, partly because it appeared on children's television and partly because it appeared on Nickelodeon. Television is conventionally understood as a "push" media, which delivers content to a passive audience.[31] Socially, there are political concerns about "television's power to corrupt children—through their commercialization, sexualisation or exposure to violent content."[32] Children's stories are often swathed in layers of censorship and controversy, whether on-screen or in print. Adults are the arbitrators of children's content, defining "what children should/should not be, or should/should not know."[33] Adults not only ensure that childhood is defined "by adults for adults" but also link childhood to "children's relationship to sexuality."[34] Children are presumed to be innocent, and sexuality transgresses that innocence, particularly female sexuality.[35] Transgressive sexuality is most often related to diverse representation.

The creators, who do not own the rights to *Avatar* and *Korra*, operate within this system, balancing their artistic work with their corporate responsibilities and audience demands. They need to collaborate with the network that owns the property and has the means to produce and distribute it. Jake Pitre summarizes the tension in the creator's role well, writing, "animators are working under constraints and limits on what they can get away with ... Animation is inherently artificial, wholly diegetic worlds that are only as representative as the artists choose them to be."[36] Handholding has subsequently been proved not to be the extent of animation's ability to produce queer content in children's television, but these perceived social and corporate restraints are barriers to progress. Fear of public disapprobation and backlash are balanced against brand name. Sometimes, as in the case of girl power, brands can capitalize and develop a reputation for progress; in other instances, it paralyzes them. The tension between diverse representation and conservatism reflects the battle between the different stakeholders, or even facing a single stakeholder, within the television industry ecosystem.

Korra into Print

Korra is unusual because it is a television sequel that migrates into comics and graphic novels, inverting the more commonly seen adaptation process of print-to-screen products. While Jan Baetens has drawn attention to "reverse" screen-to-print relationships through novelizations, such examples remain an exception to the rule.[37] *Korra* is exceptional even within this limited world of material that has moved from the screen to print because it is a continuation of the story, providing new content rather than a spin-off or tie-in as seen with the likes of *Star Wars*. In moving from screen to print, *Korra* demonstrates the increasing connections between print and screen. Synergizing content, where corporations repackage and cross-promote media, has been a common strategy of media behemoths since the 1990s.[38] In this chapter, we chronicle *Korra*'s journey across these mediums.

Comics were a preestablished pathway within the *Avatar* universe to continue the queer narrative of Korrasami. "Comics" is used as the umbrella term for the medium and the term for the smaller, flimsier paperback installments, while graphic novels refer to the larger hardcover versions. The higher production value in the material object of the graphic novel denotes a different status, a "gravitas" suggesting a "book-length, stand-alone narrative that demands attention and respect."[39] The graphic novel has led the comics incursions into bookstores and respectability. Transmediality began with mini tie-in comics, which filled in small gaps in the existing narrative, that came inside the covers of the *Avatar* DVDs. In May 2011, Dark Horse Comics published *Avatar: Relics* as part of Free Comic Book Day, an annual event that takes place on the first Saturday in May. The comics produced for Free Comic Book Day are typically short and are an easy way to test market reception to content. In 2011, the DVD mini-comics, *Relics*, and comics previously published in *Nickelodeon Magazine* were reproduced in the graphic novel anthology *Avatar: The Last Airbender—The Lost Adventures*, alongside over seventy new comics pages. It was the first move into less ephemeral comics material. *Avatar* received its first comics trilogy and graphic novel treatment, *The Promise*, in 2012. Nickelodeon had already market-tested comics as a medium and had a preestablished relationship with the publisher. Where *Avatar* laid the foundation for the move into comics and eventually picks up the television show's adventures, its move was more experimental. *Korra* comics begin with illustrations of the moment the television show closed on, showing a clear transition between one medium and the next.

Henry Jenkins, referring to *Buffy the Vampire Slayer* and *Battlestar Galactica*, argues that comics are a particularly appealing vehicle for transmediality because of their low production costs and consequently lower risk compared to other mediums.[40] In remonetizing the already-released comic trilogies as library editions, Nickelodeon maximized the potential financial gain of comics. Maintaining avid audiences and providing them with additional content is a lucrative and pragmatic marketing decision, particularly when it operates in tandem with the rest of the brand image. Lower risk, lower cost, quicker output, and maximized income are all financial benefits of comics. The *Turf Wars* trilogy was completed in fourteen months, taking less than two years to produce the three comics and the graphic novel. The next *Korra* comics trilogy, *Ruins of the Empire*, began publication with *Part One* in May 2019, with *Part Two* released in November 2019 and *Part Three* in February 2020, an even faster turn-around-time than *Turf Wars*. In some eyes, the speed of production may equate to lower-quality products and make the comics "junk material," easily produced and easily consumed for an undiscriminating audience. However, it also makes comics a more industrially appealing and accessible medium compared to more time-consuming and restrictive adaptations, tie-ins, and spin-offs like novelizations.

The lower risk of comics counterbalances the controversy surrounding many children's picture books and young adult graphic novels with LGBTQ+ content. In 2018, the comic book anthology *Love Is Love* (2016), edited by Marc Andreyko, was banned for its queer content in a Texan high school in the United States.[41] The graphic novel *Drama* (2012) is centered around a diverse group of students in a middle school drama production. In 2014, *Drama* was listed in the American Library Association's top ten most challenged books, moving up the ranks to number two by 2016 and continuing to appear in 2017 and 2018. In 2019, *Drama* was removed from the shelves of elementary schools in Ottawa, Canada.[42] Comics, like animation are often perceived as a children's medium, and thus are subject to much closer scrutiny.

Queer comics is the "fastest-growing area in comics," yet adult gatekeepers, like parents, teachers, and librarians, continue to guard children's and young adult books.[43] Comics are not free from censorship and backlash but stumbling upon queer content in comics is harder to do than passively consuming content broadcast into the living room. In media studies, different qualities are associated with particular mediums. In contrast to the "push" medium of broadcast television, comics fall under the category of "pull" media which require their consumers to demonstrate "an active interest in seeking out information."[44] The active purchase of the *Korra* comics allows parents to censor the content that reaches their children. Children watching television may passively consume queer content that parents could deem inappropriate. Parents can act as gatekeepers with comics more explicitly than with television. The expansion of Korrasami in comics was a limited victory for queer representation. It coded the mainstream children's television medium as heteronormative and comics as queer, marginalizing queer content.

While lowering risk, *Korra*'s strategic move into comics also leveraged the popularity of Korrasami and the growing interest in female superhero comics. Comics provided an avenue for maintaining the female audience, while the channel was free to focus on boys. Girls' comics are currently one of the fastest-growing segments of the comic book industry. In 2017, the year that the first installment *Turf Wars* was published, Hillary Chute noted that "in the graphic novel world, girls are the new superheroes" and particularly, "in independent comics, pairs of girls."[45] Prior industrial reports suggest a corresponding growth in female readerships. *Publishers Weekly* reported that 20 percent of new comics readers in 2013 were women aged between seventeen and twenty-six, bucking the stereotype of only men and children reading comics.[46] In 2014, women accounted for approximately 46 percent of comics readers in the United States.[47] Since the 1990s, Nickelodeon has exploited the commercial market of girl power and produced girl power content, attracting large audiences of pre-adolescent and adolescent girls.[48] The audience had already been conditioned to follow *Korra* through its moves across television and streaming. *Korra* occupies a specific niche within comics: a female-led, independently published piece of LGBTQ+ content, starring a pair of young women, which responds to the growing female demographic of comics readers and audience of *Korra* fans Nickelodeon already had.

Korrasami truly came into its own in the *Turf Wars* comics, published from 2017 to 2018. *Part One* depicts Korra and Asami's relationship openly, removing the ambiguity present at the ending of the Nickelodeon television show. The comics open with panels of Korra and Asami surrounded by yellow light holding hands, the same scene with which the television show ended, demonstrating the intention to pick up and expand Korra and Asami's relationship.[49] The long-awaited kiss between Korra and Asami occurs within the first nine pages.[50] The kiss itself is given room, its panel uninterrupted by dialogue and spanning the full width of the page. The queer content of *Turf Wars* extends beyond displays of affection. Korra comes out to her family, and her supportive father warns her that "not everyone will be so accepting" of her sexuality.[51] The coming-out narrative opens the opportunity to represent queer experiences; however, there remains somewhat of a closed-door mindset to queerness within the world the comics create.

Before Korrasami, the *Avatar* franchise had no visible sexual diversity. Every on-screen relationship and crush between the young characters were depicted as specifically and unambiguously heterosexual. Aang and Katara constituted one relationship; Toph had a crush on Sokka; Suki and Princess Yue also had relationships with Sokka. The comics provide the diversity missing in the *Avatar* universe. In *Part One*, Kya, Aang and Katara's daughter, recalls her holiday with her "first girlfriend" to Korra and Asami.[52] Kya explains that the Water Tribe "like[s] to keep family matters **private.**"[53] Kya provides further exposition on the hereto unspoken history of sexuality in the *Avatar* universe. Avatar Kyoshi, who "loved men and women," failed to bring acceptance to the four nations.[54] The Fire Nation was "tolerant" until the despotic Lord Sozin decreed that same-sex relationships were "criminal."[55] The accompanying panel depicts two women being escorted from their home by guards. The Air Nomads, and thus Aang, "were accepting of differences and embraced everyone, no matter their orientation."[56] Asami and Korra wonder whether they will be able to find acceptance.[57] The section is a neat way to deal with the lack of diversity in the universe, writing it back in under the convenient guise of the evilness of the Fire Nation and the destruction of the Air Nomads. Its lack of labeling lends fluidity to the sexuality of the universe. It also constructs sexuality within cultural constraints and acknowledges the continuing challenges of coming out—assumedly relating to its young adult readers. It is somewhat heavy-handed and moves responsibility from the real world to the text, but it does increase the cast of queer characters in the world, including Aang and Katara's own daughter, and tries to normalize the relationships it had previously marginalized.

In *Part Three*, published in 2018, Korra and Asami declare their mutual love, before holding each other on a balcony, much like Aang and Katara's similar romance scene in the original *Avatar* series.[58] With "different media attract[ing] different market niches," what was potentially too sexually subversive to depict on children's broadcast television was possible to depict in comics.[59] Narrative forms increasingly coexist, co-create, and complement each other. The queer content of comics complements the screen text. Without the screen, Korra and Asami's relationship would not have developed at all. However, the screen was limited to subtext, while the comics provided unambiguous displays of affection without the hangover of the "unwritten rule." The two mediums operate in tandem to produce queer content. Without the comics, or indeed, the social media intervention by the creators, Korrasami would never have been fully realized. However, whether Korrasami could have been depicted further on-screen and if Nickelodeon used comics to hide the content remains questionable.

Korra speaks to an era of sprawling franchises, where corporations have a plethora of mediums at their disposal and audiences who are trained to follow the content across platforms in accordance with participatory culture.

Transmedial products, like *Korra*, necessitate the "move away from medium-specific models ... to think across media platforms and to understand how they are interacting with each other in ever more complex ways."[60] *Korra* reveals that particular media are perceived as having particular attributes and can be used to package content in the most beneficial way to the owning corporation. Viacom's continued interest in *Korra* and the *Avatar* universe emphasizes the industrial reality of mediums; media are not separate in the eyes of corporations but are instead extensions of licenses and revenue, which operate to serve different commercial purposes.

Modern *Korra*

In response to the tensions surrounding queer content in the landscape of children's television, Nickelodeon has associated itself with Korrasami when it suits their commercial purposes. During 2018 Pride Month, Nickelodeon posted a picture of Korra and Asami kissing on their social media accounts for Tumblr, Facebook, and Twitter. The Twitter caption reads, "We're proud to celebrate one of our favorite LGBTQ+ couples this #Pride Month, Korrasami!"[61] Nickelodeon's public support of LGBTQ+ content still wavers according to corporate imperatives and the specific audience being alluded to at any one time.

While queer media is essential for diverse representation, it is possible to misuse it. "Rainbow-washing," otherwise known as "rainbow capitalism" and "pink washing," monetizes inclusivity and remarkets it as an exploitative practice. According to Aurea Falco and Sanjana Gandhi, rainbow-washing "connotes the practice of businesses creating products specifically marketed towards the queer community, in order to capitalize off and leverage their purchasing power" and is an attempt to be seen as "progressive, modern and tolerant."[62] Nickelodeon is reselling Pride back to the Pride community to capitalize on the purchasing power of the LGBTQ+ community. @NickAnimation's post directly targets the Pride community with the hashtag #Pride Month and the rainbow flag in the background of Korra and Asami kissing. The image reimagines Nickelodeon's relationship with *Korra* through a pinkwashed lens. The "unwritten rule" of limited affection between Korra and Asami no longer applies. With growing mainstream support for the LGBTQ+ community, the "corporate incentive of brands and companies to position themselves in sync [with] that ... sentiment" increases.[63] Nickelodeon's Korrasami marketing attempts to capitalize upon the social power of Pride Month but risks reducing the progressive power of Pride to marketing signifiers in the process.

While Nickelodeon's logo is on the spines of *Turf Wars*, it only appears on the back cover of their new 2019 LGBTQ+ *Avatar* universe novel, *The*

Rise of Kyoshi, written by F. C. Yee. The titular Kyoshi is a prior, explicitly bisexual Avatar. *The Rise of Kyoshi*'s monetization of the niche fanbase and simultaneous distancing from the Nickelodeon logo demonstrate that Viacom remains cautious about producing queer content. Print products offer a vehicle for queer content, while the mainstream television network can maintain a more conservative brand identity. The mediums serve different purposes, coexisting, complementing, and contrasting with each other to engage the attention of different niches.

While children's cable television enjoyed early success, encouraging parents to subscribe to cable television, challenges from subscription video-on-demand (SVOD) platforms with extensive investment in children's content, and from the glut of children's targeted content on YouTube, have damaged the ability of children's cable channels to reach their once mass audiences. Netflix gained the global streaming rights to *Avatar* and *Korra* in 2020, with both series arriving on the portal to great fanfare and exposing the content to new audiences. From 2010–19, Nickelodeon has lost 60 percent of its children's audience, often to services like Netflix.[64] ViacomCBS, the new conglomerate owner of Nickelodeon, is looking to original content offerings from Nickelodeon as draw cards for their rebranded SVOD service Paramount+. As such, *Avatar* and *Korra* will leave Netflix and become part of the Paramount+ lineup, with the *Avatar* universe receiving a new lease on life through evolutions in distribution. In February 2021, Paramount+ announced the launch of Avatar Studios, a production company headed by the original *Avatar* creators that would work on expanding the universe, with *Avatar*, and perhaps *Korra*'s, lineage continuing to impact upon the contemporary landscape.

Conclusion

Korra was a landmark television series, heralding in a new era of female-led animated action and queer representation, which best used new technologies as they emerged. *Korra* also saw female-led cartoons and queer representation shunted into streaming, hidden out of sight, censored, and marginalized, the network ashamed of celebrating its own achievements in representation. Both narratives about *Korra* are true—and both narratives hold a little bit of spin and myth. The narratives surrounding *Korra* are developed by fans—both for and against Korrasami, the creators, and the studios.

In between the dual narratives, we can read a changing society. *Korra* is born into a time of chaos, where ideas in industry and society are unstable. Unlike *Avatar*, there were more options for exploring the content of *Korra* than ever before. Cynically, we might say that moving *Korra* onto the nick.com platform pulled it from air and preemptively prevented the outcry of conservative parents who, unassumingly, broadcast queer content into their homes. However, there may also be some honor in moving to the nick.com platform; it was the corporation's homesite, after all, and the latest technology. Evolving social ideas about censorship and representation hover in the background of the *Korra* case study. What can children's television portray? Does children's television have a moral obligation to be diverse? The variety of industrial and social forces in play during the development and distribution of *Korra* highlights the nonhomogeneous nature of even the largest media corporation. Different stakeholders wanted different things for *Korra* and the Nickelodeon brand. *Korra* is part of the history of the development of queer representation and, as much of progressive history, is often two steps forward and one step back. Since *Korra*'s time on-air, we seem to have stepped forward.

Notes

1 Joanna Robinson, "How a Nickelodeon Cartoon Became One of the Most Powerful, Subversive Shows of 2014," *Vanity Fair*, December 19, 2014, https://www.vanityfair.com/hollywood/2014/12/korra-series-finale-recap-gay-asami.

2 Bryan Konietzko, "Korrasami Is Canon.," *Tumblr*, December 22, 2014, https://bryankonietzko.tumblr.com/post/105916338157/korrasami-is-canon-you-can-celebrate-it-embrace.

3 Sarah Banet-Weiser, *Kids Rule: Nickelodeon and Consumer Citizenship* (Duke University Press, 2007), 123–4.

4 Jake Pitre, "Queer Transformation, Contested Authorship, and Fluid Fandom," in *Representation in Steven Universe*, eds. John R. Ziegler and Leah Richards (Palgrave Macmillan, 2020), 21.

5 Marie-Laure Ryan, "Transmedia Storytelling as Narrative Practice," in *The Oxford Handbook of Adaptation Studies*, ed. Thomas Leitch (Oxford University Press, 2017), 531.

6 Chris Arrant, "*The Legend of Korra* Draws 4.5 Million Viewers, Ranks as Basic Cable's Number-One Kids' Show and the Top Animated Show for the Week," *CartoonBrew*, April 18, 2012, https://www.cartoonbrew.com/biz/the-legend-of-korra-draws-4-5-million-viewers-ranks-as-basic-cables-number-one-kids-show-and-the-top-animated-series-for-the-week-61223.html.

7 Viacom Inc., 2012 Annual Report, 7.

8 Mitchel Clow, "'The Legend of Korra' Season 3 Hits Lowest Premiere Rating of the Series," *Hypable*, June 30, 2014, https://www.hypable.com/the-legend-of-korra-season-3-premiere-low-rating/.

9 "Korra Season 3 Moves to Digital after Being Pulled from TV; Co-Creators Bryan Konietzko and Michael DiMartino Explain Why," *Venture Capital Post*,

August 16, 2014, https://www.vcpost.com/articles/25584/20140816/korra-season-3-digital-pulled-tv-co-creators.htm.

10 Jared Larson, "SDCC 2014: Nickelodeon Pulls Upcoming Legend of Korra Episodes," *IGN*, July 24, 2014, https://au.ign.com/articles/2014/07/24/nickelodeon-pulls-upcoming-legend-of-korra-episodes.
11 Viacom, 2012, 8.
12 Ibid., 8.
13 Banet-Weiser, 109–10.
14 Viacom Inc., 2015 Annual Report, 8.
15 Banet-Weiser, 123.
16 Viacom Inc., 2006 Annual Report, 8.
17 Viacom Inc., 2016 Annual Report, 10.
18 Banet-Weiser, 104–5.
19 Ibid., 138.
20 Ibid., 105.
21 Neda Ulaby, "'Airbender' Creators Reclaim Their World in 'Korra'," *NPR*, April 13, 2012, https://www.npr.org/2012/04/13/150566153/airbender-creators-reclaim-their-world-in-korra.
22 Banet-Weiser, 138.
23 For more on the Nickelodeon brand image and shows the violated it—notably, *The Ren & Stimpy Show* (Nickelodeon, 1991–5; MTV, 1996)—see: Kevin S. Sandler, "'A Kid's Gotta Do What a Kids Gotta Do': Branding the Nickelodeon Experience," in *Nickelodeon Nation: The History, Politics, and Economics of America's Only TV Channel for Kids*, ed. Heather Hendershot (New York University Press, 2004), 45–68.
24 J. Robinson.
25 Janelle Griffith, "Alabama Public Television Refuses to Air 'Arthur' Episode with Gay Wedding," *CNBC*, May 21, 2019, https://www.cnbc.com/2019/05/21/alabama-public-television-refuses-to-air-arthur-gay-wedding-episode.html.
26 Ibid.
27 Michael Dante DiMartino, "Korrasami Confirmed," *Tumblr*, December 22, 2014, https://michaeldantedimartino.tumblr.com/post/105916326500/korrasami-confirmed-now-that-korra-and-asamis.
28 Konietzko.
29 Ibid.
30 Banet-Weiser, 1.
31 Henry Jenkins, *Convergence Culture: Where Old and New Media Collide* (New York University Press, 2006), 213.
32 Anna Potter, "Regulating Contemporary Children's Television: How Digitisation Is Re-shaping Compliance Norms and Production Practices," *Medias International Australia* 163.1 (2017): 21.

33 Kerry H. Robinson, "Making the Invisible Visible: Gay and Lesbian Issues in Early Childhood Education," *Contemporary Issues in Early Childhood* 3.3 (2002): 419.
34 Ibid., 419.
35 Banet-Weiser, 108.
36 Pitre, 23.
37 Jan Baetens, "From Screen to Text: Novelization, the Hidden Continent," in *The Cambridge Companion to Literature on Screen*, eds. Deborah Cartmell and Imelda Whelehan (Cambridge University Press, 2007), 226–38.
38 Sandler, 52.
39 Justin Hall, "The Secret Origins of LGBTQ Graphic Novels," in *The Cambridge History of the Graphic Novel*, eds. Jans Baetens, Hugo Frey and Stephen E. Tabachnick (Cambridge University Press, 2018), 287.
40 Henry Jenkins, "'We Had So Many Stories to Tell': The Heroes Comics as Transmedia Storytelling," *Confessions of an Aca-Fan*, December 3, 2007, http://henryjenkins.org/blog/2007/12/we_had_so_many_stories_to_tell.html.
41 Taylor Henderson, "Comic Book Honoring Pulse Banned at School for 'Extreme Homosexuality'," *Pride*, July 17, 2019, https://www.pride.com/geek/2019/7/17/comic-book-honoring-pulse-banned-school-extreme-homosexuality.
42 Patricia Mastricolo, "*Drama* Survives Ban in Ottawa Catholic Schools," *Comic Book Legal Defense Fund*, January 17, 2019, http://cbldf.org/2019/01/drama-survives-ban-ottawa-catholic-school/.
43 Hillary Chute, *Why Comics? From Underground to Everywhere* (Harper Collins, 2017), 236.
44 Jenkins, *Convergence*, 213.
45 Chute, 188.
46 Shannon O'Leary, "Despite Early Sales Slump, Comics Retailers Remain Upbeat," *Publishers Weekly*, March 21, 2014, https://www.publishersweekly.com/pw/by-topic/industry-news/comics/article/61533-despite-early-sales-slump-comics-retailers-remain-upbeat.html.
47 Brett Schenker, "Market Research Says 46.67% of Comic Fans Are Female," *The Beat: The Blog of Comics Culture*, May 2, 2014, https://www.comicsbeat.com/market-research-says-46-female-comic-fans/.
48 Banet-Weiser, 106.
49 Michael Dante DiMartino, *The Legend of Korra—Turf Wars Part One* (Dark Horse Books, 2017), 5.
50 Ibid., 13.
51 Ibid., 20.
52 Ibid., 54.
53 Ibid., 55. Bold in the original.
54 Ibid., 56.

55 Ibid., 56.
56 Ibid., 55.
57 Ibid., 57.
58 Michael Dante DiMartino, *The Legend of Korra—Turf Wars Part Three* (Dark Horse Books, 2018), 76.
59 Jenkins, *Convergence*, 96.
60 Henry Jenkins, "Transmedia Storytelling and Entertainment: An Annotated Syllabus," *Continuum: Journal of Media and Cultural Studies* 24.6 (2010): 943.
61 Nickelodeon Animation (@NickAnimation), Twitter Post, June 29, 2018, 9:00 AM, https://twitter.com/nickanimation/status/1012697284591616000?lang=en.
62 Aurea Falco and Sanjana Gandhi, "The Rainbow Business," *Eidos* 9.1 (2020): 104–5.
63 Alex Abad-Santos, "How LGBTQ Pride Month Became a Branded Holiday," *Vox*, June 25, 2018, https://www.vox.com/2018/6/25/17476850/pride-month-lgbtq-corporate-explained.
64 Meg James, "Nickelodeon Once Ruled Kids TV. Can It Make a Comeback?," *Los Angeles Times*, November 15, 2019, https://www.latimes.com/entertainment-arts/business/story/2019-11-15/nickelodeon-brian-robbins-viacom-awesomeness.

7

Material-Spiritual Bodies: Posthuman Performativity of Avatars

Şafak Horzum and Süleyman Bölükbaş

In "The Guru" (*Avatar* S2E19), Aang's spiritual guide Guru Pathik exclaims: "The greatest illusion of this world is the illusion of separation. Things you think are separate and different are actually one and the same." To expose this illusion and convey an alternative perspective to the non-exclusionary becomings of Avatars in the franchise, we propose employing a recent philosophical approach, posthumanism, for a non-binary comprehension of Wan's, Aang's, and Korra's performances. Posthumanism, having emerged in the late 1980s and early 1990s, interrogates the alleged human superiority that was constantly given a disproportionate emphasis and legitimacy in the Western schools of thought since the Enlightenment. Such an interrogation became imperative especially after the long reign of humanism that dictated the supremacy of the human over its others and thus made use of all these others—be that animal, vegetative, material, or cybernetic—for the human's sake. In a broad sense, then, blurring the distinctions between Cartesian dualities such as mind/body, good/evil, and discourse/matter, posthumanism wonders for us all: "What is human?" In an attempt to answer this question, Pramod K. Nayar explains that "those features we take to be uniquely human—altruism, consciousness, language—are also properties exhibited by animals," referring to the proofs by biologists, zoologists, and cognitive ethologists.[1] Unable to define the human, these features cannot place the human subject above its nonhuman others, because the human is not the sole actor shaping and giving meaning to natural-cultural phenomena and whatever surrounds it. As the agency of the human is only one kind among innumerable nonhuman agencies shaping the universe, the human in the posthumanist thought has been reconfigured as a post-exclusive, post-central, and post-exceptional being.[2] For this reason, Donna J. Haraway manifests that "we have never been human," saluting Bruno Latour's famous monograph.[3] We have always been posthuman, taking into account our entanglements with several nonhuman bodies from "ecto-parasites in the hair follicles to the microbiota in the gut flora."[4]

Invalidating René Descartes's principle of "I think, therefore I am/*cognito erso sum*," posthumanist scholars have rejected the distinction between the thinking substance (mind) and the extended substance (body), arguing that mind-based Cartesian thinking amplifies binarism and provokes cognates of discrimination like sexism, racism, and speciesism.[5] They have provided a corrective to mind-centric binary oppositions, introducing materiality and nonhuman corporeal agency into the field. These new materialist and posthumanist thinkers denounce the anthropocentric ideal of subjectivity based on reason, and they argue that all the beings—be they organic or inorganic, biotic or abiotic—are dependent on their material parts, their bodies. Matter—that is, body—remains a "mesh" of tangled strings and knots made up of countless non/humans.[6] Thus, "matter matters."[7] The nonhuman and matter, in all their multiplicities, is not a "mere backdrop to what really matters"[8] to the human. "Matter is substance in its iterative intra-active becoming—not a thing, but a doing, a congealing of agency," as Karen Barad extensively discusses.[9] Not merely a linguistic or cultural construct, matter "is morphologically active, responsive, generative, articulate, and alive. Mattering is the ongoing differentiating of the world. Matter," Barad continues, "plays an agentive role in its ongoing materialization. Physical matters, matters of fact, matters of concern, matters of care, matters of justice, are not separable."[10] In this posthuman materialism, one organism or body is not superior to another since posthumanist philosophy is aware that all beings or bodies are connected to one another and built upon, as Gilles Deleuze and Félix Guattari would remind us, a thousand plateaus of relationalities and agencies since the very beginnings of existence.[11]

From the vantage of this posthumanist flat ontology, subjects in *Avatar: The Last Airbender* (Nickelodeon, 2005–8) and its sequel *The Legend of Korra* (Nickelodeon, 2012–14; nick.com, 2014) reflect the posthuman union of body and mind/spirit in the animated-realism of its imaginary world. Emphatically repeated throughout the series as well as in its official and fan sequels, inhabitants of the *Avatar* universe cannot live in mere binarism since such a separation leads only to a sort of tribalism and, hence, a distorted reality of imbalance both in a subject's personality and all around the universe. Even after Avatar Wan separates the physical and spiritual worlds due to the conflicts between the two in "Beginnings, Part 2" (*Korra* S2E08), two worlds of humans and spirits can only be situated in their intersectional conditions but not in their artificial separation. Enthused by this intersectionality in the *Avatar* universe, this chapter will explore how the union of two opposing sides, the physical and the spiritual worlds, tells the stories of mutual becomings. Underlining the story-telling capacities of the material-spiritual bodies within the animation's embrace of realities, fantasies, and im/possible existences, we will discuss the Avatars, bridges between the two worlds, as the illustrations of posthumanist performativities of human and nonhuman agencies at work. In doing so, we aim to show that the human-nonhuman relationality does not necessarily have to be a hierarchical structure positioning humans superior to all other beings. Since "nonhuman actors and supernaturally flexible bodies" such as spirits play "a prominent role" in this television series, we believe this franchise stands out as one apt manifestation of posthumanist performances.[12] Ideally, the relational performances to be discussed should align all the be(com)ings in their differences and multiplicities on a horizontal axis, as shown in the second Harmonic Convergence, which we will discuss in detail below (see Figure 7.1).

FIGURE 7.1 *The horizontal alignment of drawings, lights, and designs in the second Harmonic Convergence. Still from "Harmonic Convergence" (S2E12). Blu-ray release of* The Legend of Korra—Book Two: Spirits *(2014).*

Embodiment of Posthuman Performativity: Wan

While we think of the Avatar as the embodiment of posthuman performativity due to its harboring a human body and a nonhuman spirit within one form of existence, we also argue that the *Avatar* franchise has created its own historical folklore within the boundaries of its fantastic fictionality. This is why we follow a chronological timeline of the events in our analysis from Wan to Korra. In "Beginnings, Part 1" (*Korra* S2E07), Wan is introduced as an outcast who can tenderly share his food with nonhuman animals despite his limited means. As an othered human in close relations with other social pariahs—especially Yao, who was once possessed by a tree spirit and transformed into a hybrid being—Wan carried the common anthropocentric prejudice against the spirits after he learned to bend the element of fire. For Wan, the spirits were the "absolutely other," or *arrivant* in Jacques Derrida's conceptualization, that which is beyond his expectation and comprehension.[13] Spirits were unknowable to him before their several encounters and communications. Therefore, his attempt to enter the spirit oasis and to save Mula—a cat-deer, Wan's future hybrid animal companion—in the Spirit Wilds enabled two apparently antagonistic sides to transform each other into the familiar, the known. They and their intentions were exposed to one another and, hence, their absolute otherness dissolved in this process of familiarization. This process is noteworthy because the *Avatar* franchise presents its core idea of the horizontal alignment of non/human beings regardless of the elevation of human-centric values. In the same episode, Wan, as an example of this alignment, is named as "Stinky" by the aye-aye spirit, which upends the human's proud act of naming its others. In this regard, humanity's self-claimed norms like intellectual ability, anthropocentric physiology, consciousness, and rationality get reconfigured with the equal distribution of these norms among spirits and humans.

This reconfiguration actually reflects the world as Wan knew it. Ten thousand years before the events of *Korra*, the planet hosted two parallel planes of realities that coexisted together: the Material World, which contained nature and culture similar to the ones in the real Earth, and the Spirit World, which embodied spiritual, nonhuman entities and notions in the Material World. Revealing the animation's capability of realizing the unreal—as in the case of hybridization of nonhuman animals, two planes are connected by two portals at the poles. The crisscrossing of two distinct worlds and their inhabitants through these gates presents a large portrait of Baradian "intra-activity" between agencies of several beings. Pointing at "the mutual constitution of entangled agencies," such large-scale intra-activities showcase that the realities of Wan's world are the outcomes of a multiplicity of agencies among several beings in an assemblage which co-constitute one another and co-emerge as new becomings.[14] The interplays of these human and nonhuman agencies account for posthumanist performativities as seen in the union of Wan the human and Raava the nonhuman in "Beginnings, Part 2."

Shown to have coexisted with the nonhumans in the Spirit Wilds for two years in "Beginnings, Part 1," Wan stepped into the early phase of his posthuman subjectivity. His encounter with the battle of Raava and Vaatu furthered this becoming-posthuman as we can see in Wan's reaction to both during their battle: "Stop, or you'll destroy everything!" His response to Raava's condescending warning—"This doesn't concern you, human!"— needs a closer inspection: "It does when the lives of spirits and animals are in danger." Wan's non-anthropocentric approach to the environment and nonhuman beings is best given in this exclamation because he is unaware of any evil spirit and reacts against a possible bullying of a spirit. Wan achieved a posthuman entanglement with his nonhuman others even before mastering all four elements and becoming the first Avatar by learning to live among the spirits. Later in the following episode, upon learning that the "human and spirit realms are headed toward annihilation" due to his fault, he articulated his primary motive in life: "This world is home to all of us, and what happens here is everyone's business." For this reason, he became ready to take on the role of a bridge between these two species/realms/homes. All Wan's articulations refer to what Barad explicates in her discussions about the coexistence of materiality and discourse:

> [T]he universe is agential intra-activity in its becoming. The primary ontological units are not "things" but phenomena—dynamic topological reconfigurings/entanglements/relationalities/(re)articulations. And the primary semantic units are not "words" but material-discursive practices through which boundaries are constituted. This dynamism is agency.[15]

Underlying that the discursive and the material are inseparable, Barad suggests all agencies, both human and nonhuman, interact with one another in an ongoing process. As their entangled agencies affect their becomings, they should be acknowledged on a rhizomatic trajectory rather than a hierarchical one.

Toward the end of "Beginnings, Part 2," the story of Wan's eternal fusion with Raava provides evidence for the ongoing process of the universe where everything is connected and intra-actively takes part in each other's materiality and existence. Concerning this evidence, Wan's response to Raava during the first Harmonic Convergence recalls the Harawayan notion of "companion species": "The only way to win is together." Since becoming-avatar is accepting nonhuman-spiritual alterity into the human subject's body, Wan and Raava's eternal bonding is a chimerical phenomenon that will last "for all of [Wan's/the Avatar's] lifetimes" as confirmed by Raava at the end of this episode. From Wan to Korra, they were "training each other in acts of communication," as Haraway would contend. They have been, "constitutively, companion species. [They] make each other up, in the flesh. Significantly other to each other, in specific difference," they have engendered a divine bonding known as Avatarhood, which has come to be a natural-cultural and material-spiritual legacy.[16] This legacy has emerged out of the agential forces at work together and created their own realities; that is why Barad situates such configurations out of a multiplicity of posthuman performativities in "agential realism."[17] As another demonstration of how matter and discourse intersect in this agential reality, the Harmonic Convergence reconfigures the ontological and epistemological conditions of both humans and nonhumans as well as of portals and planets. In this regard, with an "ethico-onto-epistemological" core that "provides an understanding of the role of human *and* nonhuman, material *and* discursive, and natural *and* cultural factors in scientific and other social-material practices," agential realism emphasizes that nonhumans have much more significance in the occurrences, happenings, and emergences of phenomena in society, the world, and the universe than we believe or think.[18] The realities, in which we humans and they nonhumans survive, experience life, and engage in relations with one another, are just glimpses from unending emergent intra-actions of this posthumanist agentic realism.

Relationality of Nonhuman and Material Companions: Aang

Being the bridge between two worlds is itself an act of the Avatar's posthuman performativity. Yet again, Wan's division of the two worlds and closing the portals does not mean they are no longer connected. When Aang resumed the Avatarhood almost 10,000 years later, his 100-year unconscious residence in the iceberg was only possible thanks to the posthuman performativity of the Avatar State that, as "a defense mechanism," is explained in the episode "The Avatar State" (*Avatar* S2E01) to "empower [the Avatar] with the skills and knowledge of all the past Avatars." As seen in Aang's situation, the posthuman embodiment of the Avatar also makes a kind of posthuman temporality possible. Aang's years in the iceberg trespasses the supposed limits of a body's spatio-temporality. Reaching out to a human's—to Wan's—primordial entanglement with a spirit—with Raava—this agential reality also contains the Avatar State's spatiotemporal accumulations of physical-spiritual or material-discursive phenomena in all the Avatars' lifetimes. Every Avatar participates in this agential accumulation by means of their interactions and intra-actions with other beings during their period.

The Avatar's posthuman performativity manifests itself in other bodies related to them, such as the material-spiritual relics of past Avatars. "Matter itself," Barad argues, "is always already open to, or rather entangled with, the 'Other.'"[19] When the Avatar is regarded as a posthuman subject, their other becomes posthuman objects in relation to them. The tulku-like identification process of an Avatar is, for instance, made with the presentation of the toys of past Avatars to candidates because a material-spiritual energy from past Avatars is embedded in them. Avatars' object others are "not just in [their] skin, but in [their] bones, in [their] belly, in [their] heart, in [their] nucleus, in [their] past and future" because "[n]ot only subjects but also objects are permeated through and through with their entangled kin."[20] To give another example of this entangled kinship, we can think of Avatar statues whose eyes react and shine when the Avatar State is activated. These Avatar phenomena, as Barad would agree, "are lively and enlivened;" since "memory and re-member-ing are not mind-based capacities but marked historialities ingrained in the body's becoming."[21] Besides the material-spiritual and biological-informational memories that Avatars' posthuman performativity takes, the series reveals that the world incorporates its inhabitants' past and present experiences in itself. In "The Swamp" (*Avatar* S2E04), Huu, the protector of the Foggy Swamp, describes this area as "a mystical place" where he "reached enlightenment right under the banyan-grove tree" that is "one big, living organism, just like the entire world."[22] Putting a finer and more illustrative point on the posthumanist axiom of Rosi Braidotti, "We-are-(all)-in-this-together-but-we-are-not-one-and-the-same," Huu explicates that "this whole swamp is actually just one tree spread out over miles ... We are all living together even if most folks don't act like it. We all have the same roots, and we are all branches of the same tree."[23] Therefore, even when we are not one and the same, we are enmeshed "through the various ontological entanglements that materiality entails" as in this tree's entanglement in the world.[24] Hence, the memory of the tree is "the enfoldings of space-time-matter written into the universe, or better, the enfolded articulations of the universe in its mattering."[25] Realizing this phenomenon of agential realism, Aang as the posthuman subject traces the material-spiritual energy through the roots and branches and locates his lost animal companion Appa. Through these instances, the series makes the emergent entanglement of memory in this cosmic energy visible and tangible.

Aang's attentive communication with his nonhuman companions like Appa and Momo resembles the first Avatar's response-able performances in his relations with nonhumans and nature. Aang's treatment of his animal companions not only proves his posthumanist worldview but also underlines the Avatar's understanding of the nonhuman as a thinking, feeling, and mattering being. It is common to encounter that many nonhumans in fantasy animations and narratives are granted subject positions in their relations with humans. However, these nonhuman subjecthoods, as mere representationalist portrayals, do not go beyond anthropomorphizing. In such anthropomorphic depictions, nonhumans do not threaten human subjectivity. Yet, the *Avatar* franchise is not interested in this anthropocentric valuation; rather, anthropomorphic nonhumans in the animation "end up human exceptionalism [and morals] in question."[26] While the episode "Appa's Lost Days" (*Avatar* S2E16) reveals the nonhuman hero's subjectivity at length, "The Tale of Momo" segment in the episode "The Tales of Ba Sing Se" (*Avatar* S2E15) validates that the story of a nonhuman being does not necessarily have to be a fable and revolve around human-centered situations of life. Moreover, Momo's companionship with Appa exemplifies the becoming-together-with of two different nonhuman species. He misses, dreams about, and looks for his friend. In his quest, Momo proves to be quite an intelligent nonhuman with tool-using and communication capacities even with stranger animals. For that reason, we can claim that he, aware of being a companion of the Avatar, demonstrates ethical attitudes toward three pygmy pumas by saving them from being slaughtered at the butcher's. In a posthumanist framework, Momo's actions exhibit that ethics is not bound by human thoughts and actions. The series accordingly challenges the notion of anthropocentrism and establishes a tradition about intra-actions and performances among non/human subjects. This way, *Avatar* offers a new spectacle on the mutual sociality and co-emergent relationships of nonhumans and humans.

Dissolution of Binaries: Korra

Korra, succeeding Aang as the next Avatar, is presented in her struggles of airbending and spiritual maturity. Her posthuman performativity is wavering at the beginning of her Avatarhood. As a bridge between material and spiritual worlds, she can neither perform her posthuman subjectivity nor achieve bending all four elements just because she lacks spiritual connection with Raava. Unlike Aang, who experienced such a sorrowful event as the Air Nomad genocide committed by the command of Fire Lord Sozin and had to embrace his spiritual and emotional nature to recover, Korra relies solely on her robust physicality. She could not first comprehend her connections with nonhuman others or herself as a material-spiritual entity of the past, present, and future. Without grasping this posthuman union of her body with her Avatar spirit, she would fail to construct "a relationship of mutual supplementarity."[27] "Indeed, our very existence," as Roberto Marchesini notes, "depends on openness, because without hosting alterity ... humans would be 'sterile.'"[28] Only in the final episode of the first season, "Endgame" (*Korra* S1E12), could Korra reach an openness of mind and heart at a moment of desperation after her bending skills were paralyzed by Amon, the leader of an anti-bender revolutionary group. Only then could she connect with her spiritual self, claim her posthuman identity, and achieve becoming a full-fledged Avatar. Korra's vulnerable condition places the human not into the center of a hierarchy of beings but on a horizontal axis with other beings. Her comprehension of the fact that her physicality cannot surpass her spirituality, as they should be in balance in an Avatar, helps her perform materially-spiritually agentic actions in subsequent years.

Unappreciative of her Avatar State and her past lives, Korra fluctuates between her materiality and spirituality after defeating Amon. During the Glacier Spirits Festival held to enhance the Southern Water Tribe's spiritual connections in "Rebel Spirit" (*Korra* S2E01), she fails to seek guidance from her companions of past Avatars in her quest to restore balance to the decayed spirits. Rather, she ignores her posthuman temporality. In such a catastrophic time, as Claire Colebrook states, there happens some "exclusive disjunction" in which "the future is merely our already existing catastrophic present or a nostalgically orientalist conception of a timeless indigenous other is by way of a time that is multilinear."[29] If Korra is accepted as the future of previous Avatars, multiple coexistence of those Avatars in her body requires Korra "to think beyond what has (up until now) counted as human temporality."[30] She has to step into posthuman temporalities, which she could only manage when she washes ashore on the Bhanti Island after a gigantic dark spirit's attack in "The Sting" (*Korra* S2E06). Amnesiac at first, Korra is able to regain her historical posthuman subjectivity/memory as well as the story of the primordial division of the two worlds. Now inhabiting multiple lines of temporalities in herself, she prepares to confront Vaatu, "a timeless indigenous other."[31]

In this preparation during the episodes "The Guide" (*Korra* S2E09) and "A New Spiritual Age" (*Korra* S2E10), Korra travels to the Spirit World under the guidance of Jinora, Aang's granddaughter, and even experiences the in-between materiality of spirits while wandering around as if having no body or bending ability at all. Spirits, due to their in-between materialities, could affect and be affected by other bodies in multifarious entanglements. The balance of this entanglement is part of Korra's posthuman performativity. As a child version of herself, she realizes her negative attitude/energy turns spirits into a darker version of themselves and *vice versa*. As Iroh articulates in "A New Spiritual Age" (*Korra* S2E10), both material and spiritual worlds will give either light or darkness, depending on what one is seeking, which is a direct indicator that the world has its own agency and it engages in those of humans and nonhumans as well. Yet, even though she manages to find her way through the entanglements of the Spirit World, Korra fails to close the portals before the second Harmonic Convergence, and Vaatu is released to fuse with Unalaq, Chief of the Northern Water Tribe. As the Dark Avatar, Unalaq aims to connect material and Spirit Worlds through eternal darkness. Referring to Wan's closing both portals and creating a binary between the two parallel planes of realities, he claims in "Harmonic Convergence" (*Korra* S2E12): "You call yourself a bridge between the two worlds, but there shouldn't be a bridge. We should live together as one." Unalaq, reminding Korra of her Avatar duties of posthumanist performativities in a material-spiritual continuum, stands for a new position of the bridge through destruction, chaos, and darkness. Surely, Vaatu's and Unalaq's intentions are larger than what they have outspokenly claimed, for they yearn to colonize both planes of realities and all communities in them for the sake of their own benefits. Vaatu's transforming almost all other spirits akin to him proves this almost "liberal humanist" and expansionist ideology. However, it is Korra who, as the Avatar of peace and balance, should lead the two worlds to a coexistence in which they will live in a posthumanist harmony.

Colebrook's "exclusive disjuncture" materializes in the light blue form of Korra's inner spirit in the final episode of the second season, "Light in the Dark" (*Korra* S2E14), after Unalaq the Dark Avatar extracts Raava from within Korra's body. Raava's extraction might give the idea of the clash of the Avatar's posthuman identity since her Avatar spirit is no longer available. However, this is an aspect of posthuman temporality in Korra's case. Even though her connection to her past lives is severed, Korra consults the material-spiritual memory of the planet and, with the guidance of her mentor, Tenzin, summons the astral projection of her spirit by meditating in the hollow of the Tree of Time, which, as Tenzin explains, "had a long history long before it held Vaatu" and whose "roots bind the spirit and physical worlds together." The Tree's capacity as the merger of two worlds also demonstrates how it is able to restore "the great cosmic energy of the universe" since the "Tree of Time remembers all" in Tenzin's words. The nonhuman object's posthuman performativity relates to the banyan-grove tree in the *Avatar* episode "The Swamp," which connects all the Material World through its roots. As Tenzin's statement that "the ancients would meditate beneath this tree and connect with the great cosmic energy of the universe" indicates in the season finale, plants of this universe have deeper material-spiritual connections and performances with the inhabitants of two worlds. Korra, now deprived of Raava, sets her own agency into motion to "[f]ind the light in the dark." In doing so, her spirit gains a new form of spiritual materiality other and greater than her physicality upon which she has relied too much. She simply becomes a posthuman subject that is connected to the universe. With the help of the natural/material body—i.e., the Tree of Time—she connects to the universe to find her Avatar spirit and light, which gives her this power to fight against the liberal humanist harmony of chaos and darkness. In other words, as both sides face each other over the fate of the world, Korra meets "the universe halfway," in

Barad's expression, to become this mega-Avatar that will disallow darkness from taking over the universe.[32]

Korra's posthuman performativity has become filled with "agential cuts" like Raava's extraction, her astral spirit, and Korra and Raava's reunion. "The agential cut," as Barad details, "does not disentangle the phenomenon into independent subsystems … What the agential cut does provide is a contingent resolution of the ontological inseparability within the phenomenon."[33] Her Avatarhood as the posthuman phenomenon here resides heavily on the 10,000-year-old entanglement of the matter, the spiritual, and the meaning. Although she becomes the last Avatar of the first cycle, her posthuman performativity gets reconfigured and continues because she starts the new Avatar cycle in which the responsibilities of the Avatar change when she asks "what if humans and spirits weren't meant to live apart" while she is about to close the portals. Upon this question, Korra decides to keep portals open so that spirits and humans can coexist together and freely enter into each other's worlds. She addresses the Water Tribes and emphatically highlights the possibilities of posthuman living and mattering at the end of "Light in the Dark":

> I've realized that even though we should learn from those who came before us, we must also forge our own path. So that is why I've decided to keep the portals open. Humans can now physically enter the Spirit World and spirits will be free to roam our world. I will no longer be the bridge. Humans and spirits must learn to live together. My mission will always be to use Raava's light spirit to guide the world toward peace and balance. Harmonic Convergence has caused a shift in the planet's energy. I can feel it. Things will never be the same again. We are entering a new age.

Declaring the removal of her bridge status, Korra aims to restore the original conditions of two parallel planes that were once open to the trespassing of their unique inhabitants/species. This will enhance the entanglement of false binaries, as they were meant to be. Just like the roots and branches of the banyan-grove tree and the Tree of Time, the relationality between the two planes will freely follow a rhizomatic pattern.

As the imagery behind Korra's audience reveals, a new age that evokes an opportunity for horizontality begins. The horizontal alignment in Figure 7.1, which is meaningfully illustrated in secondary colors like purple and green, actually corresponds with the non-hierarchical becomings of hybrid and multifarious beings in both worlds. The animated nonhuman hybridities here "display such an affirmative naturalcultural emergence."[34] Furthermore, showcasing the infinite possibilities of posthumanist emergences, the polar lights or auroras that are drawn and animated during the Harmonic Convergence do not cease flowing like energy-rivers in the sky and horizon. After the convergence of two distinct worlds, *Korra*'s third and fourth seasons are enriched in terms of color spectrum used in the portrayal of the fantastic spiritual beings. Freely wandering spirits could only be given in their full vivacity by means of animation's rich color palette and cel-drawings, which prepare the spectator for forthcoming diversity, inclusiveness, and changes in future episodes. "Change," Barad affirms, "is a dynamism that operates at an entirely different level of existence from that of postulated brute matter situated in space and time; rather, what comes to be and is 'immediately' reconfigured entails an iterative intra-active open-ended becoming of spacetimemattering."[35] The change toward becoming-together-in-multiplicity in the *Avatar* franchise, as seen in the above-detailed discussions, is a condition of togetherness, a combined existence of space, time, and matter, and a diffraction of new lines and hues on both the retina/actual life and the screen/virtual platform.

The continuum of the new order by Korra has become the concomitant result of her separation from Raava. Yet again, this posthuman temporality, "this tiny disjuncture that exists in neither space nor time, torques the very nature of the relation between continuity and discontinuity to such a degree that the nature of change changes with each *intra-action*."[36] For a primary example of the proliferation of spacetimemattering during this intra-active change, spirit vines emerge in the Material World, especially amid the Republic City where Korra fought with the Dark Avatar at the second season's end. Struggling to handle these material-spiritual emergences at public demand, Korra questions her failure to cleanse the cultural space—the Republic City—from the natural entities—spirit vines—at the beginning of "A Breath of Fresh Air" (*Korra* S3E01): "I don't get it. I can vanquish Vaatu, but not a bunch of stupid vines?" Upon Jinora's confrontation by reminding Korra that "You've changed the world. We're connected with the spirits again. The Wilds are their home," we understand that Korra becomes the mouthpiece of liberal humanist perspective, according to which this urban space is the *oikos* of the human and their regular nonhuman companions, but not the nonhuman spirits. Korra's hesitation mainly stems from her self-perception as the highest entity in the world order: As the Avatar, she has to be capable of doing, fixing, winning anything.

The new world order after the Harmonic Convergence has given birth to new changes such as the transformation of some non-benders into airbenders. Whilst this transformation will assist the restoration of the balance between the four nations, especially over a hundred years after the Air Nomad genocide, it entails further iterative intra-actions between the forces of matter and mind. The Red Lotus, which, as their leader Zaheer tells Korra in "The Stakeout" (*Korra* S3E09), is supposedly "dedicated to restoring freedom to the world," keeps Unalaq's idea of a world without the Avatar and gets into action to distort the posthuman entanglements of the new order. "The natural order is disorder," as Zaheer explains his society's doctrine. In this communication, Zaheer pinpoints the main problem in the world as the political institutes and politicians that dominate people by misusing their powers. He seems to oppose certain liberal humanist ideals as well as oligarchic and plutocratic administrations. On the flip side, he proposes a kind of anarcho-capitalism, which we can grasp only at the end of the third season. Just before they poison Korra with mercury in "Venom of the Red Lotus" (*Korra* S3E13), we could learn the true meaning of their "disorderly order" doctrine: "So, we lucky few—this band of brothers and sisters of anarchy—are witnessing the beginning of an era of true freedom. Together, we will forge a world without kings or queens, without borders or nations, where man's only allegiance is to himself and those he loves. We will return to the true balance of natural order." Not hiding the anarchic nature of their group, Zaheer underlines the ideal of a Man-centric system—with a deliberate capitalization—with his use of words "man" and "his." His rhetoric seems to point at a not-so-different social order that is utterly detached from the natural order of the *Avatar* franchise. What he and the Red Lotus fail to comprehend is revealed that his "efforts to de-naturalize" social, biological, species differences are to affirm a "man-made and historically contingent structure."[37] However, these differences that contribute to the material-spiritual becomings and performances in this franchise "do exist and continue to matter."[38] "Sexualized, racialized and naturalized differences, from being categorical boundary markers under" the ideal disorder of the Red Lotus, if we appropriate Braidotti's words here, turn out "unhinged" in Korra's and other Avatars' orders, in which the multiplicity becomes "the forces leading to the elaboration of alternative modes of transversal subjectivity" beyond the human.[39]

In our view, the posthuman performativity of Avatars functions to demonstrate, reform, and reconfigure the intricate web of natural-cultural, material-spiritual interrelations among humans and nonhumans in a new materialist manner. If "man" is centered in the praxis of some philosophical thought or movement, we well know that all his others—woman, queer, animal, thing, matter, and spirit—will be subjugated, abused, and terrorized under "his" rule. By implication, Zaheer's words mean that the Red Lotus aims indeed to sever humanity's connections with nonhumanity and spirituality. However, as Max Dosser also elaborates in his chapter "From Fan Blogs to Earth Rumble VI: Disability Discourse on *Avatar: The Last Airbender*" in this volume, Korra envisions a world in which all agencies of different—and differently abled—bodies will coexist together without any supremacy of one over the other. This is how Korra differs from Zaheer and how she actualizes true posthuman performativity. "A materialist politics of posthuman differences," Braidotti argues, "works by potential becomings that call for actualization. They are enacted through collectively shared, community-based *praxis* and are crucial to support the process of vitalist, non-unitarian and yet accountable recomposition of a missing people."[40] This notion of "missing people" is Korra's ideal society consisting of humans, nonhumans, and spirits. To achieve this, necessary is "the affirmative, ethical dimension of becoming-posthuman as a gesture of collective self-styling," into which the new airbenders can join when they decide to self-style themselves as the newly emerging Air Nomads.[41] This new airbending community is not restricted "negatively by shared vulnerability, the guilt of ancestral communal violence, or the melancholia of unpayable ontological debts, but rather by the compassionate acknowledgement of their interdependence with multiple others."[42] Korra's aims to restore balance materialize with this re-establishment of Air Nomad nature-culture. This way, instead of leading the world into chaos, she intends to restore harmony by leading both material and spiritual bodies toward peace and union.

The new Air Nomads and Korra's joint victory over Zaheer and the Red Lotus is, therefore, emblematic in terms of the multiscalar relationality in the new order since it relies on "monistic affirmative politics grounded on immanent inter-connections and generative differences."[43] Because Korra collaborates with other people or forces in her victories until Kuvira, the last antagonist of the television series, we can say that Korra's final test in her material-spiritual wholeness is the little amount of the mercury left in her body. Although this moment of her poisoning illustrates the inseparability of the human from the nonhuman environment/entities as well as the human body's "trans-corporeality," in Stacy Alaimo's conceptualization, "in which the human is always intermeshed with the more-than-human world," it does not come to mean that all natural beings permeating the human body is harmless to it.[44] In Korra's case, mercury first affects her materiality, and then she is weakened both physically and mentally and finally struggles with connecting to Raava. Painted in direct contrast to how she is in the first season, her posthuman composition is temporarily tainted by both mercury and her fear of the vulnerability of her material-spiritual existence. For this reason, in "The Coronation" (*Korra* S4E03), she is surprised by old Toph Beifong's exclamations about her being "more connected to the world" during her retirement in the middle of the Foggy Swamp. First, Toph's guidance enables Korra to remove her physiological block. Then, consulting Zaheer in "Beyond the Wilds" (*Korra* S4E09) enables her to "accept what happened to [her]" and overcome her affective block. This way, she regains her power to resist Kuvira and her techno-spiritual destruction machine. In this fashion, and after performing her queer identity which is scrutinized in Emily Bauch and Oliver Eklund's chapter "A Queer Relationship: Mapping *The Legend of Korra*'s Industrial Journey across Mediums" in this volume, Korra is led to the full embodiment of her "self" as the Avatar in her relationship with Asami.

Coda: Entanglement for Good

In audio-visual materials depicting fantastic worlds, imagining, illustrating, or envisioning new philosophical and theoretical concepts like posthuman performativity and agential realism has always been possible. Noting that animation itself is a posthumanist method relying more on the combination of human creativity, paper- or cel-drawings, and storyboard designs aspired by nonhuman environs than humans' real presence, we are indebted to the *Avatar* franchise as many of us posthumans were, have been, and still are able to encounter the possibilities of togetherness and co-emergence with the nonhuman, the interconnectedness of all the earthlings, and the entanglement of the real and the virtual by pushing the bounds of probabilities. Using the theoretical notions by posthumanist and/or feminist materialist scholars like Barad, Nayar, Haraway, Braidotti, Colebrook, and Alaimo as a springboard to investigate the posthuman performativity of Avatars in this animation series, we have explored the notion of the Avatar as a posthuman subject and the actions of Avatars as posthuman performativity. Beginning in Wan's embodiment of posthuman performativity thanks to the combination of the bodily and the spiritual in him, Avatarhood has long distorted the binary thinking, being, and becoming and has opened new ways of multiple relationalities among the living and nonliving entities in the world(s). The intersectional character of the Avatar has, thus, demonstrated the possibility of a rhizomatic horizon for beings on Earth who are in desperate need of coming to terms with their environments in the twenty-first century. As witnessed in the actions of response-able nonhuman animals and objects like Momo and Avatar statues, we humans ought not to be bound in the zone of impossibility, which is assumed to be present in our communications with nonhumans and the environment. Imagine that Wan addresses not Raava, but you: "The only way to win is together."

Notes

1 Pramod K. Nayar, *Posthumanism* (Polity Press, 2014), 3.
2 Francesca Ferrando, "Posthumanism, Transhumanism, Antihumanism, Metahumanism, and New Materialisms: Differences and Relations," *Existenz* 8.2 (2013): 29–30.
3 Donna J. Haraway, *The Haraway Reader* (Routledge, 2004), 2.
4 Başak Ağın and Şafak Horzum, "Diseased Bodies Entangled: Literary and Cultural Crossroads of Posthuman Narrative Agents," *SFRA Review* 51.2 (2021): 150.
5 René Descartes, *Discours de La Méthode/Discourse on the Method*, ed. and trans. George Heffernan, Bilingual Edition (University of Notre Dame

Press, 1994), 51, 53; René Descartes, *Meditations on First Philosophy: With Selections from the Objections and Replies*, ed. and trans. John Cottingham, 2nd ed. (Cambridge University Press, 2017), 21.

6   Timothy Morton, *The Ecological Thought* (Harvard University Press, 2010), 15.

7   Karen Barad, "Posthumanist Performativity: Toward an Understanding of How Matter Comes to Matter," *Signs: Journal of Women in Culture and Society* 28.3 (2003): 803.

8   Karen Barad, "Ma(r)king Time: Material Entanglements and Re-Memberings: Cutting Together-Apart," in *How Matter Matters: Objects, Artifacts, and Materiality in Organization Studies*, ed. Paul R. Carlile et al. (Oxford University Press, 2013), 17.

9   Ibid., 17.

10 Ibid., 17.

11 Gilles Deleuze and Félix Guattari, *A Thousand Plateaus: Capitalism and Schizophrenia*, trans. Brian Massumi (University of Minnesota Press, 1987).

12 Ursula K. Heise, "Plasmatic Nature: Environmentalism and Animated Film," *Public Culture* 26.2 (2014): 303.

13 Jacques Derrida and Bernard Stiegler, *Echographies of Television: Filmed Interviews* (Cambridge: Polity Press, 2002), 13.

14 Karen Barad, *Meeting the Universe Halfway: Quantum Physics and the Entanglement of Matter and Meaning* (Duke University Press, 2007), 33. Italics removed.

15 Barad, "Posthumanist Performativity," 818.

16 Donna J. Haraway, *When Species Meet* (University of Minnesota Press, 2008), 16.

17 Karen Barad, "Agential Realism," in *Encyclopedia of Feminist Theories*, ed. Lorraine Code (Routledge, 2000), 15.

18 Barad, *Meeting*, 90, 26; italics in the original.

19 Ibid., 393.

20 Ibid., 393.

21 Ibid., 393.

22 For a detailed analysis of this episode through the lens of ecocriticism, see: Gia Coturri Sorenson's chapter in this volume.

23 Rosi Braidotti, *Posthuman Knowledge* (Polity Press, 2019), 57.

24 Barad, *Meeting*, 393.

25 Ibid., ix.

26 Heise, 309.

27 Eric Jonas, "Historicity and Alterity: Revisiting the Foucault-Derrida Debate," *Constellations: An International Journal of Critical and Democratic Theory* 22.4 (2014): 594.

28 Roberto Marchesini, "Nonhuman Alterities," trans. Elena Past, *Angelaki: Journal of Theoretical Humanities* 21.1 (2016): 161–2. Italics removed.
29 Claire Colebrook, "Anti-Catastrophic Time," *New Formations: A Journal of Culture/Theory/Politics* 92 (2017): 107.
30 Ibid., 102.
31 Ibid., 107.
32 Barad, *Meeting*.
33 Ibid., 348. Italics removed.
34 Başak Ağın, "The Ecological Posthuman in Lee's *Tarboy* and Tan and Ruhemann's *The Lost Thing*," *CLCWeb: Comparative Literature and Culture* 18.3 (2016): 6.
35 Barad, "Ma(r)king Time," 29.
36 Ibid., 29. Italics in the original.
37 Rosi Braidotti, *The Posthuman* (Polity Press, 2013), 3.
38 Ibid., 88.
39 Ibid., 98.
40 Ibid., 100.
41 Ibid., 100–1.
42 Ibid., 101.
43 Rosi Braidotti, "A Theoretical Framework for the Critical Posthumanities," *Theory, Culture & Society* 36.6 (2019): 52.
44 Stacy Alaimo, *Bodily Natures: Sciences, Environment, and the Material Self* (Indiana University Press, 2010), 2.

PART THREE

Trauma

8

"Born in You, Along with All the Strife, Is the Power to Restore Balance to the World": Exploring Representations of Children's Experiences of Trauma through *Avatar: The Last Airbender*

Joseph V. Giunta

Avatar: The Last Airbender (Nickelodeon, 2005–8) takes place in a world ravaged by a century of war. The four nations used to live together in harmony before the Fire Nation attacked. Fire Lord Sozin dealt a deadly first strike against the other nations. The Air Nomads were the first to fall. A monastic people, the Air Nomads lived scattered across the world, with no formal military, and were almost completely annihilated by the Fire Lord's ambush. At the show's onset, Fire Lord Ozai rules with the same terror and violence as his grandfather, Sozin. The Water Tribe had been surgically invaded and nearly decimated, and they have largely withdrawn from the global conflict. The Earth Kingdom is the last stronghold. The realism of this war, its casualties, and the grand scale of suffering depicted uniquely place *Avatar* amidst its animated television contemporaries, illustrating "a healthy respect for the consequences of war."[1] Viewers experience individual instances of main, recurring, and guest characters who were affected by the brutalities of the war, illustrating a complex and painful picture of the depths with which this conflict has so deeply influenced every corner of the world. A primary target of the warring Fire Nation and central figure in the series is Aang, a twelve-year-old boy who is the last remaining airbender and the Avatar, the human embodiment of peace and light whose duty is to maintain balance between the four nations. Aang has spent the past one hundred years frozen in an iceberg and emerges at the series' beginning to an entirely different world he is entrusted with saving. Tasked with finding the Avatar in order to restore his honor, an originally impossible mission now suddenly plausible, is Zuko, the sixteen-year-old banished Prince of the Fire Nation. Both Aang and Zuko undergo intensely distressing experiences as a result of the war; their personal, familial, and intergenerational ties are of significant importance to how the series explores their childhood and trauma.

This chapter focalizes the unique traumatic journeys of Avatar Aang and banished Prince Zuko, who, through their search for balance within themselves, have the power to restore balance to the world. This series' distinguishing feature is its braiding of these young protagonists' traumatic journeys of identity formation and self-discovery with the series' overall narrative arc across its three seasons. Due to the show's prioritization of children's agentic decision-making skills, anxieties, and transformative abilities, *Avatar* is able to acknowledge a "flexible and relational sense of agency," as Lucy Newby and Fearghus Roulston write of characterizations of youth and adolescence during conflict.[2] By recognizing "both the vulnerabilities of young individuals living in situations of conflict and their inventive capacity to take hold of opportunities presented by wartime disruption to create something new," the series illuminates young people's unique capacities during periods of hostility to imagine and create better futures.[3] Together with their respective primary reference groups, the people who have immediate influence over their individual explorations of self, Aang and Zuko's journeys of and through trauma result in powerful onscreen representations of posttraumatic growth, which Lawrence G. Calhoun and Richard G. Tedeschi liken to "psychological earthquakes that shake the foundations of schema that will need to be rebuilt to standards that allow resistance to future earthquakes."[4] It is precisely because of these psychological earthquakes that *Avatar* presents an extraordinary depiction of childhood: through Aang and Zuko's individual struggles with trauma, the series fearlessly tackles young people's resiliency and the power to shape their life's journeys.

During *Avatar*'s release, these representational strategies and complex constructions of animated narratives were much less commonplace. No longer is childhood trauma bounded within the confines of a singular episode, or heavily alluded to via metaphor and pacified with comedic overtones and moralistic closure. *Avatar*'s normalization of characters with disabilities and mental illness, representations of animal cruelty, and cheeky deconstructions of both character stereotypes and archetypes in children's animated media all push the boundaries of what was popularly considered acceptable for youth audiences as well as for television viewers at-large.[5] Aang and Zuko's status as young people offers an opportunity to present spectators, young and old alike, with constructions of children with agency whose nuanced journeys through trauma are scarce during this era of American children's animated television. Analyzing representations of children in post-conflict environments, Newby and Roulston argue that children can exist simultaneously at various states within the spectrums of "past/present/future" and "victimhood/perpetrator/peacemaker," able to "symbolize hope for the future and the violence of the past in roles of both victims and perpetrators."[6] Aang and Zuko consistently negotiate their positions within these spectrums, often occupying multiple roles at once, throughout their traumatic journeys across the series. Though by *Avatar*'s conclusion both characters undergo tremendous change due to their negotiations with traumatic experiences, their paths present young audiences with two disparate models of how trauma manifests itself in the minds and bodies of youth. This chapter examines Aang and Zuko's explorations of, struggles with, and transformations resulting from trauma, as well as how trauma serves as a narrative device that advances their individual character arcs and the series' overall story progression. By embracing childhood studies' call for interdisciplinarity, this analysis of *Avatar*'s two primary characters takes up multiple academic perspectives in order to highlight the series' depiction of agentic children who work through their trauma together to successfully accomplish their goals. It is as a result of their trying journeys that Aang, Zuko, and their friends are able to restore balance to their world, and present young spectators with complex models of resiliency, collaboration, and growth.

"I Know Sometimes It Hurts More to Hope and It Hurts More to Care": Children's Experiences with Trauma and Their Onscreen Representations

Childhood studies, a field emerging to rectify incomplete understandings of children from theories within developmental psychology and biological determinism, grants young people a necessary agency respectful of their particular worldviews, within their peer groups and the world at-large.[7] One of the central tenets of childhood studies is that "children must be seen as active in the construction and determination of their own social lives, the lives of those around them, and of the societies in which they live," illuminating young people's agentic ability to influence the worlds in which they inhabit.[8] When framed as capable, active, and goal-oriented, especially without the prescribed guidance of adult figures, it becomes clear that children are able to construct their own lives outside of what adults have created or assumed for them.[9] Adolescents in particular, as Michael J. Nakkula and Eric Toshalis maintain, "are in a near-constant state of constructing their lives ... actively creating development itself" apart from the boundaries of presumed developmental stages or what their environments may offer to them.[10] However, this process of formulating one's own identity in relation to multiple social worlds is an exhausting and complicated quest that often produces identity crises for young people.[11] While the support of family, teachers, and other adult community members may assist in children's constructions of identity, it is often within collectively produced peer cultures that selfhood is interpreted and created through youth's efforts to negotiate their placement within larger social hierarchies.[12] When combined with personal and generational trauma and physical and emotional danger, as in the cases of Aang and Zuko, it becomes increasingly difficult to realize one's identity and secure direction of their own lives.[13]

In his analysis of childhood in the age of media, David Buckingham asserts that media is "one of the main arenas in which the construction [of childhood] is developed and sustained."[14] Satisfying a role akin to traditional spaces of pedagogy such as school and family, these mediatic texts carry out "the same journey of disruption-solution that reinforce normative behaviors and traditional ideologies, seldom respecting children's agency or active participation that subsists at [these] narratives' ends."[15] In respecting its young audience's ability to value sophisticated themes, narratives, and characters, *Avatar* moves beyond these all too familiar narrative archetypes, appreciating children's television consumption habits and building upon their presumed base of animated television comprehension.[16] Ann E. Kaplan, in her monograph exploring representations of trauma in media and literature, stresses the "increasing importance of 'translating' trauma— that is, of finding ways to make meaning out of, and to communicate, catastrophes that happen to others as well as to oneself."[17] Kaplan believes mediatic narratives that foreground the audience as active and recognize viewers "as having agency and receiving multiple positions with which to identify," are essential to this translation process.[18] Perceiving traumatized children as too often having no voice, Joy D. Osofsky reasons, "we must help provide words as well as actions to better their lives."[19] Can children's media fulfill this role, supplying a voice for young people who have been traumatized, despite being predominantly molded by adult creators? More specifically, does *Avatar* fulfill Kaplan's call for transformative and affective "translations" of trauma for audiences, child and adult alike, even with its fictional setting and narrative? Onscreen representations of childhood, in order to adjust to childhood studies' comprehension of youth, "must begin to craft narratives of agentic children that, through their distinct subjectivities ... supersede adult-prescribed moralizations and protectionist pedagogies of yore," especially given contemporary media consumption habits.[20] Recognizing and taking into consideration children's capacity to distinguish between "the artifice and excess of cartoon language" and "the harmfulness of everyday brutalities in real life," *Avatar* is able to leverage the versatility of animation in order to portray complex constructions of childhood trauma to its informed and competent young viewers.[21]

"The Past Can Be a Great Teacher": The Difficulties of One Boy Saving the World

Aang is depicted constantly battling with his ancestral and absent past. His status as the Avatar brings with it the memories and responsibilities of his earlier incarnations as he also struggles to accept the role his absence played in the suffering experienced because of the war. Aang's trauma in the first season is primarily centered in the past, a combination of his coming to terms with the genocide of his people and his personal responsibilities as the Avatar. His trauma blends survivor guilt—a result of him being spared from the devastating harm inflicted on his people—and the generational trauma associated with both his Avatar and Air Nomad identities.[22] Aang's century of frozen statis complicates this portrayal. Though he still experiences the distress, self-blame, and difficulty grieving the loss of the Air Nomads, the temporal gap between the violent genocide and Aang's processing of trauma constructs a complex child figure who struggles to mourn his lost community, understand the events that profoundly impacted his life, and find balance within himself and the world on his own terms.[23] Portraying Aang overcoming chronic adversity that haunts him throughout the course of the series with the assistance of his new and growing chosen family, *Avatar*'s overarching narrative is pushed forward by Aang's own traumatic journey, setting up quests through which he becomes comfortable with his identity.

Aang, upon emerging from his icebound state, is reluctant to believe that one hundred years have passed and that he is the last airbender. One of Aang's primary defense mechanisms is to embrace the playful spirit embodied by his former mentor, Monk Gyatso. Across the series, he weaves fun into his life before important events, avoiding confronting the reality of his trauma. By penguin sledding in "The Boy in the Iceberg" (S1E01), building a zoo in "The Tales of Ba Sing Se" (S2E15), or teaching a group of Fire Nation students how to dance in "The Headband" (S3E02), Aang's predisposition for fun generates entertaining subplots. In "The Southern Air Temple" (S1E03), explored by Ryanne Kap in the following chapter in greater depth, Aang refuses to heed Katara's warning about the brutalities with which the Fire Nation dealt to her mother as well as around the world. He will not believe that his people were the victims of genocide. Whether in active denial or simply naïve to the grim realities he now faces, Aang decides to play a game and chase a lemur, further distracting himself from reality. After discovering Monk Gyatso's skeleton surrounded by the remains of Fire Nation soldiers, Aang has no choice but to accept what Katara has been warning him of all along. "The death of a loved one," Steven G. Little, Angeleque Akin-Little, and Matthew P. Somerville write, "can be one of the most severe forms of trauma a child can encounter."[24] Aang's emotional outburst, activating the defense mechanism that is the Avatar State, harnessing immense power from the Avatar's past incarnations, results from the intense realization that he is the last airbender. At twelve years of age, Aang is confronted with the fate of the world in his hands. Despite this, he is able to maintain his sense of joy, a central characteristic of his personality.

Aang's posttraumatic stress also materializes in the form of nightmares, whether spurred by the guilt he feels for "abandoning" the world, by his fear of losing control while in the Avatar State, or by his indecision about murdering Fire Lord Ozai. These secondary stressors and adversities further contribute to his journey. In these moments, Aang's chosen family of Katara, Sokka, and later Toph as well as his spiritual ancestors are able to help him through these acute moments of identity crisis. Confronted by a fisherman about his absence from the world in "The Storm" (S1E12), Aang's inner guilt materializes in the form of a direct and pointed aggression toward him. However, Katara encourages Aang to focus on the present moment, reminding him that he is here now so that he can restore balance to the world, instead of focusing on what may have transpired if he was present at the onset of the war. Aang realizes that he must leave the past and hypothetical situations behind him, and the fisherman reaffirms this fact after Aang saves him and Sokka from a deadly storm. This process of self-forgiveness is not resolved after just one episode and remains exceedingly difficult throughout the first season, as Aang's survival of the genocide is not a result of his heroic actions but because he ran away, creating a sense of shame and self-blame within himself, common symptoms of processing the survivor guilt that plagues Aang throughout the season.[25] Aang begins to discover that hope exists in the world when he happens upon a small community in "The Northern Air Temple" (S1E17). Aang realizes that despite his initial anger and frustration over this sheltered group's lack of understanding about the tenets of the Air Nomads and disregard for the temple, their spirit closely resembles that of the Nomads. Discovering that although he is the final remaining living airbender, the airbending ethos lives on in alternative forms comforts him, relieving, in small part, the pressure of maintaining an entire race of people, a process explored at length in

Caleb Horowitz's chapter in this part on real-world parallels with the depictions of Air Nomads in the *Avatar* television franchise. Aang's ability to embrace the Temple's new inhabitants, thereby successfully persevering through elements of survivor guilt, mitigates Aang's anger and shame as well as furthers him along his mourning process. These experiences depict Aang processing his multifaceted trauma through various moments on his journey, demonstrating how his relationship with himself and the world is changing.

The second season begins with Aang's nightmare about losing control of his power while in the Avatar State, a warning for the events of "The Avatar State" (S2E01). In this episode, Earth Kingdom General Fong attempts to weaponize Aang's powers to quickly end the war, exploiting Aang's guilt. Aang is forced to internalize an onslaught of perspectives about how his power should best be harnessed: Katara pleas for Aang to seek out bending masters; Aang's previous Avatar incarnation, Roku, explains the risks of the Avatar State; and Fong tries to force Aang into the Avatar State. After this whirlwind of emotional experiences, Aang decides that he would rather continue his journey with his new family instead of becoming a weapon for the Earth Kingdom army.

This season, Aang's arc also explores how he is able to become more attuned with his emotions after undergoing another traumatic experience. At the close of "The Library" (S2E10), Appa, Aang's sky bison, is captured by sandbenders, an emotionally devastating moment for Aang. Appa, aside from being an integral part of Aang's family and an essential form of transportation, is also one of the last living remnants of Air Nomad culture. The fury and exasperation that Aang displays during his search for Appa in "The Desert" (S2E11) concludes with a powerful outburst that mirrors Aang's response to discovering Monk Gyatso's skeleton, representative of the immense burden Aang caries as he attempts to find balance between his identity as the Avatar, his responsibilities to Air Nomad culture, and his emotional connections with his chosen family (see Figure 8.1). Unable to discern a solution to his frightening outburst, Aang retreats inward emotionally in "The Serpent's Pass" (S2E12), refusing to acknowledge his fear and grief after Appa's loss. Katara encourages Aang to reconsider this stark approach because she believes it is precisely because he cares—his innate ability to be in touch with his feelings and openly experience them— that makes Aang the person he is. Although, in certain moments, it may hurt more to care and to hope, the ability to experience the rollercoaster of emotions during these junctures is why Aang is suited to be the Avatar that the world needs at this time. As he admits at the end of the episode, "I thought I was trying to be strong, but I was just running away from my feelings." Aang's found family, this peer group of young people, supports Phillip Mizen and Yaw Ofosu-Kusi's contention that children's ability to

FIGURE 8.1 *Aang activates the Avatar State. Still from "The Desert" (S2E11). Blu-ray release of* Avatar: The Last Airbender—The Complete Series *(2018).*

understanding their own and each other's vulnerabilities and make agentic decisions in the interests of those vulnerabilities is oftentimes greater than that of adults.[26] The communities Aang does have access to, whether his tight circle of peers or his Avatar ancestors, contribute to Aang's growing sense of self-efficacy, facilitating his individual recovery as he assists in his community's manifold recoveries as well.[27]

The final step of Aang's emotional journey during the second season occurs in "The Guru" (S2E19), when he meets with Guru Pathik to unlock his chakras and obtain greater control of his body and mind while in the Avatar State. Painfully acknowledging and working through his fear, guilt, shame, identity, division, relationships, and trauma, Aang learns to become a more balanced person by forgiving himself and accepting all parts of his Avatar identity, in doing so realizing that the love felt by his former and contemporary communities will forever live on within him. This moment of growth enables Aang to process various internal traumatic experiences and mechanisms present in his psyche that have been preventing him from accessing the Avatar State on his own terms. After being struck down and nearly killed in the final moments of the "The Crossroads of Destiny"

(S2E20), however, Aang is forced to depend on his friends more than ever, as they work toward his mastery of the bending abilities and the ultimate goal of restoring balance to the world.

The final season begins as Aang recovers from a near-death experience in "The Awakening" (S3E01), realizing that the world believes him to be dead. For the first time, he feels guilt for something he could have actually prevented, the capture of the Earth Kingdom capital Ba Sing Se, and attempts to storm the Fire Nation alone. Aang's inability to accept that he does not have to stop the Fire Nation alone prompts another visit from Avatar Roku, who admits that his lack of foresight started the war and declares that Aang is destined to redeem him. Roku convinces Aang that keeping his survival a secret may be the best strategy. After finally coming to terms with his identity as the Avatar emotionally and psychologically at the end of the second season, Aang is now forced to keep his survival confidential, upending the progress he has made to this point. Whether offered illuminative glimpses of history from his Avatar lineage or assuaged of his fears of facing the Fire Lord by Katara, Sokka, and Toph, the resources Aang has access to continue to build back his confidence throughout the third season. While examining the possibilities for posttraumatic growth, Calhoun and Tedeschi note, "the degree and characteristics of growth will be influenced by the prevailing views and the types of resources of the individual's proximate cultures."[28] Even in cases where Aang's personal philosophies contrast with the prevailing views of the group, these unpleasant moments prove vital to Aang's emotional journey.

In the lead up to his climactic battle with Ozai, Aang runs away—perhaps subconsciously lured—to find another way to neutralize Ozai without committing murder. While every member of the group believes Aang must kill the Fire Lord, his journey outside of the group leads to an enlightened solution. At the same time, though, his friends and allies prepare the rest of their battle plans, confident that Aang will eventually return. Aang's ability to depend on his chosen family and spiritual ancestors, even in instances of disagreement and conflict, allows him to build unique resiliencies along his traumatic journey that is outside of individual growth processes. Adrian D. Van Breda's review of research in resiliency theory similarly "locates resiliency processes not so much within individuals, but within networks of social relationships," and that even "some individual resilience processes, such as sustained self-esteem, have been shown to be more relational than intrapsychic," emphasizing the impact that social groups have on individual's explorations of adversity and trauma.[29] It is by virtue of his tightknit peer group and connection with his spiritual ancestors that Aang works through his trauma to eventually embrace the role of the Avatar. Zuko's traumatic quests, on the other hand, offer a representation of resiliency quite different from that of Aang's community-centered course.

"You Must Look within Yourself to Save Yourself from Your Other Self": Trauma as Redemption Arc

Unlike Aang's campaign supported by similarly aged peers, Zuko's path is predominantly influenced by his relationship with his uncle, Iroh. Understanding the relationship between Uncle Iroh and Zuko is paramount to analyzing Zuko's journey through traumatic experiences, an uncommon child-adult partnership that sees both parties evolve as a result of this close-knit bond. Iroh's characterization serves as a knowing wink to the stereotyped depictions of bumbling, absent-minded adults within children's media through the slow reveal of both his competency as a father figure and his immense power as a firebender. Nakkula and Toshalis define mutually beneficial bonds like Zuko and Iroh's and the processes "through which youth and the adults who work with them promote each other's development" as "reciprocal transformation."[30] Iroh's keen sense of when to give Zuko space and when to push him in the right direction, though sometimes painful for both parties, facilitates Zuko's transformation that eventually leads to an alliance with Aang to end his father's tyrannical reign. Similar to strategies taken up by psychotherapists, Iroh is able to have a long-view of Zuko's journey through adversity, realizing that "resistance is not merely ... an interactional problem, but, rather, a starting point for exploration."[31] Iroh's patience and openness toward Zuko during moments of rage and doggedness foster a relationship where Iroh is able to get through to Zuko and guide him towards more positive and healthy growth. It is through Iroh that Zuko gradually learns to embrace the most painful parts of himself, his past, and find the strength to move forward and come to terms with his true identity.[32] Many of the key episodes discussed during earlier analysis of Aang's journey, including "The Southern Air Temple," "The Storm," and "The Avatar State," are reexamined below because of how intertwined Aang and Zuko's ameliorations of their respective traumas are, serving as mirrors for each other throughout the series.

Zuko's journey through trauma is significantly more parabolic when compared to Aang's primarily positive growth. Zuko's processing of trauma and difficulty uncovering his true purpose can be best understood through his relationships with his father, Ozai, Iroh, and his sister, Azula, his feelings toward the Fire Nation's ongoing atrocities, as well as the places from which he draws self-worth. Much of the first half of season one depicts Zuko doggedly pursuing Aang to fulfill the singular mission of restoring his honor. Banished from his own home by Ozai and visibly bearing the mark of his banishment, Zuko has been attempting to track down the Avatar. The first hint of Zuko's inner conflict over his identity occurs during his Agni Kai, or firebending duel, with Commander Zhao in "The Southern Air Temple."

Zuko seemingly recklessly challenges Zhao after the naval officer questions Ozai's love for the prince. During their fight, however, spectators are granted a glimpse into Zuko's veiled compassion. Even in victory, Zuko chooses not to permanently scar his opponent, a moment of mercy amidst his otherwise-vicious temperament. These traces of Zuko's humanity, especially amidst the brutal environment of competition within the Fire Nation, are also the impetus for his banishment.

As Iroh tells Zuko's ship crew in "The Storm," Zuko's protests against a general's suggestion of sacrificing a battalion of soldiers prompts Ozai to act. Translating this as disrespect toward his leadership, Ozai challenges his son to an Agni Kai. Refusing to fight his own father during their face-off, Zuko's pleas for mercy are ignored and Ozai deems this behavior as shameful. Ozai's violent and traumatizing actions toward his son shatter Zuko's ability to trust anyone and significantly alters his socialization processes; as Joyce Catlett writes of young people who experience incidents of severe physical abuse, these traumatic events "set up expectations of future betrayals or lead to certain blind-spots in an individual's ability to accurately judge the trustworthiness of others."[33] Zuko's struggles through trauma impede his ability to ascertain his true purpose, bringing about a significant identity crisis that he must resolve in order to work through his adversity.

Despite being a young person without peers, Zuko still draws upon his lived experiences to solve moral and social conundrums, demonstrating his unique agentic abilities. His capacity to exercise agency in manifold adverse social contexts, even when resulting in decisions that hinder his growth and lead toward compounded trauma, allow for another complex portrayal of youth atypical to US children's animated television.[34] In "The Blue Spirit" (S1E13), Zuko masks his identity in order to free Aang from Zhao. Zuko assumes that he can only be redeemed if he alone delivers the Avatar to Ozai, and he is willing to betray the Fire Nation to do so. This singular ambition continually disrupts his relationship with Iroh across the series. Iroh, who lost his only son during the war, treats Zuko as his own child, offering him guidance and compassion. The war continues to detrimentally influence not only communities outside of the Fire Nation but also those living within its borders. Zuko's prioritization of capturing Aang over heeding the advice he receives from his wholesome and restorative connection with Iroh is merely a hint of the war's ruinous effects on the world. From the sheer number of human casualties and decimated landscapes to the destruction of cultures and separation of families, the war's traumatic impact is vast and pervasive, affecting even the royal family that instigated this unwavering onslaught.

As a result of Zuko's traumatic experiences, there exist "complex feelings of vulnerability that alternate with those of optimism and pessimism," which he oscillates rashly between, upsetting the path of growth Iroh continually guides him on.[35] On the third anniversary of Zuko's banishment in "The

Avatar State," Princess Azula, under the orders of Ozai to capture Zuko and Iroh, visits her brother and disingenuously convinces him that Ozai regrets his banishment, rousing newfound hope in Zuko. Zuko lashes out at Iroh for attempting to dissuade him of his reinvigorated optimism, quickly tossing aside the bond they have built for the mere possibility of rekindling a relationship with his father. Fortunately, Iroh decides to travel with Zuko to Azula's ship and assists in Zuko's escape after Azula's ulterior motives are revealed. This episode illuminates how, regardless of Zuko's growth to this point and Iroh's enduring advice, Zuko still longs for his father's love and is particularly susceptible to Azula's emotional manipulations.

The physical and emotional scarring that Ozai inflicts on Zuko has lasting ripples in Zuko's understanding of himself and his relationships with others, causing posttraumatic stress that leads to struggles with managing emotions and negative impulses, as well as his capacity to create coping strategies for these adverse experiences.[36] Most noticeably, Zuko's relationship with Iroh is negatively impacted by the interpersonal traumas experienced at the hands of Ozai and are further heightened by Azula's manipulative tactics.[37] While on the run from Azula in "Avatar Day" (S2E05), Zuko is poorly adjusting to life as a refugee and to the trauma associated with being labeled a traitor and fugitive, an outcast to his nation (and father). Ignoring his uncle's pleas to embrace their new existence, Zuko instead steals from a nearby village. Iroh questions Zuko's actions, voicing his displeasures and challenging Zuko's motives in an attempt to prepare him for a fresh lifestyle outside of the auspices of the Fire Nation. Believing Iroh's principles to be incompatible with his own, Zuko decides to part ways with Iroh, leaving the single person who has stuck by his side all this time. Unlike Aang, who embraces his peer group in times of need, the critical inner voice Zuko develops as a consequence of his traumatic experiences dwells on and overstates the qualities in Iroh that disagree with his own self-image.[38] It is because of the genuine acknowledgment and love that Iroh shows for Zuko, in contrast to Zuko's typical adversarial relationships with others as well as his own perception of self, that disrupts their relationship.

After Zuko is reunited with Iroh, an injury his uncle suffers at the hands of Azula unleashes a wave of emotions that have been building within Zuko: guilt, sadness, fear, and, perhaps more notably, confusion over where and with whom his loyalties should lie. This inner turmoil swells as Zuko's narrative progresses, reaching a crescendo at the climax of "Bitter Work" (S2E09). Pleading with Iroh to teach him more powerful firebending techniques, Zuko must confront what has been, to this point in the series, the source of his power: anger. Though Iroh eventually relents, because of the precision and inner calm required of the dangerous technique of redirecting lightning, Iroh refuses to directly test this maneuver with Zuko by shooting lightning at him. Instead, Zuko decides to travel to the top of a mountain during a treacherous lightning storm, intent on practicing this powerful new ability. Overflowing with emotions and daring the heavens to test his resolve, Zuko explicitly acknowledges the feelings he has been struggling with, crying out, "Strike me! You've never held back before!" Zuko openly confesses his frustrations with the world, his inability to identify his purpose in life, and his difficulty locating motivation outside of the immense anger that has fueled him to this point (see Figure 8.2). This complex construction of childhood is remarkable for a US animated children's television series, leaving audiences unsure if he desperately wants to succeed in his plans to restore his honor or have the world end the pain he frustratingly cannot seem to escape.

At the end of "Lake Laogai" (S2E17), Iroh fervently interrogates Zuko's intentions as his nephew attempts to kidnap a captured Appa, asking him "Who are you? And what do *you* want?" Zuko is confronted with deciding his own destiny on his terms. His decision to free Appa, acting in a manner so inherently in conflict with how he as viewed himself to this point, leads to physical and mental manifestations of his inner turmoil, unable to digest this incredible shift in identity. Wrapped up in feelings of distress, confusion, depression, helplessness, guilt, and shame due to his traumatic past and the unfolding of recent events, Zuko's crisis materializes in literal

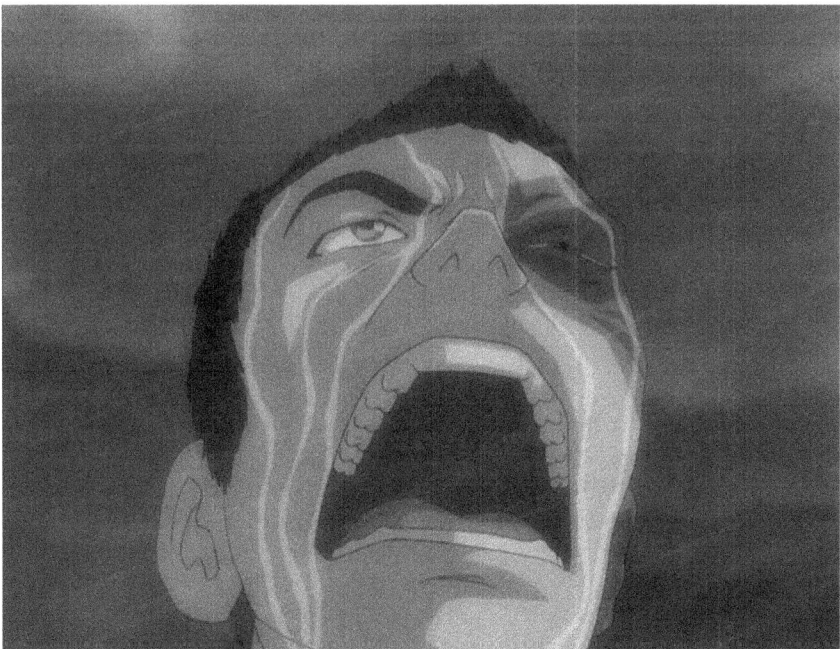

FIGURE 8.2 *Zuko finally expresses his frustrations toward the heavens. Still from "Bitter Work" (S2E09). Blu-ray release of* Avatar: The Last Airbender—The Complete Series *(2018).*

sickness during "The Earth King" (S2E18). The amalgamation of traumatic experience, physical illness, and a reformation of identity, which Nakkula and Toshalis believe to be "*the* pivotal task of adolescence," forces Zuko into rectifying the differences between his former single-minded task of regaining his honor and a new, unfamiliar version of himself removed from his Fire Nation allegiances.[39] This episode depicts Zuko experiencing hallucinations of himself with Aang's face, indicative of the series' binding of these two characters' destinies, as Zuko attempts to grapple with the shift in his core identity. The metamorphosis Zuko emerges from following this profound sickness bears witness to a version of Zuko entirely at peace, as he fully accepts his newfound identity serving tea at Iroh's shop in Ba Sing Se. This peacefulness is short-lived, however, as Azula's re-entrance in his life in "The Crossroads of Destiny" (S2E20) sees Zuko again abandon Iroh, relapsing back to his former self in a final attempt to reunite with his father.

After returning to the Fire Nation with Ozai's blessing in "The Awakening," the image Zuko had of his reunification with his father is not quite what he imagined. Battling a confluence of emotions and grappling with his unclear destiny, Zuko also realizes that, if Aang survived their final battle in "The Crossroads of Destiny," all of Ozai's praise would immediately turn to shame. Conflicted over Ozai's approval and unable to receive counsel from Iroh, Zuko is forced to search out his own answers in "The Avatar and the Fire Lord" (S3E06). This leads him to the Dragonbone Catacombs, which store the secret history of his great-grandfather, Fire Lord Sozin. After reading through this history, accounting Sozin's betrayal of his former best friend, Avatar Roku, in order to pursue dreams of world domination, Zuko returns to Iroh in prison. There, Iroh informs Zuko that though his father's grandfather was Sozin, his mother's grandfather was Roku. Zuko's combined heritage is the cause of his inner conflict. Discovering his ancestral lineage, Zuko grapples with his fate. Iroh explains to Zuko that he alone has the power to restore balance to the Fire Nation and therefore the world, but he must first find balance within himself. Like Aang, Zuko's inner doubts, emotional upheaval, and conflicts have to be resolved. The difficult process of coming to terms with the trauma of his past and present inform how he may forge his own path and identity in the future.

It is through these moments that Zuko begins to take control of his own destiny, coming to terms with his once-idealized father.[40] This leads to Zuko's direct confrontation of Ozai in "The Day of Black Sun, Part 2: The Eclipse" (S3E11) for his cruel treatment of him and the many lies that the Fire Nation has propagated. Crucially, Zuko recognizes that it is not his destiny to defeat Ozai and that he must prepare Aang in whatever ways he can to accomplish that monumental task. Breaking free from his father's iron grip over his confidence and decision-making processes, Zuko stands his ground, "having learned to accept what he wants rather than live in denial as a form of defense mechanism," while also accepting Iroh as his true parental figure.[41] Zuko's discovery of Avatar Roku's placement in his lineage assists in uncovering an entirely different understanding of the responsibilities of a Fire Nation Crown Prince. Rather than endlessly clamoring for his father's love and restoring his honor within the destructive and abusive environment Ozai has facilitated, Zuko realizes that the power his title holds encompasses far greater responsibility, including restoring the Fire Nation's relationships to other nations and returning balance to a world experiencing great suffering.

Zuko proceeds to follow the path with which he sets for himself, joining Aang and his peers in their efforts to defeat his father. Apologizing to the group about his past violent actions toward them as well as acknowledging the irredeemable damage the Fire Nation has wrought to their respective families and homelands, Zuko for the first time seeks forgiveness from those he has directly and indirectly harmed. Due to this profound transformation, he is forced to completely relearn how to firebend without depending on anger to fuel his power in "The Firebending Masters" (S3E13), further establishing the new balance he has reached on his journey through trauma. Zuko's and Aang's journeys are unified in the final episodes of the series, having directly confronted their destinies and reaching realizations of how they have the potential to restore balance to the world. Though both undoubtedly lose their way at various points throughout their journeys, it is through their trauma that they emerge as confident young people prepared to embrace their true purpose.

Conclusion—"I Don't Know If It's Because I'm Too Weak to Do It, or If I'm Strong Enough Not To": Agency, Trauma, and Children as Capable Social Actors

In "The Southern Raiders" (S3E16), Katara is given the opportunity to seek out the group of soldiers responsible for her mother's death. Despite Aang's warning to her to not give in to her vengeful desires, she and Zuko track down one of the soldiers, Yon Rha, who explains to Katara how her mother sacrificed herself to save Katara. Emotionally overwrought, Katara decides not to enact violent revenge, though she is unable to decipher if it is because of her inability to follow through on her plan or the strength to fight off these vindictive passions. This is just one example of how the rest of *Avatar*'s cast of characters and their collective quest to restore balance to the world are heavily influenced by their individual journeys through trauma, balancing their own identities in the process. It is precisely through their struggles with and growth due to adversity that they are able to eventually accomplish their goal, with the assistance of each other and in their individual endeavors.

Rather than simplistic and episodic narratives with neat and often-didactic closure, *Avatar* presents a sophisticated, interwoven story with multiple characters whose journeys through trauma push the overall narrative forward. Offering a unique media construction of young people exposed to stressors as part of their life process, the series respects its child audience and their capacity to comprehend and digest nuanced characters and narratives. Gordon L. Berry's contention that television as a medium is "both a communicator and mediator that can teach about and portray the dynamic nature of the various social roles in society … show[ing] their realistic and human foibles, balanced enough to demonstrate their strengths and weaknesses" reinforces the idea that above all, it is the content of television that determines its effects.[42] *Avatar*, by depicting complex characters and situations that involve a full spectrum of emotions as well as how various social roles adapt to adversity and work through their own and others' traumas, fulfills the role Berry believes television offers in "helping our children better understand the real and unreal, as well as the faulty and fair portrayals that are all a part of the creative process."[43] As a vessel for humanism, as Dara Poizner professes, the series demonstrates the power that young people have in solving distinctly human problems, including fear, guilt, tragedy, betrayal, crises of identity, and growing through traumatic experience.[44] These struggles and the triumphs through which Aang and Zuko accomplish major and minor feats are not often addressed in such layered accounts in US children's animated television.

Moving beyond what Ann E. Kaplan and Ban Wang problematize as the "relegating of trauma to a mystified silence," *Avatar* is able to critically examine different ways in which trauma impacts children and their identity formation processes.[45] *Avatar* actively resists the popular expectations of children's animation, while also attempting to "fill in the gaps between children's experiences and the theories of development imposed onto them," just as Hannah Dyer and Monica Eileen Patterson write of art for and by children.[46] Aang and Zuko's narrative arcs in the series constitute productive translations and depictions of trauma for young viewers that acknowledge the difficult, significant, and far-reaching nature of adverse experiences and champion child characters whose agentic decision-making processes and peer cultures contribute to their posttraumatic growth. While it would be naïve to assume that any single television series could affect change in the complex social structures of contemporary society, providing representations for young people that can assist them in coping with their own trauma, their own adversity, and offering strategies for resiliency, collaboration, and growth is essential in an increasingly ubiquitous media-centric environment. By resisting the pedagogic and moralizing structures that frequently frame children's media, the series' depictions of emotional upheaval and conflict resolution mark a significant shift in the possibilities for complex portrayals of young people. *Avatar* makes abundantly clear that, at times, life does indeed get rough, buddy, but it also attests to the fact that there is a path out of adversity leading to positive growth. Sometimes it takes surviving the dark tunnels.

Notes

1. "Award Profile: Avatar: The Last Airbender," *Peabody Awards*, n.d., https://peabodyawards.com/award-profile/avatar-the-last-airbender/.
2. Lucy Newby and Fearghus Roulston, "Innocent Victims and Troubled Combatants: Representations of Childhood and Adolescence in Post-conflict Northern Irish Cinema," in *Representing Agency in Popular Culture: Children and Youth on Page, Screen, and In Between*, eds. Ingrid E. Castro and Jessica Clark (Lexington Books, 2019), 37.
3. Ibid., 37.
4. Lawrence G. Calhoun and Richard G. Tedeschi, "The Foundations of Posttraumatic Growth: An Expanded Framework," in *Handbook of Posttraumatic Growth: Research and Practice*, eds. Lawrence G. Calhoun and Richard G. Tedeschi (Routledge, 2006), 12.
5. For further discussion of *Avatar*'s portrayal of disability and mental illness, see: Max Dosser's chapter in this collection; Amy Sue Marie Miller, "Portrayals of Mental Illness and Physical Disability in 21st Century Children's Animation," B.A. thesis (University of Louisville, 2014); Dara Poizner, "Avatar: The Last Airbender as a Moral Educator," *Footnotes* 10 (2019): 22–9.
6. Newby and Roulston, 25.
7. Joseph V. Giunta, "'Why Are You Keeping This Curiosity Door Locked?': Childhood Subjectivities and Play as Conflict Resolution in the Postmodern Web Series Stranger Things," in *Child and Youth Agency in Science Fiction: Travel, Technology, Time*, eds. Ingrid E. Castro and Jessica Clark (Lexington Books, 2019), 31.
8. Alan Prout and Allison James, "A New Paradigm for the Sociology of Childhood? Provenance, Promise and Problems," in *Constructing and Reconstructing Childhood*, eds. Allison James and Alan Prout (Falmer, 1990), 8.
9. Giunta, 35.
10. Michael J. Nakkula and Eric Toshalis, *Understanding Youth: Adolescent Development for Educators* (Harvard Education Press, 2006), 5.
11. Ibid., 5.
12. William A. Corsaro, *The Sociology of Childhood,* 4th ed. (SAGE, 2015); Giunta; Nakkula and Toshalis.
13. See Douglas Schulz's chapter in this collection on social identity theory for an in-depth examination of the series' depictions of identity, peer groups, and social worlds.

14 David Buckingham, *After the Death of Childhood: Growing Up in the Age of Electronic Media* (Polity Press, 2000), 6.
15 Giunta, 30.
16 For in-depth analysis of how children gain sophistication in their knowledge of the television medium and the ability to make distinctions between reality and fantasy aspects of this content, see Patricia Morison, Margaret McCarthy and Howard Gartner, "Exploring the Realities of Television with Children," *Journal of Broadcasting* 23.4 (1979): 453–63.
17 Ann E. Kaplan, *Trauma Culture: The Politics of Terror and Loss in Media and Literature* (Rutgers University Press, 2005), 19.
18 Ibid., 70.
19 Joy D. Osofsky, "Introduction," in *Young Children and Trauma: Intervention and Treatment*, ed. Joy D. Osofsky (Guilford Press, 2004), 4.
20 Giunta, 26.
21 Paul Wells, "Animation," in *The Television Genre Book*, ed. Glen Creeber, 2nd ed. (Palgrave Macmillan, 2008), 154.
22 Sadie P. Huston, Joanne M. Hall and Franke L. Pack, "Survivor Guilt: Analyzing the Concept and Its Contexts," *Advances in Nursing Science* 38.1 (2015): 20–33.
23 For more on the mental health and physical symptoms of survivor guilt, see: Alfred Garwood, "The Holocaust and the Power of Powerlessness: Survivor Guilt, an Unhealed Wound," *British Journal of Psychotherapy* 13.2 (1996): 243–58. For more on how youth might reach understandings of traumatic experiences, see: Hélène Berman, Marilyn Ford-Gilboe, Beth Moutrey and Sara Cekic, "Portraits of Pain and Promise: A Photographic Study of Bosnian Youth," *Canadian Journal of Nursing Research* 32.4 (2001): 21–41.
24 Steven G. Little, Angeleque Akin-Little and Matthew P. Somerville, "Response to Trauma in Children: An Examination of Effective Intervention and Post-Traumatic Growth," *School Psychology International* 32.5 (2011): 451.
25 Garwood, 246–50.
26 Phillip Mizen and Yaw Ofosu-Kusi, "Agency as Vulnerability: Accounting for Children's Movement to the Streets of Accra," *The Sociological Review* 61.2 (2013): 363–82.
27 Joy D. Osofsky and Howard J. Osofsky, "Challenges in Building Child and Family Resilience after Disasters," *Journal of Family Social Work* 21.2 (2018): 115–28.
28 Calhoun and Tedeschi, 12–13.
29 Adrian D. Van Breda, "A Critical Review of Resilience Theory and Its Relevance for Social Work," *Social Work/Maatskaplike Werk* 54.1 (2018): 8.
30 Nakkula and Toshalis, 14.
31 Sanna Vehviläinen, "Identifying and Managing Resistance in Psychoanalytic Interaction," in *Conversation Analysis and Psychotherapy*, eds. Anssi Peräkylä, Sanna Vehviläinen and Ivan Leudar (Cambridge University Press, 2008), 138.

32 Isis Cancio, Joshua Monzon and Margarita Sison, "The Iroh Effect: A Character Analysis on Zuko," *Facebook*, June 17, 2020, https://www.facebook.com/AteneoPsycheToday/posts/173500287524042.

33 Joyce Catlett, "Trust Issues: Why Is It So Hard for Some People to Trust?" *PsychAlive*, 2016, https://www.psychalive.org/trust-issues/.

34 Dorothy Bottrell, "Resistance, Resilience and Social Identities: Reframing 'Problem Youth' and the Problem of Schooling," *Journal of Youth Studies* 10.5 (2007): 597–616.

35 Joy D. Osofsky, "Perspectives on Work with Traumatized Young Children: How to Deal with the Feelings Emerging from Trauma Work," in *Young Children and Trauma: Intervention and Treatment*, ed. Joy D. Osofsky (Guilford Press, 2004), 329.

36 Sarah Hinshaw-Fuselier, Sherryl Scott Heller, Victoria T. Parton, Lara Robinson and Neil W. Boris, "Trauma and Attachment: The Case for Disrupted Attachment Disorder," in *Young Children and Trauma: Intervention and Treatment*, ed. Joy D. Osofsky (Guilford Press, 2004).

37 For further examination of how trauma affects young people's identity formation processes and relationship with caregivers, see: Maya L. Lewis and Chandra Ghosh Ippen, "Rainbows of Tears, Souls Full of Hope: Cultural Issues Related to Young Children and Trauma," in *Young Children and Trauma: Intervention and Treatment*, ed. Joy D. Osofsky (Guilford Press, 2004), 20.

38 Catlett; Lewis and Ippen, 29.

39 Nakkula and Toshalis, 18.

40 Hubertus Adam, et al., *Children—War and Persecution*, Proceedings of the Congress in Hamburg, September 26–29, 1993 (Secolo Verlag, 1995).

41 Cancio, Monzon, and Sison.

42 Gordon L. Berry, "Television, Social Roles, and Marginality: Portrayals of the Past and Images for the Future," in *Children and Television: Fifty Years of Research*, eds. Norma Pecora, John P. Murray and Ellen Ann Wartella (Lawrence Erlbaum Associates, 2007), 88.

43 Ibid., 104.

44 Poizner.

45 Ann E. Kaplan and Ban Wang, "Introduction: From Traumatic Paralysis to the Force Field of Modernity," in *Trauma and Cinema: Cross-Cultural Explorations*, eds. E. Ann Kaplan and Ban Wang (Hong Kong University Press, 2004), 12.

46 Hannah Dyer and Monica Eileen Patterson, "Editorial," *Global Studies of Childhood* 11.1 (2021): 4.

9

Lessons from the Southern Air Temple: How *Avatar: The Last Airbender* Negotiates the Trauma of Imperialism

Ryanne Kap

As a critically acclaimed children's television series, *Avatar: The Last Airbender* was never afraid to be complex. In the pilot, we meet Katara and Sokka, two young teens whose mother has been killed by the Fire Nation and whose father has left to fight in the war. The episode draws humor from this shift in the status quo, especially as Sokka attempts to make fierce warriors out of the tribe's young boys, but it just as quickly establishes the tragedy of the situation—all the men are away fighting Fire Nation soldiers, and their tribe's way of life has been severely compromised as a result. But it is "The Southern Air Temple" (S1E03) that signals the lengths the show is prepared to go to. Often referred to within the fandom as the first great episode of the series, as well as the point at which *Avatar* transcends genre, "The Southern Air Temple" addresses what being the last airbender truly means.

In addition to providing one of the most impactful moments of the series, the episode raises a fairly difficult question: How do you introduce genocide on a kids' show? And, perhaps more importantly: *why* introduce genocide on a kids' show? How are viewers, particularly children, expected to think and feel in response to this subject matter? By close-reading this episode through the lens of trauma theory, along with the vocabulary of semiotics and affect theory, we can examine how the components of the episode work together to help a young audience identify the trauma of imperialism and empathize with its victims.

"Everything Changed": Establishing the Fire Nation's Imperialist Legacy

The world of *Avatar* is shaped by many examples of both individual and collective trauma. Sociologist Kai Erikson differentiates between the two as such:

> by individual trauma I mean a blow to the psyche that breaks through one's defenses so suddenly and with such brutal force that one cannot react to it effectively ... by collective trauma, on the other hand, I mean a blow to the basic tissues of social life that damages the bonds attaching people together and impairs the prevailing sense of communality.[1]

In most circumstances, the trauma stems from the imperialist actions of the Fire Nation. As Katara narrates in the opening sequence, "Long ago, the four nations lived together in harmony. Then, everything changed when the Fire Nation attacked." The Fire Nation army—composed of massive ranks of soldiers backed by a tide of gigantic warships—is framed against a red horizon. Once the formidable scale of the Fire Nation's military has been established, the shot zooms in on the first line of soldiers, who blast fire directly at the viewer. This is our first and most constant image of imperialism within the show—a vast military set on destruction.

In his deconstruction of the Fire Nation's propaganda in "The Day of Black Sun, Part 2: The Eclipse" (S3E11), Zuko explains, "Growing up, we were taught that the Fire Nation was the greatest civilization in history. And somehow, the War was our way of sharing our greatness with the rest of the world." Throughout the series, viewers witness the Fire Nation's "greatness" as a quest for global domination, beginning with the pilot. In an extended version of the opening sequence, Katara explains, "Two years ago, my father and the men of my tribe journeyed to the Earth Kingdom to help fight against the Fire Nation, leaving me and my brother to look after our tribe." Immediately we understand the lived effects of imperialism—this is a war that has separated families and destabilized nations. The close-up on Katara and Sokka's mournful faces also creates an emotional link, effectively establishing the protagonists as sympathetic victims of a collective trauma. We also witness the temporal scale of imperialism: unlike the villain-of-the-week of more episodic television series, the Fire Nation is a consistent and gradually increasing threat throughout *Avatar*. As Aang and his friends travel through the four nations, they encounter the trauma of imperialism through refugee crises, prisons, work camps, and environmental disasters. Consequently, the show's critique of imperialist and colonialist forces has drawn attention in popular writing and within the fandom.[2]

While young viewers may not have the vocabulary to discuss and identify imperialism, the ideology and military strategies of the Fire Nation create clear parallels to any imperialist power throughout history. The Fire Nation's status as a highly industrialized nation with a formidable military echoes Japan's emergence as a military power due to its rapid industrialization in the late nineteenth century. The genocide of the Air Nomads mirrors the war crimes committed by the Chinese government against the Tibetan people; in the following chapter, Caleb Horowitz expounds on these connections in addition to other real-world examples. Meanwhile, a satirical article titled "'Avatar' Creators Not Sure How Many More Critically-Acclaimed Series It Will Take for Americans to Realize They're the Fire Nation"[3] makes a connection to American imperialism. In addition to noting that the show was developed shortly after 9/11 and during the beginnings of the Iraq War, author Thaddeus Cramer draws special attention to "The Headband" (S3E02), in which Aang poses as a student at a Fire Nation school and discovers the propaganda embedded in their education. For the younger target demographic of *Avatar*, the misrepresentation of history in the grade school curriculum may be the most accessible example of imperialism. By grounding the Fire Nation's actions in real-world history, *Avatar* implicitly communicates an anti-imperialist stance that challenges its viewers to examine the ongoing biases in their own lives. For a North American audience in particular, this challenge is set forth by encouraging them to identify not with the oppressors, but with the victims.

Negotiating the Trauma of Imperialism in "The Southern Air Temple"

By the series' third episode, viewers know little about the Air Nomads—but neither do Katara and Sokka. From the pilot, we learn that airbenders have not been seen in a hundred years, and they are thought to be extinct. When we meet Prince Zuko, we also learn that the Fire Nation has been searching for the Avatar, whom they know would have been born into the Air Nomads. Through these context clues, one can gather where the Fire Nation might have looked and what they might have done to ensure that their primary threat was eliminated. "The Southern Air Temple" unpacks these hints in a heartbreaking but ultimately hopeful episode. The A-plot follows Aang, Katara, and Sokka as they journey to the air temple to find out what happened to the airbenders, while the B-plot consists of Zuko and Iroh clashing with Zhao, a Fire Nation Commander, as they wait for their ship to be repaired.

As a twenty-two-minute episode of a children's show, "The Southern Air Temple" provides an incomplete picture of genocide. The scale and severity of the violence is only implied through the visuals of the aftermath, while the specific act itself is never named directly, but rather alluded to through plain dialogue. However, through the lens of individual trauma, Aang's grief provides an anchoring perspective that allows the viewers to engage with collective trauma, even if in a limited capacity. The complexity of the trauma of imperialism is also explored through Zuko's storyline, which provides a counterpart to Aang's story. As Joseph V. Giunta explores in the preceding chapter, the parallel arcs of these two characters provide a rich depiction of young characters encountering and transforming from trauma. This chapter takes up Giunta's investigation of how trauma is "translated" in the show and whether *Avatar*, as a piece of children's media, can help viewers make meaning out of trauma, but on a micro-level. Thus, by close-reading "The Southern Air Temple," we will explore how the medium of animation works to create meaning, and how its translation results in a unique emotional mapping of imperial trauma.

As animation scholars Kathrin Fahlenbrach and Maike Sarah Reinerth posit, "the fact that every stimulus can be controlled and may be altered to meet the desired effect" contributes to animation's "great potential to effectively address and stimulate emotions in viewers."[4] In terms of animation's affective quality, they provide the term "emotion metaphors," which "are a specific category of conceptual metaphors that have emotions as their target domain."[5] These metaphors "elaborate on an emotion by relating the depiction of prototypic emotion expressions to a different experiential domain using film style (e.g., in the use of color or camera perspective), characters …, and settings."[6] By mapping emotions in this way, emotion metaphors "convey a more complex inner state" that extends beyond an emotion expression, and in this way communicate "invisible aspects" such as "affective appraisal (e.g. pleasant—unpleasant)."[7] Affective appraisal, in turn, leads to an emotional response within the viewer based on their appraisal of the situation.[8] By understanding how various elements express and evoke emotion within the audience, we can then examine how and why *Avatar* introduces its young viewers to traumatic content.

On a structural level, the episode is full of diversions. From the juxtaposition of the A and B plot to abrupt shifts in tone for both comedic and dramatic effect, the narrative stages the viewer's journey of discovery as a gradual one, in which the enormity of genocide cannot be confronted immediately nor even directly. Thus, the visual language of the episode eases the viewer into the complexities of the trauma at its core. The use of color in particular helps establish a certain emotion, which is then contrasted or even undermined by the tension of the plot. This conflict destabilizes the viewing experience by introducing unpredictable shifts in tone, which in turn demonstrates trauma as an invasive and threatening presence. Unlike the first two episodes, which feature a white title card, the title is imposed on a close-up shot of a blazing sunrise, with a white-hot sun ascending quickly into the yellow sky to the sound of a gong. This abrupt intensity establishes a sense of unease, yet it quickly fades into a more relaxing atmosphere as the episode proper begins. The first shot shows the same sunrise, now reflected in a lake surrounded by sloping cliffs. The use of yellow subtly nods to the Air Nomads (i.e., their yellow robes) and, more generally, creates an atmosphere of optimism and happiness. A sense of tranquility is also established as a gentle pan flute plays; the shot pans left to reveal Appa, an Air Bison and Aang's animal companion, peacefully munching on his breakfast. Aang's voice reflects the brightness of the scenery as he expresses how excited he is to show Katara the temple. However, in a much more reserved tone, she gently reminds him that "it's been a hundred years since [he's] been home." However, Aang misreads Katara's reminder completely, telling her, "That's why I'm so excited!", to which she replies, "It's just … a lot can change in all that time." Her insistence sets a wary tone for the episode, but just as it threatens to darken the moment, the scene diverts to Aang pranking Sokka into waking up.

However, the lightheartedness is immediately undercut by the cut to Zuko and Iroh's storyline. The bright yellow sky is now streaked with dark clouds and pierced by the knifelike prows of huge, identical warships. In another pan to the left, we see Zuko's much smaller ship as he and Iroh disembark, their tiny figures almost indiscernible among the backdrop of an imposing armada. The emphasis on scale, particularly how miniscule Zuko, Iroh, and their ship appear, serves to highlight the shift in status quo. Prior to this episode, Zuko has been in a position of power, giving orders to his crew and even to his uncle. But Commander Zhao's entrance makes it clear that Zuko is no longer at an advantage. From Zhao towering above the two to his menacing tone, he is clearly established as the more antagonistic and powerful figure in their brief exchange. Zuko slips into a more awkward register as he offers a poorly constructed lie about the damage to his ship, thus giving the perceptive Zhao the upper hand in the conversation, but Zuko shifts back into being defiant and aggressive when Zhao challenges him on his story. Showing Zuko as the underdog is not altogether surprising given his status as a disgraced prince in exile, but in an episode that focuses on the extreme abuse of power through the Fire Nation's attack on the Air Nomads, the arc of Zuko's storyline reinforces his privileged, but also precarious position within the imperialist system. For the peoples whose persecution he is inherently seeking to perpetuate—since, by capturing the Avatar, he will ensure the Fire Nation's military success—the stakes are much higher than confronting the grownup version of a schoolyard bully. However, the decision to juxtapose these struggles ultimately expands the perspectives that the viewer is invited to identify with, as I will explore further in my analysis.

The return to the A-plot highlights two essential contrasts that continue throughout the episode. Scenes with Zuko and Iroh feature harsher, darker shades of red and gray as well as a more intense and threatening score, which create a sense of tension comparable to that of the main plot as Zuko tries to hide news of the Avatar from this menacing secondary antagonist.

Furthermore, the shift from their tense encounter with Zhao to Sokka complaining about being hungry introduces one of the episode's main strategies to navigate the trauma of imperialism: the use of comic relief. As a television show aimed at children, *Avatar* avoids a continuous stream of serious subject matter through moments of levity. Thus, Sokka's priority for most of the episode is food, which offsets the focus on what could be awaiting them at the air temple. Yet it also results in another sharp contrast when Katara tells Aang she wants to talk to him about the airbenders. These shifts in tone carry on throughout the episode, only escalating as the plot intensifies; here, they set up the pivotal turn for when Aang finally discovers the truth. But his denial is also integral to the episode. This scene introduces what is at stake for Aang and why he initially needs to protect himself— and be protected—from the truth. Although Aang fails to understand what Katara is hinting at, she makes her meaning explicit when she warns him, "I just want you to be prepared for what you might see. The Fire Nation is ruthless. They killed my mother, and they could have done the same to your people."

In this exchange, we see Katara's role in negotiating the trauma of imperialism as she demonstrates what eventually becomes a trademark habit: sharing her own trauma as a way to empathize with and support others going through similar experiences. According to trauma theory scholars such as Cathy Caruth, trauma is "impossible to understand, impossible to forget and impossible to voice. Articulating trauma and gaining linguistic control over it becomes the struggle of the traumatized."[9] However, Katara is consistently able to describe her experiences, suggesting that her emotional vulnerability is a strength that allows her to provide guidance to others. As Ruth Richards explores in her chapter on the representation of gender in *Avatar*, the caretaking role Katara inhabits is often viewed as stereotypically feminine, a reading which implies a weakness in her characterization and, more broadly, denigrates a nurturing disposition as a character trait. Yet this episode demonstrates that Katara's emotional sensitivity and supportive nature are among her greatest assets. Rather than diminishing her character, these traits help her make meaningful connections with others and model a healthier way of responding to traumatic situations. In this particular context, Katara's more practical, grounded approach establishes her as the much-needed antithesis of Aang, who denies the possibility of loss altogether by insisting that "[j]ust because no one has seen an airbender, doesn't mean the Fire Nation killed them all." To frame their respective positions through the five stages of grief, Aang occupies a state of denial while Katara represents acceptance. But here, his commitment to denial begins to waver. Despite his upbeat tone, his facial expression shifts again, with his eyebrows slightly knitted to convey doubt as he adds, "They probably escaped!" Yet when Katara tries to comfort Aang by placing a hand on his shoulder and telling him, "I know it's hard to accept," he once again assumes a happy expression and extends his denial, claiming that since the air temple is only accessible by flying bison, the Fire Nation must have been unable to find it. Aang's rationalizations are far from convincing, establishing his avoidant approach as futile in comparison to Katara's advanced emotional maturity and acceptance of the situation. Notably, this contrast allows the viewer to sympathize with both characters—just as the viewer can appreciate Katara's emotional vulnerability and empathy with Aang, they can also understand Aang's denial as a strategic coping mechanism in the face of immense loss.

As we return to the B-plot, the episode then begins to build the case for Zuko as a sympathetic figure with whom the audience can identify and eventually even root for. Through the more cartoonishly villainous Zhao, who consistently berates and undermines Zuko, we come to understand the latter as a victim of the system his father has enforced. On his part, Zuko is less than enthusiastic about the Fire Nation's impending world domination. When Zhao explains the Fire Nation's plan to claim victory in the war, Zuko angrily retorts, "If my father thinks the rest of the world will follow him willingly, he is a fool!" Notably, his hostile attitude in this moment, and throughout most of the show, stems from resentment toward his father rather than the empire his father is creating. In the same vein, his single-minded focus on capturing the Avatar is ultimately about regaining his father's approval. Yet, as Zhao coldly observes, his father does not actually want him back, and his disdain for his son is forever symbolized by the scar he inflicted on him. Through his unique relationship to the Fire Nation and its broader imperialist strategy, Zuko exemplifies Michael Rothberg's concept of the "implicated subject," which describes an individual who is "[l]ess 'actively' involved than perpetrators" but does not "fit the mold of the 'passive' bystander, either."[10] Though Zuko perpetuates colonial violence in his search for the Avatar, as seen in the following episode when he burns down the village on Kyoshi Island in "The Warriors of Kyoshi" (S1E04), "The Southern Air Temple" illustrates his simultaneous privilege and powerlessness within the imperialist system. Rothberg theorizes the implicated subject as a means of attaining "a more complete picture of the workings of violence, exploitation, and domination."[11] Accordingly, beneath the bravado Zuko is an emotionally and physically abused teenager who has been manipulated by his own father into continuing the Fire Nation's imperialist legacy. Thus, *Avatar* reveals the multifaceted nature of imperialist violence by showing how even its apparent benefiters, i.e., the son of the imperialist overlord, can still be victimized. Furthermore, by presenting Zuko as more accessible and relatable, viewers are also invited to expand their empathy even further by beginning to care for this increasingly complex character.

Yet the key moment in this scene is the confirmation of the Air Nomad genocide. When Zhao inquires about Zuko's progress in finding the Avatar, he says mockingly, "The Avatar *died* a hundred years ago. Along with the rest of the airbenders." The revelation also marks a significant shift in the narrative; the trajectory of the episode is no longer finding out what happened to the airbenders, but rather how Aang will discover the news and what effect that loss will have on him. Thus, we are given a new way of relating to the trauma at the center of this episode, as we now carry the tension of knowing what Katara and Sokka already suspect. When the episode cuts back to the A-plot, the visual relief of the lighter background and more pleasing aesthetics (particularly the unique architecture of the temple) is undermined by the knowledge that Aang is returning to what is essentially a graveyard. As Aang surveys the destitute landscape, he acknowledges the obvious evidence of abandonment when he remarks, "This place used to be full of monks and lemurs and bison. Now there's just a bunch of weeds. I can't believe how much things have changed." He is centered in the frame with withered trees on either side of him, further emphasizing the absence of life. But rather than leave him isolated, the shot pulls back to reveal Katara and Sokka, who share a concerned look behind his back. Through this subtle visual cue, the show resists positioning Aang as a solitary figure processing the drastic change on his own. He is supported by Sokka and Katara, who not only know about the pain he is going through but also actively want to protect him from it. Upon hearing the dejection in Aang's voice, they make the joint, unspoken decision to distract him. They approach him together and Sokka cheerfully asks Aang to explain an airbending game. The heavy silence is broken by a gong and upbeat percussion, with fast, dynamic shots matching the pace of the ball Aang airbends toward Sokka. When the ball sends Sokka flying into a snowdrift, Aang laughs gleefully. Sokka then quips, "Making him feel better is putting me in a world of hurt."

Yet these distractions are only temporary; the trauma of imperialism is constantly at risk of overflowing into the present. In the next instant, Sokka finds the helmet of a Fire Nation soldier. He decides that they should tell Aang. Katara calls Aang over, but as she watches him approach, still airbending the ball, she contemplates the decision and, at the last second, waterbends a pile of snow to cover the helmet. As they walk away to explore the rest of the temple, Sokka tells Katara, "You know, you can't protect him forever"; then, in the next moment when they are alone, he reiterates, "Katara, firebenders were here. You can't pretend they weren't." She walks past him, forcing him to match her pace both literally and figuratively, and replies, "I can for Aang's sake. If he finds out the Fire Nation invaded his home, he'll be devastated." Whereas Katara has, until this point, urged Aang to confront the reality of the situation, encountering the air temple for herself and witnessing his increasing discomfort causes her to change tack. Once again, Katara exemplifies a new form of empathy for the viewer. Although the demands of the narrative mean that, like the other diversions, this tactic will fail, Katara's acknowledgment of how extreme Aang's pain will be further elicits sympathy from the viewer in anticipation of what he is about to discover.

To further flesh out the impact of imperial trauma, the episode introduces the equivalent of a parent for Aang: Monk Gyatso. Before the viewer can process the loss of an entire people, the show scales it down to the loss of a single person. Similarly, Katara uses the death of her mother Kya as a way of empathizing with and mourning for all victims of Fire Nation violence. Using an individual to represent a collective trauma draws parallels to the perception of Anne Frank as the face of the Holocaust. As Holocaust survivor and writer Primo Levi suggests, "One single Anne Frank moves us more than the countless others who suffered just as she did, but whose faces have remained in the shadows. Perhaps it is better that way: If we were capable of taking in the suffering of all those people, we would not be able to live." While viewing such an extensive trauma through the lens of a single individual is undoubtedly reductive, the powerful emotional resonance of connecting with individual trauma can be viewed as a gateway to empathy for the victims of a collective trauma.

Upon encountering a statue of his old mentor, Aang describes him as the "greatest airbender in the world," explaining to his companions that "he taught me everything I know." As Aang bows to the statue, the shot zooms in to center it on the screen. In a match-cut, the statue is reanimated into the living Gyatso. To contrast the cold blue color palette of the present-day, the flashback is slightly overexposed and overlaid with a soft yellow hue, which communicates the nostalgia and warmth of Aang's memory and provides a callback to the opening of the episode. The ensuing sense of peace and security is further established by Gyatso's dialogue, which positions him as a soothing presence. When Aang wonders if the monks made a mistake in naming him as the Avatar, Gyatso replies in a calm, reassuring tone, "The only mistake they made was telling you before you turned sixteen. But we can't concern ourselves with what was. We must act on what is." The episode cuts to a panning shot, revealing the air temple in its prime, with a triumphant, orchestral score signaling the grandeur of the scene. Sunbeams cast a warm glow over the temple as sky bison and their calves graze from the trees. In the close-up shots of Aang and Gyatso, the background is almost overwhelmed by the sunlight, with the clouds and mountains softening into nearly indistinguishable outlines. They appear to be in another world altogether, one that is private and sacred. When Aang becomes frustrated with Gyatso's vague hints at the next stage of his journey as the Avatar, Gyatso lightens the mood by getting Aang to help him airbend cakes onto a group of monks below. Then, after the two bow to each other, demonstrating mutual respect, Gyatso says warmly to Aang, "Your aim has improved greatly, my young pupil" and pats his head in an added gesture of love and care.

In just a few lines of dialogue, the great love that Aang and Gyatso have for each other is perfectly expressed. Gyatso's sense of humor reads as a precedent for Aang's, further informing Aang's character by establishing how formative this relationship was in his development. Moreover, by experiencing the flashback along with Aang, the viewer is brought firmly into his point of view, such that we experience the jarring return to the present along with him. Through a slightly less aligned match-cut, the soft, warm yellow overtone of the past disappears into the cooler blue tones of the present. The abrupt shift is further accentuated by piles of snow and the visible, jagged outlines of mountains in the background. When used in reverse, the match-cut emphasizes the loss Aang feels; all brightness and warmth has been leached from the world, and what was once a kind and loving mentor is now a lifeless statue. The loss signified by this contrast, if not already evoked within the viewer, is highlighted when Katara senses Aang's grief and says, "You must miss him." Whereas Aang was previously excited to speak about his mentor, his expression is now troubled and his voice is heavier as he simply says, "Yeah" before searching for answers about his role as the Avatar in the sanctuary.

By shifting his focus to his mission as the Avatar, Aang is able to avoid dwelling in negative emotions. However, as we arrive at the emotional climax of the episode, the diversions finally fail and the unspeakable weight of trauma is encountered. In terms of comic relief, the episode often illustrates the incongruity theory of humor, in which people laugh at "what surprises them, is unexpected, or is odd in a nonthreatening way."[12] We can understand the function of this type of humor through the relief theory, which claims that "humor stems from the relief experienced when tensions are engendered and removed from an individual. Humor then results from a release of nervous energy."[13] For example, when the trio see a shadow enter the sanctuary and assume it is a firebender, suspenseful music plays as they ready for an attack. Then, when the mysterious figure is revealed to be a harmless lemur, the music shifts from the heavy bass usually associated with the Fire Nation to a short but whimsical melody. The tension is cleared, leading to another moment in which Aang excels in his element. As Sokka chases after the lemur to make it a meal, Aang quickly outruns him, laughing as he uses airbending to run on the walls and leap off a cliff. There is nothing but pure joy in the scene, especially due to the upbeat and lighthearted score. But the carefree chase leads Aang into a sectioned off part of the temple, where he pulls back the curtains to reveal a room filled with the skeletons of Fire Nation soldiers. A quick series of shots establishes the impact of the moment: first a slow zoom-in on the skeleton of an airbender; then a cut to Aang's horrified expression; and finally, a close-up on Gyatso's wooden necklace, with a dramatic musical sting signifying that these are his remains. Aang utters Gyatso's name, his pupils trembling in an exaggerated visual of shock and sadness, then falls to his knees and begins to cry. The medium-long shot shows him as a small, forlorn child in the background, the only living soul in a room of corpses. Gyatso's skeletal hand occupies the foreground, massive compared to Aang's defeated figure.

When Sokka arrives, he is still in the lighthearted mood he has maintained for most of the episode. He intrudes on Aang's mourning by asking, "Hey, Aang! You find my dinner yet?" This time, the subversion of expectations has led to a horrific discovery. The tension has been built, but cannot be released through comedic relief. Instead, we are forced to remain in the deep discomfort of this moment. In fact, the viewer knowing what Sokka does not makes his callback to the previous comedic circumstance feel perverse, with no way to reconcile or move successfully between the comedic and tragic registers. By refusing to defuse the tension, *Avatar* demonstrates trauma as deeply debilitating, and in this moment, beyond conscious expression. As Sokka realizes the gravity of the situation and puts a hand on Aang's shoulder, the latter's eyes and tattoos glow light blue (see Figure 9.1). Aang's grief is powerful on its own, but it also triggers his power as he enters the Avatar State.

Prior to this, Aang has only invoked the Avatar State out of self-preservation—first to save himself and Appa from drowning during a storm, as revealed in a flashback during "The Boy in the Iceberg" (S1E01), and then

FIGURE 9.1 *Aang enters the Avatar State. Still from "The Southern Air Temple" (S1E03). Blu-ray release of* Avatar: The Last Airbender—The Complete Series *(2018).*

a second time in the episode previous, "The Avatar Returns" (S1E02), when Zuko blasts him off his ship and into the water below. But now, instead of power as a form of protection, power becomes an expression of pain. Consumed by his emotions, Aang ignores Sokka's desperate pleas for him to "snap out of it." Instead, as he rises to his feet, he conjures a windstorm that sends Sokka flying and knocks him into the debris. Katara arrives and decides to try to calm him down, which Sokka urges her to do "before he blows us off the mountain!" She struggles against the wind to approach Aang, but as he flies into the air, his bending pushes her away. His ascent provides a frightening visual: his glowing eyes no longer look human, and he is suspended in an intense sphere of wind that threatens to hurt the only companions he has left. For the consistently happy, bright, and energetic Aang, this dramatic transformation speaks to the depths of his pain, rage, and despair at the loss of his mentor. It also provides a striking visual metaphor for trauma and grief. The initial reaction to pain on this scale can drive away those who try to offer support, to the extent that it risks hurting them as well. The intermingled feelings of despair and rage can be isolating and all-consuming.

Interrupting this tense conflict is the Agni Kai between Zhao and Zuko, which the latter initiates after Zhao disrespects him. In the duel, Zuko is once again the underdog as Zhao easily overpowers him; he quickly knocks him to the ground and prepares to finish him off with a fire blast. However, Iroh provides guidance from the sidelines, leading Zuko to break Zhao's root by sweeping his leg. This game-changing move is the so-called "money shot" of the scene—the music pauses, time slows down, and the move is shown three times, from multiple angles, so as to convey the gravity of the moment. Zuko now has the upper hand—the music resumes as he lands on his feet, emphasizing his triumph. But just as Zuko is about to deliver the final blow, he hesitates. A close-up reveals the inner struggle in his eyes, and his pause results in Zhao angrily demanding, "Do it!" But, as Giunta has noted previously, this exchange allows Zuko to become a sympathetic character in his own right. Rather than scarring his opponent, Zuko shows Zhao the mercy his own father denied him. Zuko is further aligned with a sense of morality when, as he walks away, Zhao acts disgracefully by launching a surprise attack. Iroh, continuing to be Zuko's only source of support, intervenes and shames Zhao, telling him, "Even in exile, my nephew is more honourable than you." In another humanizing moment, Zuko shows vulnerability by asking, "Did you really mean that, Uncle?" As Iroh jokingly deflects, Zuko briefly smiles before the shot cuts back to the fleet of Fire Nation ships, now bathed in shafts of light against a warm sunset. Thus, the B-plot ends satisfyingly, rewarding viewers for their identification, however strong or momentary, with Zuko. Moreover, the sentimental moment between Iroh and Zuko gestures to Zuko's own form of community. Though he does not yet have the same bonds that Aang, Katara, and Sokka are forming, his uncle's care for him reinforces the importance of kinship in recovering from trauma.

The most impactful example of this form of healing, however, comes immediately after this scene. Kept at a distance by the forceful winds, Katara calls out:

> Aang! I know you're upset and I know how hard it is to lose the people you love. I went through the same thing when I lost my mom. Monk Gyatso and the other airbenders may be gone, but you still have a family. Sokka and I! We're your family now.

Here, what distinguishes Katara's entreaty from her previous moments of empathy and connection is the reinstatement of community. Not only does she acknowledge their shared trauma, but she takes one step further and offers more than her own experiences—by presenting herself and Sokka as Aang's new family, she restores his sense of belonging and kinship. To return to Erikson's definition of trauma, the psyche-destroying effect of individual trauma, as incited by the discovery of the societal-scale collective trauma, is softened by Katara beginning to rebuild the bonds that the deaths of the Air Nomads have destroyed.

Consequently, Aang lets the wind die down and sinks back to the ground. Sokka promises that they will not let anything happen to him, and as soon as Katara takes Aang's hand in hers, the blue glow disappears and the scene's lighting becomes slightly warmer to signify a return to his natural state. Aang collapses, exhausted from the sudden surge of power, and allows himself to be held. Now that Katara has quite literally grounded him, Aang is able to name his trauma in full. Importantly, he first apologizes for disappearing into the Avatar State. Katara assures him that it was not his fault, thus making space to acknowledge victims of trauma as just that—victims, not perpetrators. Then, he finally moves into the stage of acceptance as he admits, "If the firebenders found this temple, that means they found the other ones, too. I really am the last airbender." As Aang closes his eyes in defeat, Katara tightens her embrace. But rather than lingering on this close-up shot of their literal closeness, the episode cuts to a medium-long shot (see Figure 9.2). The complexity of their expressions fades into simple dots and lines, but produces the more iconic image of Katara hugging Aang as Sokka puts a hand on her arm and stands over them. They are tiny figures against the rock and mountains, everything cast in purple by the setting sun. They are children trying to heal, and leaning on each other to do so.

As part of the narrative of a children's show, the limited depiction of genocide risks creating a standard by which the way we think about trauma is dependent on our emotional investment in its most identifiable victims. *Avatar* does offer, especially for a younger audience, is an intimate, moment-by-moment reckoning with grief, and an intimate, moment-by-moment

FIGURE 9.2 *Sokka and Katara comfort Aang*. Still from "The Southern Air Temple" (S1E03). Blu-ray release of Avatar: The Last Airbender—The Complete Series (2018).

adjustment to it. Before leaving the air temple, Aang explains to the lemur, "You, me, and Appa—we're all that's left of this place. We have to stick together." He then tells Katara and Sokka, "Say hello to the newest member of our family." By accepting Katara's extension of kinship, Aang is able to offer that sense of connectedness and community to another—even a lemur. Of course, this does not "solve" his grief. Although he and Katara laugh together in one last moment of comic relief, thanks to the newly named Momo stealing food from the ever-hungry Sokka, this isn't the note the episode ends on. A long shot shows Appa as a tiny white blip against the expanse of purple-blue sky, with the now completely empty air temple looming above him. We alternate between a shot of Aang staring at the air temple, his expression composed but neutral, then a reverse shot that shows the air temple receding into the distance. The shot remains static as Aang is pulled further toward the corner of the screen, his back turned to the viewer. Then, in the final shot, Aang is not visible at all. Instead, the angle centers the air temple to show it from a first-person point of view, as if we are watching it disappear from Aang's position. As the clouds gather to hide the temple, letting it fade into the dark night sky, it is clear that we are far from the bright yellow sunrise that opened the episode; there is no full circle moment at the end, only a color-coded acknowledgment that the tone has darkened and there is no going back.

Yet the use of framing and perspective implicates the viewer in a way that involves them in Aang's grief. By making us stand in for Aang, the final shot places us firmly in the world of *Avatar* and makes us, too, a member of the family. It is empathy through cinematography—we now belong in this somber moment, as if it was our home fading away. If we can accept the show's offer to be in community with Aang—to join his chosen family, and to stand with them against the harms of imperialism—then perhaps we can be prepared for what comes next. In this way, for *Avatar*'s young viewers, the greatest lesson from "The Southern Air Temple" may be that of identification. During their formative, identity-building years, "[c]hildren and adolescents identify with both people and characters and try on alternative ideas, images, attitudes, and identities."[14] By identifying with characters whose experiences differ greatly from their own—such as young children displaced and traumatized by war and genocide—they learn to "expand [their] emotional horizons and social perspectives."[15] Thus, it is crucial to ask ourselves, as viewers and scholars, what kinds of perspectives *Avatar* offers to its viewers. What kinds of attitudes are rewarded within the show, and which are critiqued or even dismissed? Which characters are we asked to identify with the most, and which seem to be beyond identification? By looking closely at the unique and complex language of animation, we can begin to answer these questions and explore how "even" a children's show can challenge and expand our point of view.

Notes

1 K. T. Erikson, *Everything in Its Path* (Simon and Schuster, 1976), 153–4.
2 A more detailed exploration of *Avatar*'s engagement with colonialism is available in Paola Vera's article "'Avatar: The Last Airbender': A Critique of Colonialism," *The Stanford Daily*, June 16, 2020.
3 Thaddeus Cramer, "'Avatar' Creators Not Sure How Many More Critically-Acclaimed Series It Will Take for Americans to Realize They're the Fire Nation," *The Hard Drive*, September 11, 2021.
4 Kathrin Fahlenbrach and Maike Sarah Reinerth, "Audiovisual Metaphors and Metonymies of Emotions in Animated Moving Images," in *Emotion in Animated Films*, ed. Meike Uhrig (Routledge, 2018), 39.
5 Ibid., 40.
6 Ibid.
7 Ibid., 40–1.

8   Anne Hamby and Niusha Jones, "The Effect of Affect: An Appraisal Theory Perspective on Emotional Engagement in Narrative Persuasion," *Journal of Advertising* (July 2021): 1–16.
9   Mirela Lapugean, "Speaking about the Unspeakable: Trauma and Representation," *British and American Studies* 21 (2015): 87.
10 Michael Rothberg, *The Implicated Subject: Beyond Victims and Perpetrators* (Stanford University Press, 2019), 1.
11 Ibid., 20.
12 John C. Meyer, "Humor as a Double-Edged Sword: Four Functions of Humor in Communication," *Communication Theory* 10.3 (August 2000): 313.
13 Ibid., 312.
14 Jonathan Cohen, "Defining Identification: A Theoretical Look at the Identification of Audiences with Media Characters," *Mass Communication & Society* 4.3 (August 2001): 249.
15 Ibid., 249.

10

Far from the Last Airbender: Cultural Trauma Construction and Diasporic Reimaginings in *Avatar* and *Korra*

Caleb Horowitz

Avatar: The Last Airbender (Nickelodeon, 2005–8) and *The Legend of Korra* (Nickelodeon, 2012–14; nick.com, 2014) were both hailed by critics for tackling big themes with nuance and grace.[1] Although the latter show sometimes stumbled in its depictions of complex geopolitical issues through the lens of its rapidly modernizing fictional world and has been criticized for its politics and whiteness, its engagement with the airbender genocide that defined the original *Avatar* follows through on answering important questions about recovery from genocide, intergenerational trauma, and diaspora.[2]

In this chapter, I discuss the plots of *Avatar*, *Korra*, the canonical *Avatar* comic *The Promise*—which serves as an *Avatar* sequel and *Korra* prequel—and the canonical *Korra* sequel comic *Turf Wars*. In particular, this chapter is concerned with the way the Air Nomads and Air Nation are represented across these texts and the real-world parallels these representations suggest. The challenge faced by a fictional ethnoreligious group recovering from genocide resembles the real-world struggle faced by Tibetan and Jewish diaspora groups today, and these powerful parallels can help viewers better understand diaspora, genocide, and trauma construction. Drawing from Jeffrey C. Alexander and other's *Cultural Trauma and Collective*

Identity and scholarship on diaspora by Paul Gilroy, Hyungji Park, and James Clifford, I argue that *Avatar* and *Korra* present a powerful model of diasporic belonging in the wake of human and cultural destruction.

Background

The Air Nomad genocide is not only central to *Avatar*—it defines it, from its title to its themes. Aang, the show's protagonist, is the sole survivor of the massacre of a tribe of peaceful nomads with magical air manipulation powers and a rich history of religious and cultural traditions. The Air Nomads were massacred by the Fire Nation in an attempt to kill Aang, the current iteration of the perpetually reincarnated Avatar. The Fire Nation was successful in wiping out the peaceful tribe almost entirely, but it failed to find Aang, who had fled shortly before the destruction of his people and accidentally spent 100 years alive but comatose in an iceberg. From the moment he woke back up to the moment he died, Aang's life was marked by the trauma of the loss of his entire people, a trauma that was passed down to his children and, through the complex negotiations and constructions of cultural trauma narratives, to a series of totally unrelated individuals roughly 70 years later.

In *Avatar*'s sequel show, *Korra*, Aang's son Tenzin and Tenzin's three children are initially the only remaining airbenders. However, when Korra makes a crucial decision to leave the portals to the Spirit World open in the conclusion of the show's second season, she somehow triggers a global rebalancing, in which dozens of seemingly randomly selected nonbenders from across nations become airbenders overnight. Tenzin takes on the mantle of putting together a new group of airbenders and training them in their adoptive cultural and religious history. In doing so, he makes the critical decision to rebrand the "Air Nomads" the "Air Nation," signaling a shift into modernity that aligns with the politics and industrialization crucial to *Korra*. However, Tenzin's new "nation" is not a nation-state but rather a diasporic cluster of belonging. Rather than making claims about real-world nationalist movements, *Korra*'s Air Nation plot instead focuses on movements of resilience and toward survival for dispersed diasporic populations.

Real-World Parallels: Tibet and Jews

The airbenders of *Avatar* and *Korra* are explicitly modeled after Tibetan Buddhist monks, mixed with influences from Hinduism. From their monastic lifestyle, shaved heads, and architecture to specific practices and beliefs, such as using a set of toys to find a reincarnated religious leader, the writers of *Avatar* make clear parallels between the fictional tribe and their real-world inspiration. Even the martial art associated with airbending, Baguazhang, is a technique tied to Buddhist and Taoist practice. However, I argue that, in the sequel show, *Korra*, which has notably been critiqued for being too Western and/or white in comparison to its predecessor show, the *Avatar* universe creates an additional real-world parallel for the fictional airbenders—the Jewish people (it is worth noting that many Jews are not white, but American Jewishness is often perceived as white Ashkenazi Jewishness).[3] I acknowledge that this parallel is not as explicit in the text as *Avatar*'s Buddhism. Jewishness, specifically American Jewishness, is something I brought to the text as a patrilineal American Jew from an interfaith family first experiencing *Korra* when I was in high school and reckoning with my own Jewish heritage. *Korra*'s unique perspectives on ethnoreligion, conversion, and cultural trauma recovery resonated as particularly Jewish themes. Regardless of authorial intent, *Korra* has much to say about American Jewishness.

Korra creates American Jewish parallels through the positioning of the airbender minority in a New York City-coded "Republic City" and by representing the complications of maintaining an ethnoreligion in the wake of genocide. The show simultaneously maintains the airbenders' Tibetan parallels in cultural practices, aesthetics, and the experience of being in exile in one's own homeland. These complex parallels coalesce into a potent exploration of diaspora existence, and this fictional diaspora may help viewers understand real-world diasporas better.

Cultural Trauma and Collective Identity

Central to the contemporary stories of Tibetans, Jews, and airbenders are genocide and the impact of that genocide on those who survive. Whereas the genocide of the Jewish people—the Holocaust, or *Shoah*—that resulted in the murder of more than 6 million Jews is, for the most part, well-understood globally, the cultural genocide of Tibet is less internationally recognized. As recently as May 2021, Penpa Tsering, president of the Central Tibetan Agency, hoping to pressure the international community to act in the context of the upcoming 2022 Beijing Winter Olympics, warned of the imminent threat of "cultural genocide" in Tibet.[4] This threat did not begin recently but has been ongoing for decades. In 1950, the People's Republic of China asserted its national sovereignty over the region of Tibet. Approximately 87,000 Tibetans and 2,000 Chinese government troops were killed in the resulting conflict, and 100,000 Tibetans fled by the end of March 1959 as refugees; among those who fled was the Dalai Lama himself, who found exile in India.[5] The same year, monasteries in Tibet were closed and Chinese law and custom were imposed in the region.[6] The Tibetan government in exile estimated a total death toll of 1.2 million by 1994, although this number is disputed.[7]

Both the Holocaust and the cultural genocide of Tibet mark clear examples of trauma. However, the way this trauma becomes culturally felt for a particular group is highly specific and political. In *Cultural Trauma and Collective Identity*, Jeffrey C. Alexander and the other authors outline the ways in which individually felt trauma becomes culturally significant and passed to those who did not directly experience the traumatizing event. "Cultural trauma," Alexander writes, "occurs when members of a collectivity feel that they have been subjected to a horrendous event that leaves indelible marks upon their group consciousness, marking their memories forever and changing their future identity in fundamental and irrevocable ways."[8] In outlining his theory of cultural trauma, Alexander stresses the difference between traumatic events directly experienced by an individual and the cultural construction of trauma for this collectivity. In the case of the airbenders, Tenzin and his siblings did not experience the Air Nomad genocide directly; however, its trauma was inherited. Of course, epigenetic studies indicate ties between parental trauma and altered genetics of offspring, but this scientific explanation alone does not account for the specifics of the ways second and third generation Holocaust survivors interact with and remember the Holocaust; these memories are culturally constructed.[9]

Alexander maintains that "events do not, in and of themselves, create collective trauma ... Trauma is a socially mediated attribution."[10] With regard to the Holocaust, it is worth noting that Nazi crimes against Jews were initially seen, as Alexander notes, as merely one atrocity among "a whole series of other brutalities that were considered to be the natural results of the ill wind of [the Second World War]."[11] It took work on the part of American Jews, who, for the most part, were first "enter[ing] the civil sphere as advocates for their own rather than others' causes" in 1945 to position the crimes taken against them as traumatic or at all worthy of recognition.[12] As Alexander writes:

> a claim of traumatic cultural damage ... must be established by deliberate efforts on the part of cultural carriers. ... In most cases, the process of establishing is a contested process, with different political groups divided with respect to whether a trauma occurred (historical contestation), how its meaning should be regarded (contestation over interpretation), and what kinds of feelings ... it should arouse.[13]

In this sense, Tibet proves a powerful example, with competing narratives of unity and liberation versus ethnic cleansing and genocide.

In *Avatar*, this process of historical contestation is most clearly represented in the episode "The Headband" (*Avatar* S3E02), in which Aang briefly attends a Fire Nation school in disguise. "What year did Fire Lord Sozin battle the Air Nation army?" the teacher asks the class after they recite the Fire Nation national anthem. "Is that a trick question?" Aang asks. "The Air Nomads didn't have a formal military. Sozin defeated them by ambush." Here, historical memory is clearly contested for political reasons. The language of an "Air Nation army" shifts the event that occurred from a "genocide" to a successful "war," preventing Fire Nation citizens from viewing the events that unfolded as traumatic.

In *Korra*, the Air Nomad genocide is still largely not seen by the world population for the deeply traumatic event that it was. Tenzin and his family live on a tiny island outside Republic City, the bustling capital of the newly formed United Republic of Nations and the hub of intercultural existence formed in what was once a Fire Nation colony in the Earth Kingdom. While Aang is widely admired as a world savior—a large green Lady Liberty-style statue rests on Aang Memorial Island and displays prominently in the show as a symbol of this new cultural melting pot city (it is worth noting that Jewish author Emma Lazarus penned the poem inscribed on the base of Lady Liberty about immigration and refuge)—there is little effort by the larger population to discuss reparations or the plight of the few remaining airbenders. Instead, efforts to maintain Air Nomad culture were spearheaded by Aang himself as a teenager through the creation of a group of cultural carriers known as the "Air Acolytes," individuals who devoted their lives to studying and preserving Air Nomad culture, religion, beliefs, and history in the historical Air Temples. Alexander marks this kind of maintenance as the work of "cultural specialists such as priests, politicians, intellectuals, journalists, moral entrepreneurs, and leaders of social movements."[14] The creation of the Air Acolytes occurs during the events of *The Promise*, the first of Gene Luen Yang's canonical *Avatar* graphic novels. Importantly, the Air Acolytes had no original ties to Air Nomads and emerged from multiple chapters of the Official Avatar Aang Fan Club, some of whom initially uncritically and appropriatively recreated Air Nomad culture, even going so far as to tattoo themselves with the signature Air Nomad arrows. Aang successfully taught the group why their appropriation of these tattoos was inappropriate but still chose to teach the fan club members enough about his culture to maintain Air Nomad history successfully.

When the Avatar Aang Fan Club members first appear in *The Promise*, they are wearing Earth Kingdom outfits with images of Avatar Aang on their chests.[15] The shift of the Avatar Aang Fan Club from a fun organization that mindlessly appropriated airbender tradition into a serious, even solemn group of cultural carriers mimics what Alexander describes: "Typically, at the beginning of the trauma process, most audience members see little if any relation between themselves and the victimized group. Only if the victims are represented in terms of valued qualities shared by the larger collective identity will the audience be able to symbolically participate in the experience of the originating trauma."[16] Aang's treatment of his fan club members is a strategic one. He tells them, "You already have the *hearts* of Air Nomads, so I've decided to teach you the *ways* of Air Nomads."[17] In doing so, he invites the new group to participate in the experience of his heritage. He frames this choice in terms of cultural survival. "I have to admit, I'm a little nervous about this. I love my people's culture and I don't want to see it corrupted. At the same time, it can't just belong to history. Air Nomad culture has to belong to the future, too," he explains.[18] This scene mimics contemporary Jewish conversion practices; the process of conversion to Judaism is marked by the rabbi making sure the would-be convert understands the trauma of the Jewish people and questioning why somebody would want to become a member of such an oppressed group. However, once a person decides to become a Jew, it is as if they have always been a Jew, as if "their souls were already at Sinai" (a reference to the covenant made on Mount Sinai on the last day of Moses' life).[19] This idea that the convert already has the heart or soul of an airbender or Jew is crucial in the process of creating a sense of shared culture. Aang therefore successfully navigates the process of communicating his trauma to a new generation of cultural carriers, allowing the survival of the Air Nomads.

This notion of inherited trauma is complicated by the emergence of the new airbenders in *Korra*. When nonbenders from across the globe suddenly gain airbending overnight, Tenzin successfully recruits a group of these new benders as members of his new Air Nation. His goal is to rebuild the society that was virtually destroyed by the Fire Nation 170 years prior with, essentially, new converts. The metaphor here is complex because of the shifting and sometimes contradictory symbolic function of bending within the *Avatar* universe (bending has at times functioned as metaphor for culture, religion, wealth, and martial arts). If airbenders are understood as mimicking ethnoreligion, it is worth interrogating whether bending functions as ethnicity or religion in this metaphor. Paradoxically, it can best be understood to function as neither and both. This is best illustrated by the divide between the Air Acolytes and the new Air Nation members. The acolytes have mastered the history of the Air Nomads but lack prior ethnic ties to the tribe. In this way, they resemble converts. However, the members of the new Air Nation come from disparate cultures and often lack any knowledge of Air Nomad culture or tradition, but they now have airbending. If bending is read as "ethnic," they are tied to the airbender tribe as such. If it is read as religious, they are better understood as converts. This mimics some of the real-world confusion felt by Jews in attempting to describe their positionality as "religious Jews," "secular Jews," "ethnic Jews," and converts who may have religious or secular practices. The Oxford English Dictionary definition of "ethnicity," "Status in respect of membership of a group regarded as ultimately of common descent, or having a common national or cultural tradition" makes "ethnic Jew" a nebulous distinction, because it allows for membership through ancestry *or* through nation and culture, meaning that *all* Jews are, in a sense, "ethnic Jews."[20] The new Air Nation, a combination of cobbled-together converts, benders and nonbenders, none of whom—except Tenzin and his direct descendants—have any blood ties to the Air Nomads of old, mimics this complex sense of tribe and argues for an ethnic identity that privileges difference rather than one rooted in homogeneity.

In the *Cultural Trauma and Collective Identity* chapter "Cultural Trauma: Slavery and the Formation of African American Identity," Ron Eyerman notes that antebellum slavery in America became a uniting force for African Americans as an emerging identity, regardless of "whether or not they had themselves been slaves or had any knowledge of or feeling for Africa."[21] In much the same way, the Air Nomad genocide became a memory prompting unity for the disparate peoples of the new Air Nation. In their duties as members of a new Air Nation, both acolytes and benders don the burden of the Air Nomad genocide as a central component in "their attempts to forge a collective identity out of its remembrance."[22] And just as "African American" was a linguistic designation resulting from a complex series of competing terminologies resulting from "the failure of reconstruction to integrate former slaves and their offspring as Americans, and to the new consensus concerning the past in the dominant culture in which slavery was depicted as benign and civilizing," Tenzin's choice to call his new collective the "Air Nation" is explicitly political.[23] Such a "nation" must reject the assimilationist "melting pot" nature of a unified Republic City. The airbenders, who now represent their own unified people, finally have the numbers and cultural memory necessary to distinguish themselves as separate from the United Republic.

Diasporas: Gilroy, Park, and Clifford

Although the new Air Nation has its own set of customs, laws, and practices separate from Republic City's and drawn from the long history of the Air Nomad tradition, the idea that the new Air Nation is separate politically from Republic City is one the show complicates throughout. In the third and fourth seasons of *Korra*, the new Air Nation comes to resemble a diasporic ethnic population rather than a grounded nation. This is due in large part to the Air Nation's decision to use Air Temple Island in Republic City as a central hub for training new benders rather than living in the old Air Temples and the decision made by Tenzin in the finale of season three, "Venom of the Red Lotus" (*Korra* S3E13) to refuse a state grounded in homogeneity and place. Tenzin tells the new airbenders, "[T]he Air Nation will reclaim its nomadic roots and roam the earth. But unlike our ancestors, we will serve people of all nations, working wherever there is corruption and discord to restore balance and peace." Tenzin privileges diaspora existence here as a means of recovery from genocide. It is tempting to draw further real-world conclusions about nation-states from the self-imposed statelessness of the Air Nation, but the fictional Air Nation does not resemble real-world nations sufficiently for a normative argument about nation-states to be made. (Anti-)Zionism(s), for instance, remain beyond the scope of this article and beyond the scope of the parallels presented in the source materials. Real-world nationalist movements are littered with complications for which *Korra* has no analogues; here, I argue for *Korra*'s value as a tool for showing/reflecting the workings of diaspora rather than as a text making an implicit argument about statehood.

Nonetheless, any discussion of diaspora must acknowledge that all diasporic populations require a "homeland," whether temporally or spatially removed, in order to function as such. For the Air Nomads, this homeland is the decimated Air Temples of the years prior to the genocide. Different definitions for diaspora contain a variety of perspectives toward homeland. Is diaspora rooted in a need for return or is such return a "negation" of the diaspora? James Clifford's complex exploration of diasporas and their relationship to nationalist movements leads to a definition of diaspora somewhere between the national and the universal. In contrast to William Safran's definition, which relies on an understanding of the homeland as "a place of eventual return, when the time is right," Clifford writes that "whatever their ideologies of purity, diasporic cultural forms can never, in practice, be exclusively nationalist."[24] Clifford cites Daniel and Jonathan Boyarin, who define diaspora as something between the two extremes of "Pauline universalist humanism" and "autochthonous nationalism," arguing that universalist humanism "attains a love for humanity at the price of imperialist inclusion/conversion" and "authochthonous nationalism" "gains a feeling of rootedness at the expense of excluding others with old and new claims in the land."[25] The Boyarins, according to Clifford, see diaspora as a mode of existence in which cultural distinction is maintained against the pressures of assimilation, but also a "daily converse with others" is upheld.[26] Diasporic cultural forms, Clifford argues, are "deployed in transnational networks built from multiple attachments," and they "encode practices of accommodation with, as well as resistance to, host countries and their norms."[27] Diaspora, then, constitutes the narrow space between assimilation and ethnonationalism as a way of maintaining cultural identity without total separation.

This definition of diaspora fits neatly with what is seen of the Air Nation in *Korra*. *Korra*'s Air Nation is dedicated to a life of roaming service to all peoples of the world rather than the reclusive lifestyle of the old homeland (the pre-genocide Air Temple existence). The goals of the Air Nomads are sometimes aligned with and sometimes opposed to the goals of Republic City's leadership. Although in season four, the Air Nomads help defeat the Earth Kingdom's villainous fascist leader, Kuvira, in the sequel graphic novel *Turf Wars*, the same Air Nomads find themselves at odds with the United Republic of Nations President, Raiko, when they disagree with him over how the piece of land around the new spirit portal should be used.[28] The new Air Nomads in their traditional Air Nation attire stand out against the United Republic military forces as anything but assimilated. This principled stand by Air Nation citizens against the government mirrors real-world diaspora protest movements, such as "Never Again Action," a Jewish-led movement dedicated to dismantling the U.S. Immigration and Customs Enforcement (ICE). Such diasporic movements make use of historical persecution as a tool to foster strategic unity for political reasons. These diasporic social and political movements rely on a rejection of assimilation but a simultaneous focus on social and political causes separate from a relationship to the homeland. In this way, *Korra* again mimics real-world diaspora groups with its Air Nation.

The distinction between diaspora literature and simple multiculturalism is worth noting. In *The Cambridge Companion to Asian American Literature* chapter "Toward a Definition of Diaspora Literature," Hyungji Park differentiates between Asian American literature and specifically *diasporic* Asian American literature. In Asian American texts, she argues, "[w]hen Asia is depicted, it is often seen as a source of fanciful and fictive alterity or exoticism; the Asian country is rarely given an independent or ongoing existence beyond serving as a 'source' for the Asian American."[29] She contrasts this to diaspora literature, which "might be said to provide a kind of resistance to the assimilationist or United States-centered tradition and grant the Asian country an autonomous value of its own."[30] These diasporic Asian literatures acknowledge "ongoing allegiances to nations beyond U.S. boundaries" and do not hold "'assimilation' or 'teleology' toward an 'American' future as assumed values."[31] In *Korra*, the Air Nation members function as non-assimilated citizens who maintain a strong relationship with both Republic City and the Air Nation. This doubleness mirrors the experience of diasporic groups who may feel allegiances to multiple groups, nations, or cultural traditions.[32]

Although members of any given diasporic group may share a homeland and culture, diaspora existence necessitates a focus on difference as well. Diasporas, as Clifford notes, "connect multiple communities of a dispersed population."[33] This multiplicity is an important part of diaspora existence. Throughout *The Black Atlantic*, Gilroy relies on this multiplicity as a means of combatting "ethnic absolutism."[34] Just as contemporary Jewishness must make space for a bevy of diasporic populations with traditions that have spun off from centuries of existence in exile, so too do the Air Nation members bring a multitude of traditions and cultural values with them. Although the new Air Nation of *Korra* may seem homogenous in clothing and religious and cultural activities, this apparent homogeneity is undercut by the heritage of its members. The initial crop of new airbenders are all Earth Kingdom citizens, but the goal of the Air Nation is to recruit airbenders from all nations. The new Air Nation is tied by airbending culture, clothing, and tradition, but not by total homogeneity or the obliteration of difference.

In *The Black Atlantic*, Gilroy identifies the problem of various groups' reliance on "cultural nationalism, on the differences as an absolute break in the histories and experiences of 'black' and 'white' people."[35] He argues instead for "another, more difficult option ... the theorization of creolization, metissage, mestizaje, and hybridity."[36] For Gilroy, this mixity is exciting and a rebellion against "ethnic absolutism."[37] These new hybrid forms point to "cultural mutation" and "restless (dis)continuity."[38] In the combination of "continuity" and "discontinuity," Gilroy identifies the paradox of diaspora, that culture is simultaneously obsessively remembered and also always already in flux. These ideas about mixity and cultural mutation are central to *Korra*, in which the path forward for the Air Nation post-genocide relies on embracing a diaspora built on complex ties between disparate peoples and a rejection of simple ethnic absolutism.

What does the Air Nation as diaspora teach us about real-world diasporas? What is the purpose of this parallel? *Korra*'s Air Nation serves as a rare mirror for the lived experiences of diasporic viewers. Whereas national and ethnic borders in *Avatar* remain relatively clear-cut, the messy world of *Korra* depicts something truly rare in children's television—a diasporic ethnic population recovering from genocide. This depiction of a diaspora is bolstered by the show's focus on conversations about maintaining tradition versus adaptation to modernity and/or assimilation, which can metaphorically be seen in Tenzin's attempts to recruit the new airbenders, many of whom are initially uncomfortable with their identities, in the episode "Rebirth" (*Korra* S3E02). It can also be seen in the show's complex depictions of mixed identity—whereas *Avatar* features characters of different cultures and bending backgrounds interacting and forming friendships, mixed characters (characters with parents from two different nations and/or parents who are two different kinds of benders) are not seen until *Korra*. The Air Nation serves as a powerful model of maintaining culture and tradition while leaving room for difference and change. Paul Gilroy privileges this diaspora existence as a means of preserving ethnic and cultural ties while celebrating the mixity of multicultural existence. This new cobbled-together, diverse coalition of airbenders reflects Gilroy's celebration of diaspora; while condemning the causes of diaspora, Gilroy celebrates the resulting mixture and expansion of culture.

Although the Air Nomads may not at first resemble a diaspora, their refusal to remain fixed in a single location or even within former airbender spaces reflects a shift toward diasporic, exilic belonging. The new devotion of the airbending nomads to a life of wandering and helping reflects the Jewish value of *tikkun olam*, "repairing the world," a command which must be tied to motion, to movement. "[I]n a way," Tenzin tells his children in "A Breath of Fresh Air" (*Korra* S3E01), "all airbenders are our family." Such a family offers new routes of belonging. The new Air Nation, Tenzin realizes, "repossesses" the "curse of homelessness or the cure of enforced exile" by affirming and reconstructing it "as the basis of a privileged standpoint from which certain useful and critical perceptions about the modern world become more likely."[39] Tenzin is a citizen of the United Republic and lives in Republic City, but he is also a wanderer of the Air Nation, a people rooted in diasporic exile.

The Floating Fatherland; Tibetan Diaspora(s)

"Diaspora is not only about those who depart. One need not leave home to be displaced," Chris Vasantkumar argues in "Tibetan Diaspora, Mobility, and Place: 'Exiles in Their Own Homeland.'"[40] Vasantkumar conducted ethnographic research in the Ando region of what was once Tibet and in the primary location of exilic Tibetans—Dharamsala, India—and found that both groups felt that Tibet was "absent, elsewhere."[41] In other words, whether Tibetans lived in Tibet or outside of it, they felt they were members of the diaspora. While the longing of Tibetans in exile for Tibet was unsurprising, Vasantkumar was caught off-guard by "encountering Tibetans *in Tibet* who lamented the departure of Tibet itself."[42] In order to understand the position of these Tibetans, Vasantkumar proposes, new modes of diaspora must be constructed. While Gilroy focused on diasporas rooted in the movement of *peoples*, the case of Tibet raises a powerful alternative question: what if people haven't moved, but "*home itself* [has] departed?"[43] This scenario "unsettle[s] frameworks that treat movement itself as a purely human (or animal) preserve in an otherwise static world."[44]

But how has the Tibetan homeland "moved?" The loss of Tibet, the destruction of Tibetan temples and other signs of culture, and the exile of the Dalai Lama, the "primary symbol of Tibetan unity," all contributed to the feeling of Tibet departing Tibet.[45] Or, to quote Gertrude Stein, "there is no there there."[46] As with airbenders, who freely access the old Air Temples, Tibetan diaspora exists even within Tibet. "[T]rue Tibet lies not in a territorially defined homeland, but in a body of religious and cultural practice that has traveled with the Dalai Lama and other members of the Tibetan religio-cultural elite into India and the West, and, perhaps, beyond territory itself."[47] For Tenzin, the experience of exile in the homeland was a powerful motivator for the creation of a new, floating, diasporic homeland.

How could Tenzin, the last airbender, ever feel at home within the empty temple halls of his ancestors? What is an Air Nation without airbenders? Place is not enough, *Korra* argues, culture is *people*. Vasantkumar points to the German Jewish poet Heinrich Heine as the "prototype for a nomadic, extra-territorial existence, whose home shifts beneath his feet," and who, in contrast to "Herderian territorial nationalism ... evoked what he termed a *portatives vaterland* (portable fatherland), in which belonging was not natural or grounded but the result of situationally constrained bricolage."[48] Diasporas, Vasantkumar argues, can form *in situ* when "home itself is scattered."[49] These challenges to traditional conceptions of diaspora—people do not move, places do—leave less room for the positive affirmation of diaspora central to Gilroy. Rather it points to new modes of belonging as solutions to the problem of loss. Tibet clearly shows that understandings of culture and nation are not as simple as place. *Korra*'s Air Nation successfully serves as a parallel for such a complex diaspora experience by creating a diaspora population that has a consistent relationship with and sometimes lives in, the "homeland." Although the Air Temples are treated as historical sites and an important part of Air Nation history, the Air Nation maintains its sense of diasporic identity.

Conclusion

Korra is unique as a children's show for not only addressing the aftereffects of genocide but also for showing how genocide narratives are culturally constructed and how groups can recover from this genocide. Through powerful parallels with both Tibetans and Jews, *Korra* creates resonances for diasporic viewers hoping to see themselves onscreen and for viewers who may have little experience with diasporic groups before encountering *Korra*.

Through its depiction of the new Air Nation, *Korra* points to new diasporic imaginings worth exploring. What could we achieve as the scattered peoples of genocide if we poured our energies into welcoming those of mixed heritage, those of different backgrounds, races, geographic locations, and religious leanings? *Korra* teaches us that an important survival tool for diasporic groups recovering from genocide is to embrace diaspora bonds and use them strategically. "True wisdom begins when we accept things as they are," Tenzin says in "A Breath of Fresh Air." It is an odd, almost contradictory thesis in season three, which is subtitled "Change." But Tenzin does not advocate for a static reality. His "as they are" is fluid, constantly changing. "You started a new age," he tells Korra. "There's no going back to the past." And what do we have to lose if we ignore the changing and complex realities of diaspora groups? Creating diasporic consciousness takes work, but it is work upon which our survivals rest. Celebration of diaspora existence rooted in culture, pluralism, and peoplehood allows post-genocide populations a way to maintain culture while evolving. This process relies on the continual (re)construction of trauma memory for new group members and celebrating the ties that bring us together in distant lands.

Notes

1. Joanna Robinson, "How a Nickelodeon Cartoon Became One of the Most Powerful, Subversive Shows of 2014," *Vanity Fair*, December 14, 2014, https://www.vanityfair.com/hollywood/2014/12/korra-series-finale-recap-gay-asami; Oliver Sava, "*The Legend of Korra:* 'Day of Colossus'/'The Last Stand,'" *The AV Club*, December 19, 2014, https://www.avclub.com/the-legend-of-korra-day-of-the-colossus-the-last-st–1798182260.
2. Jeannette Ng, "The Inescapable Whiteness of *Avatar: The Legend of Korra* and Its Uncomfortable Implications," *Medium*, July 25, 2020, https://medium.com/@nettlefish/the-inescapable-whiteness-of-avatar-the-legend-of-korra-and-its-uncomfortable-implications-debc76bbf7f.
3. Eli Horowitz, "Ashkenormativity in the Jewish Community," *Sefaria*, August 25, 2020, https://www.sefaria.org/sheets/258180.3?lang=bi&with=all&lang2=en.
4. Sanjeev Miglani and Cate Cadell, "'Running out of time': Tibetan President-Elect Warns of Cultural Genocide," *Reuters*, May 21, 2021, https://www.reuters.com/world/asia-pacific/running-out-time-tibetan-president-elect-warns-cultural-genocide-2021-05-21/.
5. "China/Tibet (1950–present.)," *University of Central Arkansas*, https://uca.edu/politicalscience/dadm-project/asiapacific-region/chinatibet-1950-present/
6. Ibid.
7. Valerie Strauss and Daniel Southerl, "How Many Died? New Evidence Suggest Far Higher Numbers for the Victims of Mao Zedong's Era," *The Washington Post*, July 17, 1994, https://www.washingtonpost.com/archive/politics/1994/07/17/how-many-died-new-evidence-suggests-far-higher-numbers-for-the-victims-of-mao-zedongs-era/01044df5-03dd-49f4-a453-a033c5287bce/.
8. Jeffrey C. Alexander, "Toward a Theory of Cultural Trauma," in *Cultural Trauma and Collective Identity*, eds. Jeffrey C. Alexander, Ron Eyerman, and Bernard Giesen (University of California Press, 2004), 1.
9. Tori DeAngelis, "The Legacy of Trauma: An Emerging Line of Research Is Exploring How Historical and Cultural Traumas Affect Survivors' Children for Generations to Come," *Monitor on Psychology* 50.2 (February 2019): 36.
10. Alexander, "Toward," 8.
11. Jeffrey C. Alexander, "On the Social Construction of Moral Universals: The 'Holocaust' from War Crimes to Trauma Drama," in *Cultural Trauma and Collective Identity*, eds. Jeffrey C. Alexander, Ron Eyerman, and Bernard Giesen (University of California Press, 2004), 197.

12 Ibid., 217.
13 Alexander, "Toward," 38.
14 Ibid.
15 Gene Luen Yang, *The Promise*, Library Edition (Dark Horse Comics, 2013), 95.
16 Alexander, "Toward," 14.
17 Yang, 224.
18 Ibid.
19 Aish, "A Convert's Soul," *Aish*, n.d., https://www.aish.com/atr/A_Converts_Soul.html.
20 Oxford English Dictionary Online, s.v. "ethnicity (n.)," accessed June 20, 2021, https://www-oed-com.liblink.uncw.edu/view/Entry/64791?redirectedFrom=ethnicity#eid.
21 Ron Eyerman, "Cultural Trauma: Slavery and the Formation of African American Identity," in *Cultural Trauma and Collective Identity*, eds. Jeffrey C. Alexander, Ron Eyerman, and Bernard Giesen (University of California Press, 2004), 60.
22 Ibid.
23 Ibid., 63.
24 William Safran, "Diasporas in Modern Societies: Myths of Homeland and Return," *Diaspora: A Journal of Transnational Studies* 1.1 (Spring 1991): 83–4; James Clifford, "Diasporas," *Cultural Anthropology* 9.3 (August 1994): 307.
25 Daniel Boyarin and Jonathan Boyarin, "Diaspora: Generation and the Ground of Jewish Identity," *Critical Inquiry* 19.4 (1993): 693–725; Clifford, 322.
26 Clifford.
27 Ibid., 307–8.
28 Michael Dante DiMartino, *The Legend of Korra: Turf Wars*, Library Edition (Dark Horse Comics, 2019), 83–9.
29 Hyungji Park, "Toward a Definition of Diaspora Literature," in *The Cambridge Companion to Asian American Literature*, eds. Crystal Parikh and Daniel Y. Kim (Cambridge University Press, 2015), 156.
30 Ibid.
31 Ibid., 157.
32 For an exploration of the concept of "dual loyalty" and why having multiple allegiances or contradictory ties is a common experience that should not cause us to "question the justifiability of a plurality of political loyalties," see: Ilan Zvi Baron, "The Problem of Dual Loyalty," *Canadian Journal of Political Science/Revue Canadienne de Science Politique* 42.4 (2009): 1025–44.
33 Clifford, 304.
34 Paul Gilroy, *The Black Atlantic and Double Consciousness* (Verso, 1993).
35 Ibid., 2.

36 Ibid.
37 Ibid.
38 Ibid.
39 Ibid., 111.
40 Chris Vasantkumar, "Tibetan Diaspora, Mobility and Place: 'Exiles in Their Own Homeland'," *Theory, Culture & Society* 34.1 (January 2017): 115.
41 Ibid.
42 Ibid., 116.
43 Ibid.
44 Ibid.
45 Ibid., 119.
46 Gertrude Stein made this remark in *Everybody's Autobiography* (1937), in regards to how her Oakland childhood home no longer existed. Gertrude Stein, *Everybody's Autobiography* (Cooper Square Publishers, 1971), 289.
47 Vasantkumar, 119.
48 Ibid., 120–1.
49 Ibid., 122.

PART FOUR

Fandom and Reception

11

From Fan Blogs to Earth Rumble VI: Disability Discourse on *Avatar: The Last Airbender*

Max Dosser

After buying tickets for an event called Earth Rumble VI, you walk into an arena and see two muscular men facing off on an elevated stone platform. All around you, fans scream at the competitors to start fighting, but the men merely toss taunts at one another. It might strike you as odd that no one is sitting in the bottom three rows of seats. Before being able to give it much thought, the starting bell rings, and it all becomes clear. Rather than wrestle traditionally, these men "bend"—control through a combination of martial arts and the mind—earth and stone at one another. The men "throw" rocks the size of mini-vans across the arena at each other, with their competitor often redirecting the boulders, slamming them into the bottom three rows. Mystery solved. The purpose of the sport is not to pin your competition to the ground like in the WWE; rather, it is to knock them from the ring, an extreme version of sumo wrestling. After multiple bouts of larger and larger men knocking one another out of bounds, another thing might strike you as odd. The last competitor, the reigning champion, the Blind Bandit, is not yet another muscular man. Instead, she is a blind, twelve-year-old girl (see Figure 11.1). Some in the audience ask if the "blind thing" is just a part of her act. Others worry about her: she's just a little girl! And she's blind! Still others cheer for the Boulder—the man who has won match after match that day—to take her down. Then it happens. An exchange of taunts, a ringing of the starting bell, and with only two steps and an arm movement, the Blind Bandit is victorious.

FIGURE 11.1 *Reigning champion Toph enters the ring. Still from "The Blind Bandit" (S2E06). Blu-ray release of* Avatar: The Last Airbender—The Complete Series *(2018).*

This is the viewer's introduction to Toph Beifong, one of the main characters in the animated series *Avatar: The Last Airbender* (Nickelodeon, 2005–8), in "The Blind Bandit" (S2E06). The world of *Avatar* is inhabited by people of many races, creeds, and abilities; Toph is just one of the many characters with physical and/or cognitive disabilities. Prominent characters like Princess Azula and Prince Zuko exhibit signs of posttraumatic stress disorder, which can often manifest as mental illness.[1] Disability is also seen in tertiary characters such as Teo, who is paraplegic, and Combustion Man, who has a prosthetic arm and leg. Unnamed background characters are physically disabled as well, using their own prosthetics and mobility aids. Fans have latched onto these characters, and many argue over the quality of the representation, often directly or indirectly using disability studies theories. I argue that through engaging with how fans discuss academic concepts, scholars will be better equipped to study media representations of disability.

In this chapter, I draw from Elizabeth Ellcessor's work on online audiences and respond to Sami Schalk's call for scholars to engage in fan studies to explore audience reception of disability representation. To do so,

I turn to various Tumblrs, wikis, and personal websites of *Avatar* fans that feature discussions of *Avatar* and disability. From these posts, I analyze fan-generated content that deals with the "supercrip" and "narrative prosthesis" disability studies concepts. Through examining how fans—disabled and not—react to disability representation in *Avatar*, I illustrate how many fans rebel against the traditional academic stigmas attached to these disability studies concepts and reveal that there is more nuance to these concepts than many scholars suggest.

Avatar: An Animated Fantasy

Disability representation in animated television series and films is growing. Series such as *South Park* (Comedy Central, 1997–present), *Adventure Time* (Cartoon Network, 2010–18), and *Rick and Morty* (Adult Swim, 2013–present) all feature characters and storylines involving cognitive disabilities, and there are primary and secondary characters in series such as *Big Mouth* (Netflix, 2017–present), *The Dragon Prince* (Netflix, 2018–present), and *Undone* (Amazon Prime, 2019–present) who are physically disabled. In writing about *BoJack Horseman* (Netflix, 2014–20), Kevin Pabst argues that the medium of animation allows for more honest depictions of disability—mental illness, in particular.[2] The fact that all but one of the series listed above premiered in 2010 or later is likely due to the growing awareness of disability in the United States. Persons with disabilities (PWDs) make up more than 26 percent of America's population, and, when you consider family members and caregivers, over half the population is impacted by disability.[3]

Avatar predates most of these series and exists at the intersection of animation and fantasy—a genre that is historically known for "exploiting disabled people by presenting them as embodiments of terror and evil."[4] Fantasy depictions of disability have often been problematic, either casting disabled characters as evil and resentful of their disability or having the characters seek cures to overcome their disability.[5] Ria Cheyne writes that while fantasy series may depict their protagonists as temporarily disabled, this is often a stage on the heroic journey and will typically be remedied later in the narrative. Cheyne continues, "Fantasy narratives generally affirm that the protagonists or viewpoint characters, at least, will get what they deserve. Disability disrupts the genre's affective trajectory because the feelings of loss and grief associated with disability in the western cultural imagination undercut the affirmative sense of hope and optimism fantasy aims to evoke."[6] This, of course, is not always the case in fantasy as evidenced by series like *Game of Thrones* (HBO, 2011–19), *Shadow and Bone* (Netflix, 2021–present), and *Avatar*. In fact, *Avatar* has multiple characters who reject "cures" for their disabilities when they are offered, and for Toph, her blindness actually enhances her abilities, which gives some fans pause.

Avatar has accrued a large and lasting fandom. Many fandoms often engage in "crip fanfics" where they employ disability to heighten the characters' vulnerability.[7] While this type of fanfic may appear insensitive, Francesca Coppa argues that "fandom has a high percentage of disabled participants and is concerned with issues of accessibility (both digital and meatspace) and positive disability representations."[8] Often, blog posts by fans engage with critical theories, even posting their sources at the end like one would for an academic paper. Ellcessor explains that "people with disabilities marshal digital media in order to explore disability identity and form communities. This is seen in blogs and message boards, where users may be introduced to academic and activist conceptions of disability identity or use their experiences to produce original formulations that complicate these definitions."[9]

While there has been much literature written in fan studies and disability studies, little has been written on *Avatar*. In focusing on fan responses to *Avatar*, I build on previous scholarship through centering non-academic fan discourse that deals with academic concepts. Through this approach, I illustrate not only the fan reception of *Avatar* but also fan reception of these theories. To do so, I first turn to the central character of this chapter, Toph, who, as the most prominent disabled character in *Avatar*, is of particular interest to fans.

Is Toph a Supercrip?

Toph is a twelve-year-old blind girl and the only child of one of the wealthiest families in the Earth Kingdom. The professional wrestling-type scenario in which Toph is introduced evokes associations with disability, as there are many connections between wrestling and disability.[10] In "The Blind Bandit," there are two versions of the character presented: "Toph the Beifong" and "Toph the Bender." While Toph the Bender is the reigning champion at Earth Rumble VI, none of the characters realize she is a Beifong. In fact, the Beifong family has hidden her existence from the world, as if having a disabled daughter is a source of shame. Filmmakers have the "tendency to characterize disabled people as isolated,"[11] and that is exactly how Toph the Beifong is presented. She has no contact with anyone outside of her home other than a bending instructor, who tells her parents that he is "keeping her at the beginner's level. Basic forms and breathing exercises only." Ato Quayson terms this representation as "Disability as Normality" as it is a fantasy depiction of disability that deals with real issues, such as social isolation and infantilization due to her blindness.[12]

Toph as Bender, however, proudly displays her disability, even using it as her moniker—the Blind Bandit. This leads to others underestimating her, like the Boulder does moments before she knocks him from the ring. Speaking in the third person, he says, "The Boulder feels conflicted about fighting a young, blind girl," emphasizing not only her disability, but her youth and gender. Toph, however, does express the ability to "see." She tells Aang, "Even though I was born blind, I've never had a problem seeing. I see with earthbending. It's kind of like seeing with my feet. I feel the vibrations in the earth, and I can see where everything is" (see Figure 11.2). The supercripping dimensions of these comments lead to the discussions I found in many blog posts, as Toph appears to imply her earthbending negates her disability.

The conception of the supercrip is used differently by different authors. Schalk provides history on the concept, writing that "the term supercrip seems to have emerged colloquially within the disability rights community in the mid-to-late 1970s as a pejorative term for overachieving people with disabilities, though it's unclear if the term originally applied specifically to representations or to individual disabled persons directly."[13] Joseph P. Shapiro describes the supercrip as a disabled person who is glorified for

FIGURE 11.2 *Toph "seeing" with earthbending. Still from "The Blind Bandit" (S2E06). Blu-ray release of* Avatar: The Last Airbender—The Complete Series *(2018).*

doing things considered normal or mundane for an able-bodied person and is more about how nondisabled people view "inspirational" disabled people.[14] Eli Clare uses the term in a similar way when he describes various supercrips: "A boy without hands bats .486 on his Little League team. A blind man hikes the Appalachian Trail from end to end. An adolescent girl with Down's syndrome learns to drive and has a boyfriend."[15] Jay Dolmage, however, argues a supercrip is a "person with a disability [who] overcomes their impairment through hard work or has some special talent that offsets their deficiencies."[16] While Shapiro and Clare's definitions do not apply to Toph, it seems that Dolmage's does. That said, while Toph describes what she experiences as *seeing*, her powers do not completely negate her blindness—she is unable to "see" when cut off from her element—such as while flying on Appa or when standing on sand, like in "The Library" (S2E10)—and she cannot "see" people's facial features, and, as such, mistakes Suki for Sokka in "The Serpent's Pass" (S2E12) after the former saves her from drowning. These moments demonstrate how Dolmage's definition is complicated when considering that *Avatar* is a fantasy series.

Schalk also argues that using supercrip as a category for individual PWDs "makes us complicit in the ableism that constructs such low expectations for people with disabilities that all achievements are considered extraordinary."[17] Instead, we should refer to supercrips as a narrative form that is constructed around PWDs. Amit Kama developed two types of supercrip narratives, and Schalk added a third. The first is the "regular supercrip narrative," which focuses on the PWD (real or fictional) who gains attention for "mundane accomplishments, which because of their impairment are considered exceptionally successful."[18] The second is the "glorified supercrip narrative," which focuses on a PWD who "achieve[s] feats that even non-disabled persons rarely attempt."[19] Schalk's addition is the "superpowered supercrip narrative," which "is primarily a fiction, television, or film representation of a character who has abilities or 'powers' that operate in direct relationship with or contrast to their disability."[20] Superpowered supercrip narratives are more common in speculative fiction genres, as seen in Josefine Wälivaara's description of Chirrut Îmwe from *Rogue One: A Star Wars Story* (2016).[21] Much like Toph, Chirrut is a blind character who is a capable warrior due to his special ability—in his case, his connection with the Force.[22] Wälivaara argues that Chirrut can actually be understood as an empowering portrayal of a PWD. Rather than fall back on tropes associated with blind characters, Chirrut "proposes an alternative to these ableist fears by showing that disability does not necessarily make one neither weak nor dependent" through his capabilities and seemingly superpowered skills.[23]

Wälivaara's description of Chirrut being a supercrip and a positive, empowering portrayal of disability may strike many as odd. As Schalk notes, "at the very word [supercrip], disability studies scholars sharpen their critical claws to rip to shreds what has now become quite the infamous figure."[24] This, however, is an issue that Schalk attempts to address with her reevaluation of the term, because "disabled people generally do not always find supercrip representations to be entirely oppressive or problematic."[25] While academics may point out all the negative associations and ramifications of supercrips, of which there are many, PWDs can feel differently, even empowered by larger-than-life representations of disability.[26] The blog posts I analyze reveal the conflicted feelings of many PWDs.

On a Tumblr titled "Disnability," run by a group of four people who call themselves R2J2, there is a post arguing, "Toph is a supercrip but that is not a bad thing."[27] They write that due to Toph's "unhuman-like ability to be able to 'see' with her feet" and her "unhuman ability to hear," she "is a perfect example of a 'Supercrip.'" In R2J2's definition of a supercrip, they focus on the inspirational messages nondisabled people may take from supercrip narratives and how "ordinary disabled people are made to feel like failures if they haven't done something extraordinary." R2J2 then states that *Avatar* plays into stereotypes of disability; they believe, however, "the message swings towards the more inspiring spectrum for children as they are taught that even if they have a disability such as blindness, 'You can accomplish anything, despite what people may say.'" The post concludes that *Avatar* provides a message that persons with disabilities should be accepted and treated with normalcy. While one could push back against their statement that *Avatar* features stereotypical portrayals of disability as they provide no examples, R2J2 believes that, even if Toph is portrayed as a supercrip, she is also associated with positive messaging.

Stacy Whitman, publisher of Tu Books, authored a post entitled "Toph: 'Supercrip' stereotype or well-rounded disabled character" on her personal website. In it, she asks her followers if Toph is a supercrip and, if she is, how she may be reconceived as a better character. Whitman writes, "I don't see Toph in the same way that I see those emotionally manipulative stories [of other supercrips]," and she questions how fantasy could feature disability without playing into the supercrip concept, as "one of the main tropes of fantasy protagonists is that the reason they're the protagonist is that they stand out in a crowd, whatever their unique talent is."[28] Whitman identifies as "a mostly-able-bodied person who doesn't always get it," so she turns to her followers, many of whom identify themselves as disabled in their comments. The comments range from "I wouldn't think of Toph as a Supercrip only because her blindness isn't completely negated and it does affect her throughout the show" to "I think, without a doubt, that Toph is a 'supercrip' as it has been defined … Odd that this is much of a question at all."[29] Despite the disagreement over whether Toph is a supercrip, all the commenters concur that she is a positive representation of disability and that they hope to see more characters like her.

This raises the question of what makes Toph a positive representation. While her prowess as a bender is evident almost immediately upon her introduction as evidenced by my opening description of Earth Rumble VI, Toph is seen as a positive representation largely due to her complexity of a character. Her blindness is only one aspect of her character, not her entire personality. While Toph is independent and has agency, she also acknowledges moments when she needs assistance, like in "The Earth King" (S2E18) when she asks Katara to read a letter for her. The representation is strengthened by how none of the characters view Toph as a liability. While they do help Toph, Toph also helps them in large ways—such as preventing the Spirit Library from plunging into the desert in "The Library"—and small, like making sure they are not scammed in "The Runaway" (S3E07). Perhaps most importantly, Toph never expresses the wish to not be blind. She is comfortable with her disability to the point of making jokes about it, such as in "The Drill" (S2E13) when Sokka and Toph are in a tunnel and he says, "It's so dark down here. I can't see a thing," and Toph replies, "Oh no. What a nightmare." As discussed by the "Representative Character" Tumblr, Toph "frequently [jokes] about her disability in a way a lot of disabled people do in real life."[30]

Two readings that complicate the praise showered on Toph's character come from blogger Joanie Davis, who runs a WordPress blog titled "Challenging Bodies: Disability, Gender & Culture," as well as Corinne Duyvis, who identifies as autistic and is the co-founder of the website *Disability in Kidlit*. Davis engages with scholarship by Shapiro and Dolmage to illustrate how the many myths of disability, such as disability as an object of pity, are harmful to PWDs as well as how Toph's narrative successfully disrupts those myths. The final line in Davis's post, however, aligns with what Schalk describes as a typical academic move: "The effectiveness of this argument is, of course, diminished by the fact that Toph's unique way of 'seeing' pushes her into the category of a 'supercrip' or overcoming her disability rather than simply living with it."[31] For Davis, the mere invoking of the term "supercrip" undercuts the entirety of the positive impacts from disrupting harmful myths of disability.

Duyvis, on the other hand, has a bit more nuanced approach to the discussion of Toph. Instead of evoking the supercrip, Duyvis describes how Toph fits into the "disability superpower category."[32] Duyvis praises the writers for making Toph have "an identity and personality outside of The Blind Girl. She's respected as a character, and while her blindness informs her personality and skills, it doesn't dominate those things." The problem Duyvis has with Toph is "for all the things [*Avatar*] did right with Toph's character, in the end, she's still got a superpower that conveniently negates a lot of her disability." Duyvis notes that Toph could have been a waterbender, firebender, or non-bender, but instead the writers chose to make her an earthbender, where she can adapt to her blindness. These adaptations go so far as to become nearly superpowers, such as how Toph can tell when characters are lying in "Lake Laogai" (S2E17). In the same post, Duyvis' co-founder Kody Keplinger compares Toph's "seeing" to blind people using "sonar-like sound perception." Keplinger argues, "Do some blind people do it? Yes. There is a clicking technique. But the vast, vast, vast majority of us do not and could not." Despite many criticisms, Duyvis concludes saying, "It's difficult not to slot Toph in the disability superpower category as a result, even if she's one of the better takes on that trope … [However,] disabled people actually exist in this fantasy universe, they're capable, and they have agency. That's a damn good start."

Each post debated how Toph fit into the supercrip category, with some saying yes and others saying no. How the animated, fantasy setting impacted these representations was something brought up by multiple posters. The consistent theme, however, was that Toph—supercrip or not—is an example of empowering disability representation. While academics have tended to place all media featuring supercrip narratives into the negative representation pile, fans think differently, at least when it comes to Toph Beifong, the Blind Bandit.

Narrative Prosthesis in Teo's, Azula's, and Combustion Man's Histories

Similar to the supercrip, narrative prosthesis is viewed as harmful in narratives featuring PWDs. David T. Mitchell and Sharon L. Snyder argue that "disability pervades literary narrative, first, as a stock feature of characterization and second, as an opportunist metaphorical device."[33] What this means is that disability in media is often used as a metaphor to communicate something about a character or as a plot device. Mitchell and Snyder posit that when a body is deemed too far from the norm or too aberrant, stories provide "a prosthetic intervention" that attempts to either erase all difference or, when that is impossible, lower the degree of difference. While a "cure" is too frequently used as narrative prosthetic, this is also accomplished through providing an explanatory narrative. By providing a narrative of *how* one became disabled—a narrative prosthesis— the degree of difference, while still high, can be lessened.[34] This idea can be seen in any number of media texts featuring disabled characters where an explanation is given for *why* a character is disabled or *how* they became that way.

An interesting example of *Avatar* as a series engaging with the concept of narrative prosthesis occurs with Teo. Teo was originally a guest character in "The Northern Air Temple" (S1E17) before returning as a recurring character in the third season. He is paraplegic, and he is visibly marked as disabled not only by being in the wheelchair, but from the fact that his legs are wrapped in white bandages—a contrast to the bright green and yellows worn by him and by the rest of his community. Despite this, none of the main characters mention his disability apart from Sokka, who compliments his wheelchair, which is able to glide on air currents. As soon as Teo's father is introduced, however, he explains how Teo was hurt in a terrible flood as a child, with the implication that the flood is the cause of Teo's disability. What stands out about his explanation is that no one asked for it. Teo's father's explanation evokes narrative prosthesis: Teo's body, which his able-bodied father deems "lacking, unfunctional or inappropriately functional," must be explained in order to be accepted.[35] This use of narrative prosthesis is important to note. Similar to Toph's experience, it is the parent who denigrates the disability, while the younger characters make little to no comment on it. As *Avatar* is aimed at a younger audience, this rhetorical gesture could suggest that while children may witness their parents or other adults react to PWDs in certain ways, they do not need to see people with mobility aids, blindness, or other disabilities as separate.

What is interesting in looking to fan usage of narrative prosthesis and the supercrip is that, while the latter has become a term many fans invoke, I did not see any fan write "narrative prosthesis." While the applicability of the concept has crossed over, the actual name has not. This may reflect how fans think about narrative prosthesis. While academics rail against it as harmful, disabled fans seem to employ the concept in fan fiction. Fandoms and fan fictions often engage in speculation about what came before the series or what comes after. Looking through posts, I found speculation centered on two characters central to the final season of the show, one with backstory and the other with virtually none, Princess Azula and Combustion Man.

Azula is not properly introduced in *Avatar* until the final episode of the first season, "The Siege of the North, Part 2" (S1E20). A firebending prodigy at only fourteen, Azula becomes a main antagonist during season two before growing increasingly paranoid after her brother's and best friends' betrayals in season three. Azula's mental disability is first seen through how other characters refer to her. During a flashback in "Zuko Alone" (S2E07), Azula's mother asks "What is *wrong* with that child?" upon hearing how flippantly Azula refers to her grandfather's possible death. Two episodes later in "Bitter Work" (S2E09), Zuko says he needs more training in case he has to fight Azula again. He continues, "I know what you're going to say: She's my sister, and I should be trying to get along with her." Iroh, a level-headed and sage character, responds, "No, she's *crazy*, and she needs to go down." In the four-part series finale "Sozin's Comet" (S3E18–21), Azula begins to experience delusions and her paranoia and anxiety become evident. By this point, Azula's two best friends have betrayed her, her brother has tried to kill her, and her father has left her—a fourteen-year-old—to rule a kingdom. The animation in these episodes plays up her mental state, exaggerating her features: her mouth and eyes are wider than before, her hair is illustrated in jagged lines, and her previously fluid movements are now jerky and staccato. In her final scene, she is physically chained to a metal grate, tears scalding her eyes (see Figure 11.3). Normally an eloquent speaker, she is unable to do anything but grunt, laugh manically, and weep.

Many users were quick to diagnose Azula, wanting to provide a more concrete narrative for her actions. This is similar to other online forums that discuss topics such as whether the eleventh doctor in *Doctor Who* (BBC, 1963–present) or Sheldon from *The Big Bang Theory* (CBS, 2007–19) are autistic as well as the various mental illnesses and posttraumatic stress disorders on *Homeland* (Showtime, 2011–20) and *Jessica Jones* (Netflix, 2015–19).[36] A post by a Tumblr user Vanessa begins by establishing that they identify as mentally disabled and are knowledgeable about psychology and mental illness. In their opinion, though Azula "showed a few signs of early psychopathy, those signs are not sufficient for a psychiatrist to diagnose her with psychopathy—or, as it is now called, antisocial personality disorder."[37] Vanessa spends the rest of the post laying out the symptoms Azula displays and explaining why those may exist, shooting down other posited conclusions, such as Azula's delusions indicating schizophrenia. Vanessa's

FIGURE 11.3 *Azula in tears after being defeated and chained. Still from "Sozin's Comet, Part 4: Avatar Aang" (S3E21). Blu-ray release of* Avatar: The Last Airbender— The Complete Series *(2018).*

penultimate paragraph is her own diagnosis: "In my opinion [Azula] is neither a psychopath nor suffering from schizophrenia. A true psychopath has no capacity for compassion, his ability to feel anything (happiness, sadness, remorse etc) is severely reduced and there is an apparent lack of self-reflection. Azula suffers more from a pervasive development disorder." Rather than end there, however, Vanessa continues and ends with a final thought: "Princess Azula remains one of the most fascinating villains I ever came across watching cartoons or anime. She's my unchallenged favourite."[38]

A post by the user porluciernagas links to the "meta" by Vanessa in their discussion of Azula. Like Vanessa, porluciernagas identifies as disabled, but they do not claim the psychological expertise Vanessa does. porluciernagas agrees that "we can't accurately diagnose Azula with a mental illness" but claims her actions primarily are "extreme reactions of parental neglect."[39] What is fascinating about porluciernagas's post is that they state "*Avatar* doesn't treat [Azula] with the same respect as it does its other characters with disabilities. Azula ends the series in a straitjacket."[40] While Azula is shown institutionalized in a straitjacket in the graphic novel continuation of the series, many fans have disavowed those comics as "non-canon" due to contradictions found in the characterizations and plots. porluciernagas observes that unlike many other characters in the series, Azula is not given a chance at redemption. This chance is also not given to the Fire Lord, Combustion Man, or a number of other villains; but porluciernagas concluded that, as a disabled villain who was a product of her upbringing, Azula deserved that chance.

Unlike Vanessa and porluciernagas, blogger Anima Irenea, who also identifies as disabled, does not waffle about Azula's diagnosis. Irenea first applauds the series, as both Zuko and Azula are mentally disabled and traumatized, yet show "very different symptoms as a result of directly-related emotional traumas … a rarity in television."[41] Continuing, Irenea declares Azula "is clearly unstable in a deeper way" and "identifiable as sociopathy."[42] In diagnosing Azula, Irenea creates a causal link between Azula's disability and her actions. This is evocative of narrative prosthesis, as Irenea uses Azula's diagnosis to explain her aberrant behaviors.

In contrast to Azula, Combustion Man—which is not his real name but a nickname he is given by Sokka in "The Runaway"—is neither well-developed nor a consistent presence throughout the series. Combustion Man is a hitman hired by Zuko early in the third season to kill Aang. Combustion Man's introductory scene in "The Headband" (S3E02) is particularly important, as he is introduced in a series of five shots. When he arrives to a shady, late-night meeting with Zuko, viewers initially see his prosthetic metal leg, then there is a cut to Zuko's face. Next, we see his prosthetic metal arm, then it cuts to Zuko again. Only on the fifth shot is his face shown. Here, his disability is foregrounded. After Combustion Man's bending backfires and he explodes in "The Western Air Temple" (S3E12), the last trace we see of Combustion Man is his prosthetic arm falling through the air. In this sense, his prosthetics/disability acts as synecdoche for the man. Though whether Combustion Man is actually disabled in the world of *Avatar* is an interesting question. When Luke Skywalker loses his hand in *The Empire Strikes Back* (1980), it is surgically replaced by a prosthesis that functions just as a hand of flesh and bone would. According to Ralph Covino, the severing of limbs in the *Star Wars* universe is not equivalent to becoming disabled.[43] As Combustion Man's prosthetics function just as well as non-prosthetic limbs, there is an argument to be made that he is not disabled. The fan content, however, takes his disability as a fact.

On a fan-generated wiki page, Combustion Man is credited as "the third known character to have a physical disability."[44] The post states he is one of three characters to have a prosthetic, but it does not include the other characters with prosthetics in the list of physically disabled characters, so there is some internal inconsistency, which can be expected from a wiki. The wiki also includes a popular theory about how Combustion Man became disabled. The page mirrors language seen on the "Avatar Parallels" Tumblr. In a post on disabled characters in *Avatar*, the poster wrote "#if anyone asks me how is combustion man disabled #he discovered his firebending abilities as a child #and accidentally blew his right arm and leg off."[45] The wiki also includes this information, using the same language as it explains Combustion Man was unable to control his power as a child "and accidentally blew his right arm and leg off, which he replaced with his trademark metal prosthetic limbs."[46] The wiki backs the information up with a citation to "The Lost Lore of Avatar Aang," a Tumblr from the now-defunct official *Avatar* page on the Nickelodeon website. While this citation implies that the theory is true, the fact that the information is provided on a Tumblr and not the actual series suggests the narrative prosthesis for Combustion Man's disability was driven by online fan desire.

Narrative prosthesis is often seen as a negative when it comes to disability representation in media. Typically, narrative prosthesis is invoked when characters' narratives are focused on their disability and there develops a compulsive need to explain their disability. The disabled characters in *Avatar*, however, all have narrative arcs focused on things other than their disabilities. *Avatar* largely foregoes providing a narrative for how characters became disabled. Instead, fans—both abled and disabled—are the ones to provide those characters' narratives. *They* debate diagnoses for Azula, and *they* argue over Combustion Man's history. The series provides the viewers space to do just that, both crafting nuanced representation of disability and providing room for polysemic fan interpretations.

Conclusion

Avatar experienced great success while it aired, and, since concluding, it has produced graphic novel continuations, a sequel series, a live-action reboot at Netflix, and more. While the disability representation is only part of the reason for *Avatar*'s success, the series deserves to be lauded for rejecting traditional fantasy tropes and using its popular medium and genre to promote positive ways of thinking about PWDs to children. As more disability studies scholars discover *Avatar* and its successors, it would be easy to focus on the supercrip aspect of certain characters, even though Schalk states that "by taking note of medium and genre context, scholars may find that other theoretical frameworks besides the supercrip are more applicable to certain representations."[47] Even so, the fans, who vary on the topic of Toph as a supercrip, find her to be a positive representation. Many even refer to Toph and other disabled characters on the series as inspirational.

Too often inspiration is used as a negative when it comes to dealing with disability studies. Wendy L. Chrisman calls for "a consideration of inspiration as a valuable, rhetorically strategic emotion," which may be employed by PWDs amongst themselves in productive ways.[48] Schalk writes that not "all inspiration narratives are supercrip narratives" and not "all supercrip narratives are targeted at a nondisabled audience."[49] Through examining fan responses to the series, scholars will be able to see how PWDs react to disability representation. There will likely never be agreement, such as how Vanessa and Anima Irenea loved the portrayal of Azula's mental disability while porluciernagas found it problematic. This, however, only makes sense, as PWDs are not a monolith. Through engagement with fans, scholars will be better equipped to study media representations of disability, regardless of if the media is realistic or if it is set in an animated fantasy where five children hold the fate of the world in their hands.

Notes

1   For more on trauma in *Avatar*, see: the previous part in this volume, especially Caleb Horowitz's chapter.

2   Kevin Pabst, "Why the Long Face? Narratives of Depression in Netflix's *BoJack Horseman*," MA thesis (Wake Forest University, 2017). For more on how animation is an effective medium for depicting disability, see: Annabelle Honess Roe, "Evocative Animated Documentaries, Imagination and Knowledge," *Studies in Documentary Film* 15.2 (2021): 127–39.

3   "Disability Impacts All of Us," *Centers for Disease Control and Prevention*, September 16, 2020, https://www.cdc.gov/ncbddd/disabilityandhealth/infographic-disability-impacts-all.html.

4   Colleen Elaine Donnelly, "Re-visioning Negative Archetypes of Disability and Deformity in Fantasy: *Wicked, Maleficent* and *Game of Thrones*," *Disability Studies Quarterly* 36.4 (2016).

5   For examples of the former, see: the Nessarose in the musical *Wicked* (2003), Ephialtes in the comic book *300* (1998) and its 2006 film adaptation, and Howard Clifford in the film *Detective Pikachu* (2019). For examples of the latter, see: Colin in the novel *The Secret Garden* (1911) and its various adaptations, Curt Connors in the film *The Amazing Spider-Man* (2012), and Morbius in the film *Morbius* (2022). For analysis of these particular texts, see Beth Haller, "*Wicked* Gives Disability an Evil Name," *Disability Studies Quarterly* 24.2 (2004); Michael M. Chemers, "'With Your Shield, or on It': Disability Representation in *300*," *Disability Studies Quarterly* 27.3 (2007); E. Young, "Detective Pikachu Had So Much Going for It. Then the Ableism Showed Up," *Global Comment*, May 21, 2019, https://globalcomment.com/detective-pikachu-had-so-much-going-for-it-then-the-ableism-showed-up/; "'Wheel Me Over There!': Disability and Colin's Wheelchair in *The Secret Garden*," *Children's Literature Association Quarterly* 41.3 (2016): 263–80; Angela M. Smith, "Dis-affection: Disability Effects and Disabled Moves at the Movies," in *The Matter of Disability: Materiality, Biopolitics, Crip Affect*, eds. David T. Mitchell, Susan Antebi and Sharon L. Snyder (University of Michigan Press, 2019), 118–39. For more on disability as evil and fantasy's tendency to search for a "magic cure" see: Robert Bogdan, Douglas Biklen, A. Shapiro and David Spelkoman, "The Disabled: Media's Monster," *Social Policy* 13.2 (1982): 32–5; Jane Stemp, "Devices and Desires: Science Fiction, Fantasy and Disability in Literature for Young People," *Disability Studies Quarterly* 24.1 (2004).

6   Ria Cheyne, *Disability, Literature, Genre: Representation and Affect in Contemporary Fiction* (Liverpool University Press, 2019), 113.

7   Derek Newman-Stille, "From Slash Fan Fiction to Crip Fan Fiction: What Role Does Disability Have in Fandom?" *Canadian Journal of Disability Studies* 8.2 (2019): 73.

8   Francesca Coppa, "Fuck Yeah, Fandom Is Beautiful," *Journal of Fandom Studies* 2.1 (2014): 78.

9   Elizabeth Ellcessor, "Cyborg Hoaxes: Disability, Deception, and Critical Studies of Digital Media," *New Media & Society* 19.11 (2016): 1772.

10 Max Dosser, "Throw in the Tune: Musical Characterizations of Disability in Wrestling Films," *Journal of American Culture* 43.4 (2020): 300–11.

11 Martin F. Norden, *The Cinema of Isolation: A History of Physical Disability in the Movies* (Rutgers University Press, 1994), 2.

12 Ato Quayson, *Aesthetic Nervousness: Disability and the Crisis of Representation* (Columbia University Press, 2007), 52.

13 Sami Schalk, "Reevaluating the Supercrip," *Journal of Literary & Cultural Disability Studies* 10.1 (2016): 74.

14 Joseph P. Shapiro, *No Pity: People with Disabilities Forging a New Civil Rights Movement* (Times Books, 1993), 16–17.

15 Eli Clare, *Exile and Pride: Disability, Queerness, and Liberation* (South End Press, 1999), 2.

16 Jay Dolmage, *Disability Rhetoric* (Syracuse University Press, 2013), 35.
17 Ibid., 78.
18 Amit Kama, "Supercrips versus the Pitiful Handicapped: Reception of Disabling Images by Disabled Audience Members," *Communications* 29.4 (2004): 454.
19 Ibid., 454.
20 Schalk, 81.
21 Josefine Wälivaara, "Blind Warriors, Supercrips, and Techno-Marvels: Challenging Depictions of Disability in *Star Wars*," *Journal of Popular Culture* 51.4 (2018): 1036–56.
22 While I do not have space to go into it in this chapter, there is a deliberate evocation of the blind warrior trope from East Asian fiction, as seen in *The Tale of Zatoichi* (1962) and *House of the Flying Daggers* (2004), with both Toph and Chirrut.
23 Wälivaara, 1049.
24 Schalk, 71.
25 Ibid., 75.
26 Kama, 453.
27 R2J2, "Avatar: The Last Airbender," *Tumblr*, March 17, 2011, https://r2j2.tumblr.com/post/3919449340/avatar-the-last-airbender. R2J2 comes from the authors names: Roxanne Roxas, Ralph Li, Jennifer Snow, and Joline Chen.
28 Stacy Whitman, "Toph: 'Supercrip' Stereotype or Well-Rounded Disabled Character," *Stacy Whitman's Grimoire*, September 4, 2010, http://www.stacylwhitman.com/2010/09/04/toph-supercrip-stereotype-or-well-rounded-disabled-character/.
29 TS, September 4, 2010 (11:48 p.m.), comment on Stacy Whitman, "Toph: 'Supercrip' Stereotype or Well-rounded Disabled Character," *Stacy Whitman's Grimoire*, September 4, 2010; seeme, October 4, 2010 (3:16 a.m.), comment on Stacy Whitman, "Toph: 'Supercrip' Stereotype or Well-rounded Disabled Character," *Stacy Whitman's Grimoire*, September 4, 2010.
30 Representative Characters, "Toph Bei Fong," *Tumblr*, December 30, 2019, https://representativecharacters.tumblr.com/post/189959952131/character-toph-bei-fong-from-avatar-the-last.
31 Joanie Davis, "Disability in Avatar: The Last Airbender," *Challenging Bodies: Disability, Gender & Culture*, January 24, 2018, https://challengingbodies.wordpress.com/2018/01/24/disability-in-avatar-the-last-airbender-joanie-davis/.
32 Corinne Duyvis, "What Do You Think of the Disabled Representation in the Avatar Series?" *Tumblr*, August 11, 2014, https://corinneduyvis.tumblr.com/post/94438038932/what-do-you-think-of-disabled-representation-in.
33 David T. Mitchell and Sharon L. Snyder, *Narrative Prosthesis: Disability and the Dependencies of Discourse* (University of Michigan Press, 2001), 47.
34 Ibid., 6.

35 Ibid.
36 Leslie Manning, "Negotiating *Doctor Who*: Neurodiversity and Fandom," in *Media, Margins, and Popular Culture*, eds. Einar Thorsen, Heather Savigny, Jenny Alexander and Daniel Jackson (Palgrave Macmillan, 2015), 153–65.
37 Vanessa (goannavanessastuff), "Mental (In-) Stability: *Princess Azula*," *Tumblr*, January 18, 2014, https://goannavanessastuff.tumblr.com/post/73665562869/mental-in-stability-princess-azula-lately.
38 Ibid.
39 porluciernagas, "In Brightest Day: Disability in the *Avatar* Universe," *Lady Geek Girl*, September 18, 2015, https://ladygeekgirl.wordpress.com/2015/09/18/in-brightest-day-disability-in-the-avatar-universe/.
40 Ibid.
41 Anima Irenea, "Representation of Disabilities and Persons with Disabilities in Avatar: The Last Airbender (and Legend of Korra)," *Anima Irenea*, October 23, 2014, https://animairenea.wordpress.com/2014/10/23/representation-of-disabilities-and-persons-with-disabilities-in-avatar-the-last-airbender-and-legend-of-korra/.
42 Ibid.
43 Ralph Covino, "Star Wars, Limb Loss, and What It Means to Be Human," in *Disability and Science Fiction: Representation of Technology as Cure*, ed. Kathryn Allen (Palgrave Macmillan, 2013), 110.
44 "Combustion Man," *Avatar Wiki*, accessed October 29, 2021, https://avatar.fandom.com/wiki/Combustion_Man.
45 Avatar Parallels, "Disabled Characters in Avatar," *Tumblr*, June 12, 2014, https://avatarparallels.tumblr.com/post/88585860368/disabled-characters-in-avatar.
46 "Combustion."
47 Schalk, 83.
48 Wendy L. Chrisman, "A Reflection on Inspiration: A Recuperative Call for Emotion in Disability Studies," *Journal of Literary & Cultural Disability Studies* 5.2 (2011): 184.
49 Schalk, 75.

12

Ships at the Edge

Ashley Hendricks

The Covid-19 pandemic has caused a shift in the way that we interact with media. A months-long lockdown ushered in not only changes to what media we consume but also how we consume and respond to it. Binging streaming media no longer seemed so irresponsible. That judgmental Netflix question—"Are you still watching?"—was easily brushed aside. What else would we be doing in the midst of a panic-inducing lockdown? In addition to binging, viewers also started to create, leading to a renaissance in online fanfiction.

For some, the pandemic created quiet and space for making and remaking as they tackled artistic issues of identity, aesthetics, and authorial voice. Henry Jenkins, in a nod to Michel de Certeau, writes that "like poachers of old, fans operate from a position of cultural marginalization and social weakness"; during a pandemic, these vulnerabilities are exacerbated.[1] Modern fan culture, that tenuous amalgamation of texts, community, and creativity thrived under lockdown. *Avatar: The Last Airbender* (Nickelodeon, 2005–8) is a children's television show that aired for three seasons roughly fifteen years before Covid-19. While there are offshoots of the franchise, those available sequels and prequels are sparse in comparison to the sprawling multiverses that this era of US film and television banks on. Nevertheless, its fandom spiked in activity during the pandemic, as seen in the creations and updates of fanfiction; as measured by Archive of Our Own (AO3), *Avatar* fans posted or updated 13,997 out of 29,102 recorded fanfictions between March 11 and December 14, 2020. The first stories were posted tagging the fandom on multiple fan sites in 2005 (and transferred to Archive of our Own in 2008)—which means 48 percent were updated or posted during the height of pandemic.[2]

In May 2020, Netflix began streaming all three seasons of *Avatar*—it stayed in the top ten for sixty days, a record at the time and is still the most watched children's show on the platform.[3] On July 27, 2020—right in the midst of the fandom designated "Zutara Week"—Netflix tweeted out: "Okay time to settle something, Zuko and Katara would have made a good couple, right? Am I crazy?"[4] The fans responded to this first and then a series of tweets from Netflix identifying and co-signing major fanon (fan canon) pairings. The number of fanfictions that originated that day and soon after also jumped; roughly 37 percent of the fanfictions dedicated to *Avatar* are shipping fics focused on noncanon pairings. I have only taken the major fanon ships into consideration, though there are certainly less popular ships present on AO3 that would expand that percentage. It is worth noting that voice actors associated with the show, Dante Basco (Zuko) and Mae Whitman (Katara), are long-time shippers of their characters, both hyping Zutara Week on their respective social media accounts particularly during the pandemic.[5] While Netflix's prodding of an already committed fandom might account for some of the resurgence, it does not seem to be enough to account for the ongoing fan investment; viral marketing is ubiquitous and is a given for any release of a television show or film. The generative possibilities of *Avatar*'s worldbuilding and imaging of racial otherness are productive spaces not only for more traditional reads but also offer pressure points to a fandom incredibly responsive to elements of aesthetics and race in their making and consuming.

Race in *Avatar*

Avatar remains a turning point in children's television programming and, as such, has a somewhat elevated place in discussions on popular culture. It offered an example of a children's show that appealed to its demographic with rather complicated characters and the use of ellipsis, the removal of certain exposition and diegetic time which leads to more work on the viewer's end to fill in gaps in the narrative, unusual for children's media which so often works to clarify and simplify all plot points. Beyond its storytelling, *Avatar* also captured our attention and scrutiny over the ways that issues of race were handled as the franchise grew and served as a ground to debate both authenticity and appropriation. While those discussions are at the forefront of popular media, there is also no doubt that the characters of *Avatar* are meant to reference Asian bodies, and, perhaps more importantly to this argument, they exist in a geography that does not acknowledge whiteness as the default subjectivity. The terrain of *Avatar* has been described as a collapse of different cultures and locations by both fans and more scholarly critics, but there is something of the animation that resists amalgamation and disavowal.[6] *Avatar* opens with a quick exposition of the diegetic four nations and the elements attributed to each. They are shown mostly in silhouette, and there is a cut to the map which depicts a world unlike ours but still very much recognizable. Through the use of cosmic zooms, a term coined by Garrett Stewart and teased out by Jennifer Barker as "ontologically puzzling: neither a 'zoom' nor a 'travelling' or 'tracking' shot in the conventional senses of those terms, it exists somewhere in between the two."[7] Barker's discussion is situated within the discourse of where we might the body in film and the ways in which technology might assist and restrict our search. In *Avatar*, as in other fantasy show openings, the impossible movement traveling both through space and time might gesture to the very impossibility of being able to separate our constant bird's eye view of Asianness, our insistence on seeing the whole in every singular iteration. This mapping is also notable for its reliance on movement of the viewer rather than a character as it overlaps real and fictive understandings of Asian geographies. If "space is a practiced place" and made of mobile elements it seems that even while the map of *Avatar* condenses fixed Asian identity, the movement through renders that read anachronistic and demanding a different sort of interaction.[8] I am interested most in the episodes that rupture and turn places into spaces that allow multiplicity, deviation, and, perhaps, subversion. The places on *Avatar*'s map do not circulate around one shared body of water or a particular reverence for a creature, instead bending is the constant in the *Avatar* world. Not every culture is in awe of the power nor do they have the same reverent relationships with bending; in other words, the relationship that each nation or tribe has to bending is unique and complicated. I believe this is more reflective of how Western audiences have come to understand Asian places and spaces. Third Space, as identified by Westphal and Tally, collapses the real, the historical, and the fictive onto one site—the geographical locations of *Avatar* hint at the real bodies and histories associated with island nations, northern tribes, and landlocked cities.[9]

   It makes narrative sense, then, that each group would view bending in different capacities. The airbenders treat bending religiously, the waterbenders as a boon for daily life and survival, the earthbenders are often showed using their powers to either support the governmental authority or thwart it, and the firebenders associate firebending as a gift bestowed to the chosen and worthy. The cultures are visually coded through costuming to correlate with an amalgamation of Asian identities; it was one of the first children's shows to celebrate Asian identity or to children eating rice for breakfast or even a strict vegetarian diet that stemmed from spiritual belief rather than ethical concerns. Fans rejoiced. But they also began correcting and revising through digital mediums as early as 2005.

   Beyond its early digital presence, the *Avatar* fandom has always operated with an acknowledgment of the complexities of race, aesthetics, and appropriation. The debate that so often most famously attached to the show comes in response to the casting of the live-action film, *The Last Airbender* (2010). Lori Kido Lopez chronicles the ways in which fans turned political activists as a reaction to the whitewashing of the characters and explains the ways in which fans view race and identity of the characters, landing on the concept of "*mukokuseki*, or 'lacking any nationality' (Iwabuchi, 2004), many fans actively searched for proof that these characters were actually Asian."[10] Rukmini Pande takes up Lopez's argument in *Squee From the Margins* in a chapter notably titled "Aang Still Ain't White," and points out that the privileging of white subjectivity is often present around texts and, in particular, their more palatable adaptations.[11] Both Lopez and Pande speak directly to the real—the desires of real fans searching for scraps of authenticity and the desires of a production company to return to a default baseline of white spectatorship; however, the phenomena of the absent Asian body has been theorized by scholars, as well. In her book *Ornamentalism*, Anne Anlin Cheng lays out the project of constructing Asian femaleness through objects and modes of production—a connection that replaces the body with the ghost, something already long passed. She posits that "flesh that passes through objecthood needs 'ornament' to get back to itself."[12] Cheng's provocative examples span different mediums, moving from literature, to film, to actual court cases and she often uses the terms "animate" and "animation" in terms of a more material understanding of racialized gender but she does not discuss animation directly. Cheng notes that "we do not need the presence of a yellow woman to invoke the logic of yellow femininity."[13] It is here that I think we might understand how and why the arguments that surround Avatar and Asian identity arise in fan art; revision and, through some perspectives, correction grounds the existence of fanfiction, in the case of *Avatar* there seems to be a desire to recall the body, to animate it further.

In her discussion of the *Fast & Furious* franchise, another narrative that features a racially ambiguous cast, Mary Beltran cites Teresa Kay William's article in which Williams rejects fixed constructions of racial identity and argues that racial identity is always in a state of flux, particularly in America where a large part of the population recognizes their own racial ambiguity.[14] In relation to *Avatar*, the fandom seems to respond to that friction, reflecting that the construction of Asian identity through objects is not enough. Traditional film studies has not always been kind to fan studies, which are often more personal, in response to lived experiences, and the motivation to attempt to deconstruct this particular kind of otherness and displacement through representation is familiar. The trouble, of course, with examples of ambiguous Asian identity is that those in the dominant and default position would very much like if we accepted this pieced together version of ourselves and our identities and readily agree to place all nuances under an umbrella of Asian-ness that, at its very best, can pass as white when necessary or transcending into a big budget Hollywood film.

That problematic desire is one that is at the center of both critical race studies and post-colonial thought. The same aesthetic and psychology phenomena of racial melancholia—as identified by Cheng and stemming from the similar instance that Frantz Fanon identified as being seen as only as a raced body—seems to permeate this intervention from the fandom in response to the live-action film.[15] The film was a financial and artistic failure. There are not many fan works that spun off from the film, prompting the conclusion that the television show seems to enable the creators in the fandom in ways that only animation might provide paths from, even when the show offers problematic depictions of otherness. Cheng posits that the stereotype, or even the outline, can still disrupt structures of power and of looking and "how the very deployment of the stereotype already traces the impossibility of its desires."[16] This echo chamber that Cheng describes and identifies in *Flower Drum Song* (1961) might be applicable here to *Avatar* as well—the performativity of the voice actors (mostly white) and the creators (also white) offer something of an homage to and a fetishization of Asian experience that circles back to how Asian representation is constituted in relation to whiteness, emphasizing what of Asian identity is worth replicating and what is not. Representation has become a redundant word in pop culture; while media companies have begun to understand the buy in of non-white fans and have responded to grow their audiences, there is also a valid scholarly concern over what kind of representation is available and to what end. On our utopic hopes surrounding representation, Herman Gray writes that it is the quality of representation matters.[17]

While *Avatar*'s characters are, as Lopez points out, amalgamation of different Asian cultures, they are more pronounced than more modern iterations. There is a slippery texture and the text might open just where it seems to shut down as well as offer spaces of making. The construction and placement certainly caused a fissure stemming from its placement as neither a fully American animated television show but not quite an anime either; like its racially ambiguous characters and the impossible movement through the diegetic map, the show has roots in both worlds, calling attention, again, to its instability as a text—and this instability is further compounded by the show's aesthetic.

The animation style of *Avatar*, mentioned above as also a sort of amalgamation that collapses Western-style animation and anime, is quite different from its sequel *The Legend of Korra* (Nickelodeon, 2012–14; nick.com, 2014). From the vantage point of a fan, it may be more enjoyable to view the world of *Korra* as the style is more contemporary, heightened, and dramatic, but it is more fun, productive, and possible to play in the less aesthetically precise world of *Avatar* when it comes to fanfiction. *Korra* pieces on AO3 amount to roughly only 30 percent of *Avatar* fanfics. While *Korra*'s narrative responds to fissures in the fandom stemming from the canonical relationships as well as narrative holes when it comes to politics, *Avatar* is still the more generative when it comes to fan texts—a deviation that might be explained by their differences in animation aesthetics.

In his part-analysis of and part-response to Sergei Eisenstein's essay on Walt Disney, Matthew Solomon emphasizes the subversive potential that Eisenstein identified in American animation of the time period, using the term "plasma" to describe Disney's 2D animation. Solomon points to the "unbounded capacity for metamorpheses."[18] Perhaps what makes *Avatar* so generative is the plasmaticness that the animation invokes. Though Solomon notes that Eisenstein never mentions *Dumbo* (1941), the pink elephant sequence serves as example par excellence of potential subversion that Eisenstein ruminates about and notes that though the elephants have a definite form they act like the "primal protoplasm" that Eisenstein so admires.[19] In comparison, Solomon points out that, in *The Adventures of Tintin* (2011), the 3D computer animation is constantly accentuated by reflection, by the use of reflections in mirrors and backwards glances, particularly when movement is involved; it is within these scenes of animated movement that the differentiation of the planes is forced. He looks to a scene of Tintin driving and looking into the rear-view mirror, a forced point-of-view shot that frames both the 2D background and 3D foreground while offering little narratively and showing off the technology. We might see this as evident in the lush design of movement in *Korra*; the series is set in a revised 1920s, and the cars, planes, and tech move fast. The speed and movement grounds the characters and stories in a real and mappable space because of the ways that the cinematography taps into a phenomenological response.

This argument may be best situated in some ways within discussions of potentiality as posited by Scott McCloud, who notes that, in comics, the gutter is a place of both literal negative space and figurative imaginative space were the "invisible accomplice" takes part in the narrative.[20] McCloud points out that film uses this technique less often than comics, but there certainly are gutters rupturing multiple places *Avatar*; aesthetically, narratively, and through its use of ellipses. Thomas LaMarre affixes this attribute to anime in general, and he lists *Avatar* as having the particular quality of forcing a gap between planes that forces a multiplicity.[21] The show's aesthetic then opens up yet another point of multiplicity felt not only in the narrative constructive of characters and nations but of the animated space itself. Everything fits within the panels in *Korra*, even the subtexts are identified and defined in the narrative. There is little room for a multiplicity of narratives. Aesthetically, *Korra* is figuratively checking itself in the mirror by using slow pans of its gorgeous scenic design and the speed of cars and motorbikes, creating juxtaposition to accentuate its aesthetic—and it is a beautiful show. Animators use far more point-of-view shots than the original *Avatar* though the perspective does not shift from person to person, implying there is a grounded and fixed reality even for those of different subjectivities within the diegesis. There is also an overuse of object-perspective shots attached to speeding anchoring ropes or bullets, and lines are constantly being drawn with precision over the geographical space, grounding a spatial temporality.

Avatar has no such way or reason to alert its audience that something novel is happening in the animation (see Figure 12.1). Perhaps a type of gutter opens up in the absence of a reflection, that double-checking to see if the audience is appreciative of the artistry; and, while *Korra* has been celebrated and critiqued for providing a kind of closure or fan service in its ending and might address the desires of the fandom, it does not quite fulfill them. There is a rigidity to the narrative as well as the visual setting (see Figure 12.2). With Asami's backward glance, the pull in rack focus shifts, but it is most obvious that the character chooses to see, to investigate closer, and to discern something indisputable. The space created between the viewer and the couple viewed is easily traversable, mappable, and moving in a static direction; Asami sees herself and the evidence of intimacy between Korra

FIGURE 12.1 *Azula faces her mother's reflection. Still from "Sozin's Comet, Part 3: Into the Inferno" (S3E20). Blu-ray release of* Avatar: The Last Airbender—The Complete Series *(2018).*

FIGURE 12.2 *Asami spies on Korra and Mako. Still from "When Extremes Meet" (S1E08). Blu-ray release of* The Legend of Korra—Book One: Air *(2012).*

and Mako. Azula's glance in the mirror, by contrast, offers a literal shifting of panels and her gaze is reflected back to her through the visage of someone else, a mother who, of course, left long ago. If Asami's mirror sequence reflects a sort of truth then Azula's opens up a multiplicity of narratives, remembrances, and questions in a splitting open of sorts that offers multiple panels in which viewers might play through different possibilities. The color saturation of *Korra* is vivid and, beside it, there is an almost-dinginess to the coloring of *Avatar*, seemingly nostalgic in its fadedness. Considering the innovation in animation of the time period, *Avatar* is strangely situated. Nickelodeon's offerings targeted at the same age group from the early 2000s were brightly colored and offered purposefully crudely drawn characters, and the episodic anime featured magical girls and the Pokémon duels. Studio Ghibli and, more specifically, Miyazaki Hayao's *Howl's Moving Castle* (2004) may offer the most productive comparison. While *Avatar*'s animation does not quite encapsulate the plasmaticness that I would argue *Howl's Moving Castle* openly courts in terms of age and material space, the aesthetic is not static, and the world of *Avatar* was constantly unfolding, doubling back on itself, and expanding without the rigidity that could be attributed to its sequel.

That there may be an inherent aesthetic multiplicity to *Avatar* is interesting, particularly when we now pair it with certain narrative episodes that then push the concept of multiplicity further. *Avatar* is not quite anime, but the phenomena that Lamarre brings up prove to be incredibly generative for the fandom precisely because the potential for multiplicity is connected directly to the phenomenological assertion that there is space to move. McCloud's "gutters" as envisioned in *Avatar* are not necessarily empty, but they are flanked by meaning and context. Fanfiction seems to be a logical response to a text that offers so many fissures for the audience to enter and cross the threshold.[22] In other words, it stands to reason that *Avatar* is precisely so generative because there is more space for the readers/watchers to find themselves and shift between planes, between racial subjectivities, and between art styles in a way that allows for more ruptures than traditional or even more technologically advanced animated fare. This invitation is provocative as it not only allows fans to move through, to experience, but to also cross boundaries and come out the other side changed.

AO3 and *Avatar* Fanfiction

Playing in any fictional world, whether through creating visual art, fanvids, fanfictions, or even consuming those fan works, demands a certain level of commitment that is usually affixed to more lofty artistic engagements. Solomon notes:

> "For those who are shackled by hours of work and regulated moments of rest, by a mathematical precision of time, whose lives are graphed by the cent and the dollar," the infinite possibilities of pure protoplasm, Eisenstein argued, offer a figurative revolt.[23]

Eisenstein's words resonate quite differently when taken in relation to a strange locked-down landscape where lives are not necessarily regulated and more open to infinite possibilities. On the possibility of fan fiction, Abigail Derecho writes that it opens up potential to engage in "a different perspective on the institutional and the social" that might be taken up by "any writer interested in doing the job."[24] Fanfiction, as described by Derecho is democratizing and, in some ways, the pandemic released time for individuals who would have otherwise been racing to work or other responsibilities.[25] While I do not contend that this is an argument built upon methods of the social sciences, it is difficult to ignore what the data says about fanfiction and, in particular, about *Avatar* fanfiction during the pandemic. The work of scholarly analysis does not often hinge on the value of an object but rather the possibilities; digital fandom, in general, is potentially capable of yielding a numerical value if not an aesthetic or artistic one.

Reflecting upon their generous data dumps, AO3 seems as invested in making theory as inclusive and democratized as fanfiction.[26] This article leans heavily on AO3 as a definitive archive, one that is self-reflexive and interested in creating safe spaces for fans as well as engaging in scholarly research. Here is a space, they seem to say, that values fanfiction for everything it is: boundary-pushing, beautiful, terrible, embarrassing, worthy of canon, and worthy of dissection. The fact that they have so readily made their statistics and figures available is significant, and, while this analysis does not fit into a true quantitative mode of research, it does help to focus how and where fans were entering into the conversation. While several of the *Avatar* episodes might serve to illustrate the engagement with the fandom, the three that I focus on in this chapter have been particularly stimulating in the fanfiction community, both in the proliferation of how many fics were posted and tagged on AO3 as stemming from the episodes as well as from the number of kudos (AO3's version of likes) they accrued.[27]

Of the 290 tags mentioning "The Blue Spirit" (*Avatar* S1E13), 243 were originated or updated from the pandemic onward, and it makes sense that this episode lends itself to various narratives. The plot of the episode begins with a mysterious illness that incapacitates both Sokka and Katara; they hallucinate through the entire episode. While searching for the cure, Aang is captured by Admiral Zhao and subsequently freed by the Blue Spirit, a masked and conflicted Zuko. The tables turn rather quickly, and Aang goes from prisoner to savior, taking Zuko to safety and away from the Fire Nation soldiers. When the literal smoke clears, we are met with an aerial shot of a crossroads and no sign of Aang or Zuko. When Zuko wakes, Aang asks, "If we knew each other back then, do you think we could have been friends, too?" Zuko has not yet embarked fully on his redemption arc, so his answer is a fire blast; but he has exhibited that he is morally gray enough that a character shift is possible. This episode functions almost as a gap in the narrative, one that offers possibilities to fanfiction writers who might identify the motif of the crossroads as an encouragement to take a different narrative path.

This episode also kicks off the alter egos and vigilante-versions of the characters as well as the narrative hallucinatory, allowing the fans to speculate. In the stories with the most hits and kudos, this presents a turning point and a break with the canonical relationships. In this hallucinatory and free-form space, what bonds might be allowed to form? Aang himself asks an unmasked Zuko of things could have been different if they met at a different time.

Fans seem to answer yes, and from here Zuko and Sokka become a relationship favorite; many of the best loved fanfictions with this fanon pairing utilize the mask to signify Zuko's internal struggle not only with his morality but with his sexuality as well. Kristina Busse and Karen Hellekson point out that, sometimes, a sexual relationship is "all but an extension of canon."[28] Of the 2,911 fanfictions as of December 2020 that tag a Sokka/Zuko relationship, 2,407 were updated or created during the pandemic. Similar to other fanon pairings, the pieces range from tracing the evolutions of epic relationships between the two, to smutty one-shots, to crack fics meant to amuse or dislodge the ship from its originating source; the most accessed Sokka/Zuko fic, as understood by the tracked hits from AO3, features Zuko's turn as the Blue Spirit. "Blue" is rated as a teen fic and starts with what might happen in a cut scene, a chance meeting and blossoming friendship between the two teenagers.[29] Katara and Zuko fics that originate with "The Blue Spirit" also have an impressive following, as evidenced by a pandemic-timed "Rumour Has It: The Festival of Molten Sun," a sequel to one of the fandoms most lauded and re-read works, "Rumour Has It," both by FictionIsSocialInquiry.[30] The pacing and release of fanfics often pain readers as they wait for the next installment to drop, in contrast to the accessibility of all the episodes of *Avatar* on Netflix. The waiting on fan forums seems to underline the care that the authors treat both themselves and audiences with; and, while neither author tags their works as "slow-burn," there is an element of restraint in both of the fanfictions.[31] If "The Blue Spirit" sets up the crossroads and the possibility of multiple paths for identity to evolve, both of these works follow that lead.

The fandom antithesis to the slow-burn fic is a one-shot. These texts usually center on one instance and are usually "extreme," offering extreme fluffiness, smut, or violence. "The Tales of Ba Sing Se" (*Avatar* S2E15) functions in similar ways. In the later half of season two, the main characters have gathered in the capital of the Earth Kingdom, where they will spend many pivotal episodes. The city itself offers an appealing prospect for fanfiction writers—out of the 339 tags for "Ba Sing Se," 269 originated or updated during the pandemic—but it is the format of "The Tales of Ba Sing Se" that provides the most obvious multiplicity. In this episode, composed of several vignettes spotlighting the different characters, the gutters are pronounced. The different storylines never cross while the literal stammers separating them diverge and converge within the same space.

Each of the vignettes flirts with forging new identities, complete with the success and failures that entails, and provides a glimpse of the people that the characters could be if life was just a bit different or if the context was changed. The first slice of life vignette follows Toph and Katara who opt for a spa day only to be met with cruelty from other girls. The second picks up with Iroh who spends the majority of his story parenting and mentoring children who are not his own; he soothes a baby with a song, helps a group of street urchins get out of trouble, and reforms a would-be mugger all while he goes about his day shopping. He ends the vignette at a makeshift altar honoring his dead son, singing and weeping. The third vignette belongs to Aang, whose empathy for animals and talent in bending coalesces as he dabbles in urban planning and literally reshapes land just outside of the city to create a zoo. Sokka stars in the fourth as he stumbles in an all-female haiku slam and, though he keeps his recognizable humor, he is beaten by a stronger contender. In the next, Zuko goes on a date with regular customer Jin, an outing that his uncle sets up. He is awkward and uncertain, and, though viewers can easily guess it will not end well, he displays slight kindness to a girl he has been taught to hate. The last vignette follows the nonhuman storyline of Momo, recasting Ba Sing Se as an unknowable place with storylines bubbling under the surface, stretching into multiplicity. Thirty-nine percent of the fanfictions feature noncanon ships set against a city that allows for the play through of different identities and subjectivities. Zuko, the Blue Spirit himself in a city where he can become anonymous, is the most popular character to ship with either Sokka, Katara, or Jet. The choice of Zuko's partner is, of course, important, but most of these fics, regardless of the coupling, offer instances of resisting the institutional gaze. In the case of Zuko's relationship with Sokka, the narratives are often coming-of-age love stories; with Katara, they are confrontations of Zuko's past actions and inactions; and, with Jet, they are an acknowledgment of desire. In short, they are all stories that the animated show did not have the space, time, or allowance to tell but whose subtexts are, as Busse and Hellekson might point out, there all the same.

The show acknowledges as much with "The Ember Island Players" (*Avatar* S3E17), which also saw a jump in fanfiction content created during the pandemic, with 275 of 331 "Ember Island" tags originated or updated during the time frame. The tagging system of AO3 seems, at first, intricate; the tagging functions by making fics searchable by main characters and relationships—similar to a site like Fanfiction.net—but also allows searchers to view the way in which authors to tag with other warnings, comments, or tropes in one place. Beyond that, readers can then tag stories into their own collections, declaring a fic "god tier" or anything else. By this logic, it makes sense that Ember Island as location, episode, and even vibe might be searchable and consumable. By the third season, Ember Island has been referenced several times, with the Fire Nation teens making an angsty detour there in "The Beach" (*Avatar* S3E05), before Zuko decides to train Aang to battle his own father ahead of the series finale. The island, the teens are told in that earlier episode, is a place to find yourself; but "The Ember Island Players" depicts something quite different and offers ruptures into the real with an unmistakable glance to the fandom itself. Team Avatar decide to take a break from training and buy tickets to "The Boy in the Iceberg," an in-universe dramatization of the series that acknowledges the show's own narrative devices and manipulations as well as the processes of fanfiction itself. The creators seem to admit that the subtext is already present through the use of camp. Susan Sontag's definition of camp privileges a certain taste profile, and there are countless instances of children's media that meander close to being full-blown camp.[32] However, "The Ember Island Players" suspends the full effect in ways that perhaps the creators did not intend. The characters are in the duplicated position of acting as viewer and being viewed, a nod to the fiction of the diegesis and also of the metatexts surrounding the show. It seems no mistake that both stage-Aang and stage-Toph are played in drag, Sontag's most famous example of camp. The audience is made up of Fire Nation citizens, and, even though there is the understanding that no one is white in the *Avatar* universe, Katara and Sokka are the characters with darker skin and come from a tribe murdered mercilessly by their would-be colonizers. With this in mind, the promiscuity of the stage-Katara—her noticeably bigger breasts, lips, and rouged face—is as much a racist statement as stage-Sokka's buffoonery, reduced to slapstick on stage. The creators seem to posit that perhaps fans see things this particular way in their fan works and cite the near ubiquitous focus on Katara and Sokka as romantic leads with several partners. In the fanfictions I have come across, the sexuality of the Water Tribe siblings is referenced about as many times as everyone else. Racial difference and cultural context are more often than not a part of most *Avatar* fanfictions. There are certainly other tropes present but not the racist and sexist ones put forth on the Ember Island stage in this episode. It makes sense, in relation to this episode, that the live-action film was completely whitewashed, a nod to the belief that the othered bodies of Asian actors were somehow deficient to tell a story about resisting colonizing forces in a particularly meaningful and identifiable way, especially when their own recast versions operate in just the way that Anne Anlin Cheng suggested to reflect back upon the default and white subjectivity. The utilization of racist stereotypes without noting from where these stereotypes originate is jarring in a context of resisting a brutal colonizing force. *Avatar* is a children's show, made up of episodes with 24-minute runtimes; however, presenting the colonizing gaze, particularly the colonizing gaze that demands to define othered bodies in relation to its own desire, without reflecting back on it, feels like a disservice to fans as well as the narrative. The play serves to unreservedly fetishize and focus in on stage-Aang and stage-Toph's gender duality; the desire is coupled with the expectation for stage-Katara's body to overflow its bounds, both with her tears and her breasts. While the real Katara in the stands rejects the idea of being overemotional, her companions do not dispute the depiction. Stage-Katara's sexuality becomes her only notable attribute, and her role as a woman, caretaker, and nurturer will follow her counterpart doggedly throughout the series. This is not a case of the creators responding to fanfiction but rather creating their own and recasting their leads with what seems to be a feasible replacement. While many of the fanfictions with the "Ember Island" tags focus on the group as a whole rather than solely on romantic relationships, the Katara and Zuko ship is the most popular, even surpassing the canon ships. Thirty-nine fics originated during the pandemic starring the couple while the next fanon ship of Sokka and Zuko yielded only nine. The fics mostly focus on dismantling the tropes from the play, referencing more canon events than not in order to offer more complex characters with reflection. The episode and the island are referenced heavily in fanfiction, and this particular episode is in constant correction and revision, a notable intervention as these texts is usually slotted between the play episode and the series finale, which will usher in the ending to the narrative and to any possibilities of diverging storylines.

Conclusion

Certainly, this chapter and others like it privilege *Avatar* as a media text, art object, and popular cultural artifact extraordinaire. Looking at the sheer number of fan interventions, *Avatar* falls behind franchises with huge worlds, multiverses, and different iterations. It seems strange that a children's animation series that ran for only three seasons remains so relevant, so accessible from different fan points. The fact that such fan activity spiked during the lockdown can be understood alongside discourse of fandoms and fan studies—but it also lends itself to discussions that cross over into aesthetics and film theory. I believe that it is here that the value of *Avatar* expands and multiplies as a media object and allows the series to stretch beyond its categorization as an enjoyable television series—it demands analysis that is varied and constantly flanked and juxtaposed with other paths of inquiry. The fandom, able to tease many of the show's nuances, long before academic scholarship picked it up, is an integral piece that was in discussion with the actual creation of the show. At the of this writing, Netflix has officially cast its live-action remake of the series; there is, as of now, a strong Asian presence both in front and behind of the camera, a decision certainly made with a fandom engaged in the art of making, revising, and questioning the authorial voice in mind.[33]

Notes

1   Henry Jenkins, *Textual Poachers* (Routledge, 1992), 28.
2   In comparison, the number of fanfictions posted to AO3 in that time frame—March 11, 2020 to December 14, 2020—categorized under *Marvel* accounted for 51,324 of the 424,689, roughly 12 percent; in the *Harry Potter* fandom, 42,341 of the 255,654 fanfictions were posted within the given dates amounting to 16.5 percent. Other Netflix holdings of interest might include *Stranger Things*, whose fanfiction numbers hit 3,459 of the 17,405 or around 20 percent; *Supernatural* (who had a significant fanbase prior to becoming a Netflix mainstay), 18,182 of the 221,520 or less than 10 percent; and *Lucifer*, whose fanfictions posted during the pandemic account for 2,298 of 8,050 or 28 percent.
3   For a sense of the conversation arising from the popularity of *Avatar* fifteen years after its debut, see: Samuel Spencer, "'Avatar The Last Airbender'

Just Broke a Major Netflix Record," *Newsweek*, July 20, 2020, https://www.newsweek.com/avatar-last-airbender-show-netflix-chart-top-10-record-1519004; Kari Sonde, "How 'Avatar: The Last Airbender' Became One of the Summer's Most Popular Shows—15 Years after Its Debut," *Washington Post*, August 7, 2020, https://www.washingtonpost.com/entertainment/how-avatar-the-last-airbender-became-one-of-the-summers-most-popular-shows-15-years-after-its-debut/2020/08/06/e368e740-d803-11ea-aff6-220dd3a14741_story.html.

4   Netflix (@NetflixGeeked). Twitter Post, July 27, 2020, 6:24 PM, https://twitter.com/netflixgeeked/status/1287876539216887810.

5   Dante Basco (@dantebasco), Twitter Post, July 27, 2020, 7:11 PM, https://twitter.com/dantebasco/status/1287888251701714944; mae Whitman (@maebirdwing), Twitter Post, August 19, 2016, 11:32 PM, https://twitter.com/maebirdwing/status/766855447336751104.

6   The closest thing to compare the kind of geography that *Avatar* poses is the Disney film, *Raya: The Last Dragon* (2021). While differences between a Nickelodeon franchise of the mid-2000's and a recent big budget Disney film that streamed through Disney+ are vast from an industry stand point, the content, however, does overlap in certain places.

7   Jennifer Barker, "Neither Here Nor There: Synesthesia and the Cosmic Zoom," *New Review of Film and Television Studies* 7.3 (2009): 311–24.

8   Michel de Certeau, *The Practice of Everyday Life* (University of California Press, 1988), 117.

9   Bertrand Westphal and Robert T. Tally, *Geocriticism: Real and Fictional Spaces* (Palgrave Macmillan, 2011), 69.

10 Lori Kido Lopez, "Fan Activists and the Politics of Race in The Last Airbender," *International Journal of Cultural Studies* 15.5 (2011): 431–45.

11 Rukmini Pande, *Squee from the Margins: Fandom and Race* (University of Iowa Press, 2018), 86.

12 Anne Anlin Cheng, *Ornamentalism* (Oxford University Press, 2019), 156.

13 Ibid., 117.

14 Teresa Kay Williams, "The Theater of Identity: (Multi-) Race and Representation of Eurasians and Afroasians," in *American Mixed Race: The Culture of Microdiversity*, ed. Naomi Zack (Rowman and Littlefield, 1995), 79–96; Mary Beltran, "The New Hollywood Racelessness: Only the Fast, Furious, (and Multiracial) Will Survive," *Cinema Journal*, 44.2 (2005): 50–67.

15 Anne Anlin Cheng, *The Melancholy of Race* (Oxford University Press, 2001), xi; Frantz Fanon, *Black Skins, White Masks*, rev. ed. (Pluto Press, 2008), 92.

16 Anne Anlin Cheng, *The Melancholy of Race* (Oxford University Press, 2001), 40.

17 Herman Gray, *Cultural Moves: African Americans and Politics of Representation* (University of California Press, 2005), 792.

18 Matthew Solomon, "Sergei Eisenstein: Attractions/Montage/Animation," in *Thinking in the Dark: Cinema, Theory, Practice*, eds. Murray Pomerance and R. Barton Palmer (Rutgers University Press, 2015), 101.
19 Ibid., 84.
20 Scott McCloud, *Understanding Comics: The Invisible Art* (William Morrow, 1994), 68.
21 Thomas Lamarre, *The Anime Machine: A Media Theory of Animation* (University of Minnesota Press, 2009), 36.
22 Walter Benjamin, "A Glimpse into the World of Children's Books," in *Walter Benjamin: Selected Writings, Volume 1: 1913–1926*, eds. Marcus Bullock and Michael W. Jennings (The Belknap Press of Harvard University Press, 1996), 435.
23 Solomon, 83.
24 Abigail Derecho, "Archontic Literature: A Definition, a History, and Several Theories of Fan Fiction," in *Fan Fiction and Fan Communities in the Age of the Internet*, eds. Karen Hellekson and Kristina Busse (McFarland & Co., 2006), 76.
25 The pandemic led to a significant number of people leaving their jobs in search of more meaningful and fulfilling pursuits; the connection with more fan interaction seems to correspond to this phenomenon. For more insight on the job quitting trend, see: Derek Thompson, "The Great Resignation Is Accelerating," *The Atlantic*, October 15, 2021, https://www.theatlantic.com/ideas/archive/2021/10/great-resignation-accelerating/620382/.
26 Admin, "Selective Data Dump for Fan Statisticians," Archive of Our Own, accessed March 21, 2021, https://archiveofourown.org/admin_posts/18804.
27 All data referenced in this part comes from the AO3 Selective Data Dump and from running terms through the site's search tools: https://archiveofourown.org/works/search.
28 Kristina Busse and Karen Hellekson, *The Fan Fiction Studies Reader* (University of Iowa Press, 2014), 79.
29 bealeciphers, "Blue," Archive of Our Own, completed November 15, 2020, https://archiveofourown.org/works/24376396.
30 FictionIsSocialInquiry, "Rumour Has It," Archive of Our Own, completed March 29, 2019, https://archiveofourown.org/series/1799311; FictionIsSocialInquiry, "Rumour Has It: The Festival of Molten Sun," Archive of Our Own, completed November 11, 2020, https://archiveofourown.org/works/24867220.
31 In FictionIsSocialInquiry's "Rumour Has It: Festival of the Molten Sun," the narrative is focused on the deteriorating mental health of an aged-up Zuko. This sequel to an earlier story, in which Katara and Zuko's relationship evolves through canonical events, takes into account the despair that the pandemic caused, and several commenters reference not only their own struggles with mental health but the ways in which this particular fiction and

author have captured the distress they felt due to the pandemic. The real-time self and community reflexivity reflect how author notes and warnings reinforce the kind of care that fan communities can cultivate, particularly in times of duress (https://archiveofourown.org/works/24867220).

32 Susan Sontag, "Notes on 'Camp'," *Partisan Review,* 31.4 (1964): 515–30.
33 Netflix (@NetflixGeeked). Twitter Post, August 12, 2021, 10:30 AM, https://twitter.com/NetflixGeeked/status/1425826986195394560.

13

Fans, Gender, and the Sequel: Analyzing Audience Reaction to *The Legend of Korra*

Brecken Hunter Wellborn

"Being a huge fan of Aang, I admit my expectations were a bit high for Korra (yes, korra ... I refuse to accept her as Avatar)"[1]

The comment above is from a "user review" of *The Legend of Korra* (Nickelodeon, 2012–14; nick.com, 2014), the sequel series to *Avatar: The Last Airbender* (Nickelodeon, 2005–8), posted on the Internet Movie Database (IMDb). This excerpt introduces the reviewer's position as a fan of *Avatar*, acknowledges their high expectations for the sequel, and suggests a negative reaction to the new female protagonist, Korra. Taken on its own, this comment provides insights into the views of one particular viewer of the series *Korra*. What can be understood about reaction to the series if more reviews are analyzed in conversation with one another?

As a sequel, *Korra* continues to provoke divisive reactions in casual audience members and fans of the franchise alike. Simply the word "sequel" can prompt wildly different responses in media consumers. As evidenced by several recent high-profile examples, from the new *Star Wars* trilogy (2015–19) to *Ghostbusters* (2016), sequels can incite intense emotional reactions, particularly among a fandom. For this reason, *Korra* is an apt case study for understanding audience reaction. As a high-profile continuation of a franchise with a dedicated fandom, *Korra*'s fan reviews provide insight into the intense reaction fans have to new entries in a beloved media series.

Since the series' initial airdate through to the time of this writing, audiences have continued to post reviews of the series on two of the most popular film and television websites, IMDb and Rotten Tomatoes.[2] On IMDb, audience members can post "user reviews" to a television series' content page. On Rotten Tomatoes, users can post "audience reviews" to the landing page for each season of the series. As Mattias Frey notes, Rotten Tomatoes claims to increase the democracy of criticism by including audience reviews on their site but relegates user reviews away from the professional critics.[3] More reviews are published on IMDb, perhaps for this reason. Regardless of platform, user reviews are subjective, and no one site's reviews speak to the film's "actual" quality, an unquantifiable value.[4] This study thus focuses entirely on the content of the reviews at the time of this writing.

For the purposes of this chapter, both the user reviews of IMDb and the audience reviews of Rotten Tomatoes are referred to as "fan reviews." As this chapter argues, fan reviews constitute a form of fan practice, and, therefore, the *fan* component of the review is integral for understanding its contribution to the fan community. Furthermore, this term allows for future studies to incorporate other forms of fan criticism into one identifiable term. This chapter draws from fan studies to contextualize fandom and situate fan reviews as a form of informative fan practice. Through an analysis of the user reviews posted to IMDb and Rotten Tomatoes, this chapter addresses the patterns that appear throughout the polarized reactions to *Korra*. This chapter then examines how fans perceive and react to *Korra* as a sequel, focusing on how audience reactions communicate cultural responses to gender. Finally, this chapter introduces the concept of "expectational standards," metrics fans use to measure a new textual entry in a fandom.

Fan Reviews as Fan Practice

The fandom which produces user reviews on IMDb and Rotten Tomatoes are not, perhaps, what comes to mind when one thinks of fandom. As Henry Jenkins identifies, though, "there is nothing timeless and unchanging about [fan] culture; fandom originates in response to specific historical conditions [...] and remains constantly in flux."[5] The rise of digital media and the popularization of entertainment fandoms give rise to less labor-intensive forms of practice that should absolutely be considered within conversations of fandom.

Contemporary digital media platforms also allow fans to feel like their unique points of view are part of the community. Fan reviews both contribute to an overarching community of reviews and are representative of the particular perspectives of each individual reviewer. These platforms work in direct conjunction with the "personalization of media content and media use" as identified by Cornel Sandvoss, Jonathan Gray, and C. Lee Harrington.[6] With the increase of personalized media, it is unsurprising that media consumers would also wish to contribute their personal perspective to the fan community. As both IMDb and Rotten Tomatoes prominently display the username of the review's author, their personal stamp is marked onto the review community.

A crucial component of any sector of fandom is the opportunity for engagement. Jenkins claims that "fan reception does not and cannot exist in isolation, but is always shaped through input from other fans and motivated, at least partially, by a desire for further interaction with a larger social and cultural community."[7] IMDb and Rotten Tomatoes provide excellent case studies then for analyzing fan reception, as they both provide the appearance of community and conversation. The collection of different fan perspectives allows the fan reviews to represent a collected discourse about a particular media object. There is also some evidence that some reviews are direct responses to the other reviews in the community. One reviewer asks, "Guys are y'all dumb?!??" in response to the negative reviews, and instructs other fans, "DON'T LISTEN TO THE HATE COMMENTS."[8] Another reviewer also makes a plea to the community, asking, "What is wrong with everyone? [...] I'm so confused."[9] Another reviewer states, "What really disappoints me is how people have these awful 'opinions.'"[10] Though these websites do not offer a great deal of interactivity from review to review, fans still address the community through appeal.

If the network of fan reviews is understood as a sector of fandom, then those who contribute to these networks are fans themselves. Jenkins notes, "the difference between watching a series and becoming a fan lies in the intensity of [a fan's] emotional and intellectual involvement"[11] There is a distinct difference between the viewer who passively watches a media object and the one who is activated to create, which requires emotional and intellectual involvement.

Following the lead of Matt Hills, this chapter wishes to avoid the common academic practice which "transforms fandom into an absolute Other."[12] Referring to the user reviewers of *Korra* as fans does not serve to Other the fans' practices and perspectives but to make the case that those who post reviews are likely fans of the media object. Action is thus the key to fan practice. When a series provokes an audience member to create, it can be called "fan activation." Therefore, the viewers who took their activation to IMDb and Rotten Tomatoes to create fan reviews should be considered fans. Both IMDb and Rotten Tomatoes feature reviews of *Korra* dated between 2012 and 2021, which supports Nicholas Rombes' claim that media "stories are continually in a 'present' state."[13] When audiences can discover a series at any point in time, they can experience fan activation at any point in time, as well.

Fan reviewers can be understood as "fan critics." As Jenkins states, fan criticism serves to "provide a public forum for evaluating and commentating" on all aspects of a given fan object.[14] The popularity of IMDb and Rotten Tomatoes shift the fan forum to a more popularized space, one which offers the presumption of more cultural capital than a message board. According to Hills, "internet-enabled fan practices will no longer be set apart from broader cultural norms, practices and processes."[15] As the internet exponentially grows in its ubiquity as a daily practice, the act of engaging online as a fan practice is not exclusively for the nonmainstream. IMDb and Rotten Tomatoes bring with them a built-in audience, namely those interested in the same program. Internet fan practices may be moving from out of the counter-normative shadow, but that does not mean that they still do not require specific intention and labor to complete.

In some ways, fan reviews are disrupting traditional notions of what constitutes fan labor. As Suzanne Scott overviews, "media producers all contribute to the construction of a narrowly defined, and often rigidly gendered, vision of fan identity."[16] One way in which these representational depictions of fans shape the imagined fan image is by their depictions of what constitutes fan practice. It is unlikely, for many people, that writing a user review on an entertainment website constitutes fan practice. However, the intensity of passion and appreciation depicted in the user reviews speaks to their existence as works of fan practice. Some fans declare their fan identity directly, and others' admiration appears in their assessment. One fan's review passionately begins, "How do you make a sequel to arguably the greatest animated show of all time?"[17] Another review addresses other reviews directly as fans, writing in their mixed review, "Fanboyism is distinct from the true fan base. The true fan cares more deeply for the quality of the content."[18]

The primary goal of a fan review is to communicate the fan's evaluation of the media object to the greater fan community. This is also situated within the confines of performing a reception study, as the reviews analyzed reveal each fan's assessment as well as the evaluative make up of this sector of the *Avatar* fandom at a specific point in time. Derek Johnson argues that "fan interpretation is constantly shifting, never unified or maintaining the same valences over time."[19] This is a limitation, since performing a reception study cannot account for future changes within the fandom. Fortunately, fans often acknowledge their own shifting perspectives in their reviews. One fan writes, "I used to love this show [...] but eventually I realized that I was deluded."[20] Another fan writes, "rewatching it, I see a lot more of the complexities of Korra's character."[21] Reviews such as these do help to account for the inability of a reception study to account of future variance, as they acknowledge the ability for evaluation to change over time. There is more to glean from these reviews than simple assertions about *Korra*'s quality or that opinions change over time. These reviews demonstrate fans making a case for their assessment, and their insights, whether in support of positive or negative readings, are often the key to understanding fan reviews as informative fan practice.

Melissa A. Click claims "dislike and hate play important roles in fan communities," and must be understood alongside the increased visibility of fan practice in digital media.[22] Fan practices that communicate dislike are just as important to study as practices that communicate admiration. For this reason, this chapter pays particular attention to the negative reviews of *Korra*. These tend to better illustrate the cultural messages found within the fan reviews of *Korra*, which allows them to provide insight into the competing cultural values of the fandom alongside or within users' evaluations of program merit.[23] The following parts thus analyze that messaging, assessing how fans react to *Korra* as a sequel, as well as assessing how fans react to a new female protagonist.

Infringements and Inherent Comparison

At the textual level, fan reviews of *Korra* demonstrate how fans react to the serialization of a beloved media object. Constantine Verevis finds the key characteristic of the sequel to be serialization, or, the sequel's expansion of narrative or of political elements found in the original text.[24] Serialization can also refer to the transformation of the object from one iteration to multiple. Multiplicities, as defined by Amanda Ann Klein and R. Barton Palmer, are "textual pluralities [that] take a number of distinct but hardly mutually exclusive forms, including adaptations, sequels, remakes, imitations, trilogies, reboots, series, spin-offs, and cycles."[25] Applying multiplicity to fan studies is a symbiotic mission, as many of the fan objects that inform fan studies are multiplicities. With so many terms, both popular and academic, for the various kinds of multiplicities, it is important to define *Korra* as a sequel, specifically, for this analysis. According to Carolyn Jess-Cooke and Verevis, a sequel seeks to recharge audience investment in a particular series rather than just replicate it.[26] *Korra* certainly fits this definition, as its setting, cast of characters, and narrative events recharge fan interest in the *Avatar* franchise, rather than simply repeat the experience of the first series.

Attempts to recharge fan engagement, though, create opportunities for fans to reject the multiplicity's forms of serialization. Fans' displeasure in creative decisions that reframe what they hold dear about the program exemplifies what Jenkins calls "unjustifiable infringements" on fan pleasure.[27] Unless a sequel literally replicates the experience of the predecessor, the sequel always carries the potential to change what is known and understood about a particular media object. These infringements appear to be the primary crime that negative reviewers believe *Korra* commits. While a few criticize perceived production quality, far more fan reviewers view these infringements as direct violations of the pleasures established by the predecessor. Infringements disturb the world's coherence, which disturbs a fan's connection to the object and reminds them that the object itself is constructed that it is not real.[28]

Another reason fans oppose infringements is because they connect with an object at a personal level, transforming it into what William Proctor calls a "totemic object."[29] Fans thus perceive multiplicities as "threats to self-identity, self-continuity, and self-narrative."[30] The infringements on a totemic object are rendered as personal assaults, as challenges to the self. Connections with the original text shape not only fan identity, but also fan perception. Jess-Cooke and Verevis suggest that sequels exist "always in relation to [their] heritage and that both [their] meaning and entertainment value ultimately derive from a negotiation" of previous entries in a series or franchise.[31] The presence of the sequel, therefore, when received either positively or negatively, denotes "reciprocal interest," or, encouraging audiences to look backward within the franchise.[32] Nearly every single fan review of *Korra*, whether positive or negative, makes reference to *Avatar*. The reciprocal interest generated by *Korra* yields a critical observation in the reception of multiplicities: inherent comparison.

More specifically, the fans express disappointment based on their expectations from watching *Avatar*. These negative reviewers may not be quite "anti-fans" (those whose fan practices are informed by their dislike of a fan object) of *Korra*, but they certainly are fans of *Avatar*, as they state in many reviews.[33] One writes, "While watching 'Avatar: The Last Airbender' left me with a warm feeling in my heart, 'The Legend of Korra' took that and crushed it. Hard."[34] Though not all are as dramatic, many repeat a similar sentiment: *Avatar* is a good show, but *Korra* did not live up to it. These are not fans who are just disappointed by certain elements of a particular media object but are disappointed with a multiplicity within the object's franchise. The fans of the *Avatar* franchise could therefore be deemed "selective fans." They are fans of only select objects within the larger franchise. Based on the reviews, this threat is perceived primarily in the form of infringements that do not do justice to the original series.

Many of these infringements specifically identify ways in which *Korra* directly reacts to *Avatar*. One fan writes, "The characters from ATLA are disrespected and half are gone [...] the show is NOT a worthy successor to the first series."[35] Another writes, "They might as well have just changed every rule of bending and all the aspects of everything else from the original."[36] One more reviewer explains this position even more plainly, writing, "I especially hate this season for making changes to the franchise."[37] Each of these reviews exemplifies fans' reluctance to accept series elements that threaten their established knowledge of and connection to the predecessor. Changes to the knowledge established by the original text are not always viewed as infringements, though. Many of the positive reviews of *Korra* highlight the ways in which the sequel expands the mythology of the *Avatar* franchise. A positive reviewer writes, "This series does not use The Last Airbender as a crutch—it evolves past it [...] expanding the Avatar universe."[38]

Fan reviews reveal not just audience perceptions of a particular sequel, they also allude to how audiences watch. For many *Korra* fans, watching the series is shaped by the practice of "hopeful hatewatching," the practice of watching a series with the hope that the show better meets expectations for the program.[39] Though several *Korra* viewers express disappointment with the show, they also declare their intent to continue watching. Before completing the series, one fan writes, "praying it gets better" at the end of their review.[40] Other fans allude to their hopeful hatewatching in the past. One writes, "season 1 was terrible and 2 not much better but I was literally suprised [sic] how well everything in 3 was ... the plot the villains the comedy ... very awesome job and I'm glad they got it together."[41] Hopeful hatewatching can be identified as an intentional practice of fans, as well as an effort to continue comparison. Hopeful hatewatchers continue watching the series expressly intent on appraising *Korra* in relation to *Avatar*. This also suggests a secondary layer of comparison. The hatewatcher is now comparing the series not only to the original media object, but also to what they have seen of the sequel.

The negative reviews of *Korra*'s hopeful hatewatchers also speak to one of Johnson's observations about fan culture: "fans may hate the current status quo, but their intense feelings and continued contribution to fan discourse stem from pleasurable engagement with the diegetic past."[42] *Korra*'s situation is unique in the fact that this "diegetic past" may refer to either the series itself or the *Avatar* series that came before it. The longing for the diegetic past alludes to the feelings of nostalgia that stem from engaging with a totemic object. Sometimes, this takes a more literal form, where viewers express their nostalgic positioning, such as when one fan writes, "I loved growing up with Avatar the last Airbender."[43] Far more frequently, though, it is understood that passion for a fan object is bound in an unspoken nostalgic connection. Fans are thus not reviewing *Korra* to negate its quality but to advocate for their totemic object.

In addition to the patterns of reception and the insight into fan practice that analyzing the fan reviews yields, this study also uncovers the "discursive mantra" of *Korra*'s fans, that repeated phrase asserting a fan object's value in the face of criticism from external parties.[44] Based on the show's multiplicity context, the inherent comparison found within the reviews, and the practices fans engage in to watch the series, it is clear the discursive mantra of the *Korra* fandom can be summarized by one individual's review: "You cannot compare this to ATLA."[45] By their nature, fan reviews seek to publicly declare one's assessment of a program's quality. By either publicly lauding or condemning the series, these reviews add to the discourse around the program, attempting to sway the way other fans perceive the series in order to better align with their specific interpretation. Fans repeatedly instruct readers of their reviews to not compare *Korra* to its predecessor. However, while fans continually instruct others not to compare the two series, they typically spend the bulk of their reviews doing just that. Most intriguingly, these claims do not seem to be aligned exclusively with either positive or negative reviews. As the mantra then suggests, whether or not fans enjoy the series, they both cannot escape comparison and stress that others find a way to avoid it.

In addition to the discursive mantra discussed above, one other repeated phrase stands out from the research: "Korra is unlikable." Various forms of the phrase appear throughout the fan reviews. Forms of "Korra is unlikable" could thus be thought of as discursive *anti*-mantras, repeated phrases that assert a fan object's *lack of* value in the face of *appreciation* from external parties. This discursive anti-mantra also prefaces the analysis of the next part: fans' reaction to Korra as a female protagonist.

Coded Language and Expectational Gender

The most pervasive cultural messages that recur throughout the fan reviews of *Korra* are related to the series' female protagonist, Korra. *Avatar* focuses on the journeys of Aang, an incarnation of the Avatar as a young boy who is hesitant to take on the Avatar mantle. Though female characters do exist in the *Avatar* series, their narrative purpose is to support Aang's narrative.[46] *Korra* thus represents a departure from the original series in the fact that the protagonist is now a teenage girl who is confident in her ability to take on the Avatar mantle. While the original series references female Avatars, fan reviews point to Korra as a significant infringement on their fandom:

Korra is just NOT a likable character.[47]

Korra too is unlikable [...] constantly whining and very hard to sympathise with.[48]

The weakness of the show is that Korra is not as likeable as Aang was.[49]

Though many fans react negatively to Korra, adding a new type of protagonist is not an isolated trend within multiplicities. In his analysis of franchises, Daniel Herbert correlates franchising with increased in-series diversity.[50] Having a female protagonist rather than a male one is thus one way in which the series may be actively attempting to increase the franchise's points of identification.

In many cases, misogyny takes form in fan communities as a response to more inclusive gender representation. Scott summarizes:

> Perceived shifts at the micro level of media textuality and target demographics are thus deeply bound up with macro cultural concerns that conflate legitimate criticisms of systemic and intersectional forms of oppression with a censorial rise in "PC culture."[51]

Even a positive review alludes to this trend when they write, "I thought making avatar a female character was asking the show to be just for the girls."[52]

Negative reactions to identity-based alterations in media are, of course, nothing new. As Peter Cullen Bryan and Brittany R. Clark uncover in their analysis of the 2016 *Ghostbusters* reboot, many male fans react to multiplicities introducing female protagonists as an intentional effort by producers to take the object "away from them."[53] The presence of a female protagonist infringes on the totemic object's nostalgic past. Nostalgia may play a great part in fan identity, but the identity of the characters in a fan object also plays a great part in nostalgia. Though the messages that appear in *Korra's* fan reviews are far less violent than the discourse surrounding *Ghostbusters*, they are no less important for understanding fan discourse on gender. As Jeffrey A. Brown writes, "political issues are made visible through popular culture and the struggle over the popular is tantamount to a struggle over the ideological."[54]

The discursive anti-mantra about Korra's unlikability signals a specific response to the character's gender. More specifically, describing Korra as "unlikable" is a coded way for reviewers to critique the character at a gendered level. Though a variety of definitions exist for coded language, it can simply be understood as language with an implied ideological appeal. Historically, coded language repeatedly appears in the political arena as a means to target messages to specific audiences without disrespecting ideological consensus.[55] As the contemporary Western political arena and work force feature more visible women, issues of gender are also discussed in coded language, such as concern about "likability."[56] In both contexts, likability is tied to expectations about how women should behave or act. This can be understood as "expectational gender," or how one interprets someone of a particular gender to behave.

Expectational gender is also seen in other fan reactions. Holly Willson Holladay and Click's analysis of fans' dislike of Skylar White, the most prominent woman in *Breaking Bad* (AMC, 2008–13), reveals much of the dislike for the character comes from a conflict between how fans expect her to act and how the character actually does.[57] Unsurprisingly, these expectations reveal "deep-seated biases [...] about gender and sex roles."[58] While much of the dislike expressed about Skyler White is explicitly sexist and violent, the biases revealed in the fan reviews of *Korra* are more subtle. The use of coded language gives the negative reactions to Korra the appearance of being non-misogynistic.

While audiences can and do have legitimate complaints about fictional female characters, the repetition of specific terms that demonstrate issue with expectational gender suggest an underlying misogyny. Even fan reviews that support Korra deploy coded language. One reviewer refers to her as a "confident young lady" who "is likable throughout."[59] "Korra is a really likable main protagonist [...] She is very identifiable and connect to the audience members," writes another.[60] Though both examples react favorably to Korra, they still contribute to Korra's evaluation through "likability."[61]

The coded language is not exclusive to this one term, as revealed by other repeated words implying that Korra does not behave as expected. One fan review, in particular, best summarizes this point, including many of the coded words in a lead up to unlikability: "arrogant, brash, rude, hot-headed, stubborn, and just plain unlikable."[62] Misogynistic language, coded as a behavioral disconnect, further the evidence that fans take issue with the actions that disrupt their interpretations of Korra's expectational gender.

As fan reviews build on the network of those that precede them, the wide-ranging reach of coded misogyny demonstrates its spreadability. Though the user reviews of *Korra* do not demonstrate, save for a few, the level of violent language found in other fan communities, the consistent devaluing of Korra as a protagonist works as a form of "spreadable misogyny," though aimed more at a female protagonist rather than at female fans.[63] That being said, the consistent devaluing of the female protagonist certainly makes the fan space seem less likely to embrace female fans, especially when considering that Aang receives no equivalent backlash in fan reviews.

Expectational Standards

Analyzing the most predominant messages found within fan reviews of *Korra* on IMDb and Rotten Tomatoes reveals the primary reasons fans take issue with the series. Firstly, sequels are received through inherent comparison, which reveals infringements committed by the sequel on the original fan object. Secondly, serializing gender is also viewed as an infringement if it disrupts the expectational gender that a fan projects onto the female character. Both of these themes demonstrate the overarching evaluative measure fans use to assess a multiplicity's value: expectation.

Even though comparisons to *Avatar* and spreadable misogyny were the most prevalent examples of unmet expectations, fan reviews of *Korra* demonstrate concerns of expectation across textual and cultural lines. Many fans express trouble connecting with the series because of how it disrupts generic expectations. In one fan's description of their disappointment, they write, "The Last Airbender truly felt like a perfect marriage between Japanese style Anime (serious) and American Cartoon (relaxed). On the contrary, The Legend of Korra feels like I am watching a badly done American teenager soap opera."[64] Another fan writes, "Too many times I felt like watching a typical soap."[65] One more writes, "Remove the melodramatic romances. This is suppose[d] to be an Avatar sequel, not the Winx club."[66] Fans who are particularly attached to the generic construction of *Avatar* read the romance of *Korra* as a disruption to their expectations for animated action series.

A number of fans also express unmet expectations in regard to how the criticized romances achieve narrative completion. One of *Korra*'s more noteworthy narrative moments is the final scene of the series which implies that Korra and her female friend, Asami, end the series in a romantic relationship. Many fans, whether they reviewed the series positively or negatively, take issue with the sudden appearance of identities they did not expect in the series. One fan's critique of the pairing reads, "the writers thought pandering to a minority community was better than sticking with the story and relationships they had been developing."[67] Another review titled "Amazing until the end" reads, "the writers just fell into the pressure of politics [...] they changed who the character was."[68] The identity-based disruption to fans' expectations alters their perception of the series, and also potentially exposes coded homophobia within the fans, as well.

Whether unmet expectations are related to textual factors, such as multiplicity comparison or genre, or to cultural factors, such as expectational gender or queerness, the level of dissatisfaction with the unmet expectation seems to be the primary informant of the fan's perception of the series. For this reason, this analysis uncovers what can be called "expectational standards," metrics for determining how a multiplicity compares when assessed against an internal expectation that fans hold. Expectational standards can refer to textual, cultural, or even industrial elements. As the fan reviews of *Korra* demonstrate, patterns do occur in the expectational standards of fans, and these patterns reveal how those fans interpret new multiplicities.

Notes

1   redherringr, September 19, 2015, user review of "The Legend of Korra," *IMDb*, https://www.imdb.com/review/rw3319643/?ref_=rw_urv.

2   As of spring 2021, over 190 fan reviews for *Korra* have been published on Rotten Tomatoes and over 350 on IMDb.

3   Mattias Frey, "The New Democracy?: Rotten Tomatoes, Metacritic, Twitter, and IMDb," in *Film Criticism in the Digital Age*, eds. Mattias Frey and Cecilia Sayad (Rutgers University Press, 2015), 92.

4. Walt Hickey, "'Ghostbusters' Is a Perfect Example of How Internet Movie Ratings Are Broken," July 14, 2016, https://fivethirtyeight.com/features/ghostbusters-is-a-perfect-example-of-how-internet-ratings-are-broken/.
5. Henry Jenkins, *Textual Poachers: Television Fans and Participatory Culture*, 20th Anniversary ed. (Routledge, 2013), 3.
6. Cornel Sandvoss, Jonathan Gray and C. Lee Harrington, "Introduction: Why Still Study Fans?" in *Fandom: Identities and Communities in a Mediated World*, eds. Jonathan Gray, Cornel Sandvoss, and C. Lee Harrington, 2nd ed. (New York University Press, 2017), 9.
7. Jenkins, 76.
8. saudmishaal, February 20, 2021, user review of "The Legend of Korra," *IMDb*, https://www.imdb.com/review/rw6617216/?ref_=tt_urv.
9. B. Doug, July 12, 2020, audience review of "The Legend of Korra: Season 2," *Rotten Tomatoes*, https://www.rottentomatoes.com/tv/the-legend-of-korra/s02/reviews?type=user.
10. G. Roger, June 15, 2020, audience review of "The Legend of Korra: Season 1," *Rotten Tomatoes*, https://www.rottentomatoes.com/tv/the-legend-of-korra/s01/reviews?type=user.
11. Jenkins, 56.
12. Matt Hills, *Fan Cultures* (Routledge, 2002), 5.
13. Nicholas Rombes, "Before and after and Right Now: Sequels in the Digital Era," in *Second Takes: Critical Approaches to the Film Sequel*, eds. Carolyn Jess-Cooke and Constantine Verevis (State University of New York Press, 2010), 192.
14. Jenkins, 95.
15. Matt Hills, "Defining Cult TV: Texts, Inter-Texts, and Fan Audiences," in *The Television Studies Reader*, eds. Robert C. Allen and Annette Hill (Routledge, 2004), 520.
16. Suzanne Scott, *Fake Geek Girls: Fandom, Gender, and the Convergence Culture Industry* (New York University Press, 2019), 51.
17. vidarmostad-67587, February 18, 2021, user review of "The Legend of Korra," *IMDb*, https://www.imdb.com/review/rw6608595/?ref_=tt_urv.
18. Reviewer746, January 9, 2016, user review of "The Legend of Korra," *IMDb*, https://www.imdb.com/review/rw3391746/?ref_=tt_urv.
19. Derek Johnson, "Fantagonism: Factions, Institutions, and Constitutive Hegemonies of Fandom," in *Fandom: Identities and Communities in a Mediated World*, eds. Jonathan Gray, Cornel Sandvoss and C. Lee Harrington, 2nd ed. (New York University Press, 2017), 375.
20. ibrahimctit, December 20, 2017, user review of "The Legend of Korra," *IMDb*, https://www.imdb.com/review/rw4008180/?ref_=tt_urv.
21. dalzelljack-94653, August 30, 2017, user review of "The Legend of Korra," *IMDb*, https://www.imdb.com/review/rw3793713/?ref_=tt_urv.

22 Melissa A. Click, "Introduction: Haters Gonna Hate," in *Anti-Fandom: Dislike and Hate in the Digital Age*, ed. Melissa A. Click (New York University Press, 2019), 6.
23 Jenkins, 95.
24 Constantine Verevis, "Redefining the Sequel: The Case of the (Living) Dead," in *Second Takes: Critical Approaches to the Film Sequel*, eds. Carolyn Jess-Cooke and Constantine Verevis (State University of New York Press, 2010), 18–21.
25 Amanda Ann Klein and R. Barton Palmer, "Introduction," in *Cycles, Sequels, Spin-Offs, Remakes, and Reboots: Multiplicities in Film & Television*, eds. Amanda Ann Klein and R. Barton Palmer (University of Texas Press, 2016), 1.
26 Carolyn Jess-Cooke and Constantine Verevis, "Introduction," in *Second Takes: Critical Approaches to the Film Sequel*, eds. Carolyn Jess-Cooke and Constantine Verevis (State University of New York Press, 2010), 5.
27 Jenkins, 104.
28 Ibid., 115.
29 William Proctor, "'Bitches Ain't Gonna Hunt No Ghosts': Totemic Nostalgia, Toxic Fandom and the *Ghostbusters* Platonic," *Palabra Clave* 20.4 (2017): 1112.
30 Imdb., 1120.
31 Jess-Cooke and Verevis, 3.
32 Verevis, 23.
33 Jonathan Gray, "New Audiences, New Textualities: Anti-Fans and Non-Fans," *International Journal of Cultural Studies* 6.1 (2003): 70.
34 Trixie_reviews, October 4, 2018, user review of "The Legend of Korra," *IMDb*, https://www.imdb.com/review/rw4376925/?ref_=tt_urv.
35 unicornvsdragon, August 30, 2017, user review of "The Legend of Korra," *IMDb*, https://www.imdb.com/review/rw3793891/?ref_=tt_urv.
36 ninjamaster08, March 9, 2014, user review of "The Legend of Korra," *IMDb*, https://www.imdb.com/review/rw2976444/?ref_=tt_urv.
37 B. Nikolas, August 18, 2020, audience review of "The Legend of Korra: Season 1," *Rotten Tomatoes*, https://www.rottentomatoes.com/tv/the-legend-of-korra/s01/reviews?type=user.
38 lukeloganvladimir, November 4, 2019, user review of "The Legend of Korra," *IMDb*, https://www.imdb.com/review/rw5234736/?ref_=tt_urv.
39 Jonathan Gray, "How Do I Dislike Thee? Let Me Count the Ways," in *Anti-Fandom: Dislike and Hate in the Digital Age*, ed. Melissa A. Click (New York University Press, 2019), 35.
40 M. Kevin, June 15, 2020, audience review of "The Legend of Korra: Season 1," *Rotten Tomatoes*, https://www.rottentomatoes.com/tv/the-legend-of-korra/s01/reviews?type=user.

41 H. Joshua, April 24, 2020, audience review of "The Legend of Korra: Book Three—Change," *Rotten Tomatoes*, https://www.rottentomatoes.com/tv/the-legend-of-korra/s03/reviews?type=user.
42 Johnson, 378.
43 chelseajmbelehar, January 8, 2018, user review of "The Legend of Korra," *IMDb*, https://www.imdb.com/review/rw4026985/?ref_=tt_urv.
44 Hills, *Fan*, 67.
45 H. Jack, August 23, 2020, audience review of "The Legend of Korra: Book Three—Change," *Rotten Tomatoes*, https://www.rottentomatoes.com/tv/the-legend-of-korra/s03/reviews?type=user.
46 For more on gender in the *Avatar* television franchise, see Ruth Richards' as well as Emily Baulch and Oliver Eklund's chapters in this collection.
47 ryan-73023, November 7, 2016, user review of "The Legend of Korra," *IMDb*, https://www.imdb.com/review/rw3576487/?ref_=tt_urv.
48 jk384-949-142166, March 16, 2014, user review of "The Legend of Korra," *IMDb*, https://www.imdb.com/review/rw2980435/?ref_=tt_urv.
49 sylvainmolinier, September 1, 2020, user review of "The Legend of Korra," *IMDb*, https://www.imdb.com/review/rw6053649/?ref_=tt_urv.
50 Daniel Herbert, *Film Remakes and Franchises* (Rutgers University Press, 2017), 87–101.
51 Scott, 3.
52 saints_spider, July 26, 2014, user review of "The Legend of Korra," *IMDb*, https://www.imdb.com/review/rw3056382/?ref_=tt_urv.
53 Peter Cullen Bryan and Brittany R. Clark, "#Not My Ghostbusters: Adaptation, Response, and Fan Entitlement in 2016's *Ghostbusters*," *The Journal of American Culture* 42.2 (2019): 154.
54 Jeffrey A. Brown, "#wheresRey: Feminism, Protest, and Merchandising Sexism in *Star Wars: The Force Awakens*," *Feminist Media Studies* 18.3 (2018): 338.
55 For more on this subject, see: Ian Haney López, *Dog Whistle Politics: How Coded Racial Appeals Have Reinvented Racism and Wrecked the Middle Class* (Oxford University Press, 2013); Jessica Autumn Brown, "Running on Fear: Immigration, Race and Crime Framings in Contemporary GOP Presidential Debate Discourse," *Critical Criminology* 24.3 (2016): 315–31.
56 Claire Bond Potter, "Men Invented 'Likability.' Guess Who Benefits," *The New York Times*, May 4, 2019, https://www.nytimes.com/2019/05/04/opinion/sunday/likeable-elizabeth-warren-2020.html; Pragya Agarwal, "Not Very Likeable: Here Is How Bias Is Affecting Women Leaders," *Forbes*, October 23, 2018, https://www.forbes.com/sites/pragyaagarwaleurope/2018/10/23/not-very-likeable-here-is-how-bias-is-affecting-women-leaders/?sh=35c41b60295f.
57 Holly Willson Holladay and Melissa A. Click, "Hating Skyler White: Gender and Anti-Fandom in AMC's *Breaking Bad*," in *Anti-Fandom: Dislike and Hate in the Digital Age*, ed. Melissa A. Click (New York University Press, 2019), 150.

58 Ibid., 164.
59 Carlotta 4, December 26, 2017, audience review of "The Legend of Korra: Book Three—Change," *Rotten Tomatoes*, https://www.rottentomatoes.com/tv/the-legend-of-korra/s03/reviews?type=user.
60 johnmichinock, March 31, 2013, user review of "The Legend of Korra," *IMDb*, https://www.imdb.com/review/rw2775541/?ref_=tt_urv.
61 These fan reviews also exemplify community responses to other fans.
62 blutraine, September 13, 2013, user review of "The Legend of Korra," *IMDb*, https://www.imdb.com/review/rw2869078/?ref_=tt_urv.
63 Scott, 84.
64 ryan-73023, November 7, 2016, user review of "The Legend of Korra," *IMDb*, https://www.imdb.com/review/rw3576487/?ref_=tt_urv.
65 d_3434_d, May 20, 2013, user review of "The Legend of Korra," *IMDb*, https://www.imdb.com/review/rw2800155/?ref_=tt_urv.
66 CynicOwl, December 28, 2012, user review of "The Legend of Korra," *IMDb*, https://www.imdb.com/review/rw2727108/?ref_=tt_urv.
67 pownjesus-78518, August 31, 2020, user review of "The Legend of Korra," *IMDb*, https://www.imdb.com/review/rw6050925/?ref_=tt_urv.
68 loganholliday-10728, June 15, 2020, user review of "The Legend of Korra," *IMDb*, https://www.imdb.com/review/rw5825837/?ref_=tt_urv.

EPISODES INDEX

"Appa's Lost Days" (*Avatar* S2E16) 30, 122

"Avatar and the Fire Lord, The" (*Avatar* S3E06) 148

"Avatar Day" (*Avatar* S2E05) 146

"Avatar Returns, The" (*Avatar* S1E02) 87, 166

"Avatar State, The" (*Avatar* S2E01) 120, 141, 144–6

"Awakening, The" (*Avatar* S3E01) 23, 143, 148

"Bato of the Water Tribe" (*Avatar* S1E15) 67

"Beach, The" (*Avatar* S3E05) 36, 218

"Beginnings, Part 1" (*Korra* S2E07) 4, 118–19

"Beginnings, Part 2" (*Korra* S2E08) 4, 117, 119

"Beyond the Wilds" (*Korra* S4E09) 128

"Bitter Work" (*Avatar* S2E09) 26, 66, 84, 146–7, 198

"Blind Bandit, The" (*Avatar* S2E06) 12, 16, 190, 192–3

"Blue Spirit, The" (*Avatar* S1E13) 145, 216–17

"Boy in the Iceberg, The" (*Avatar* S1E01) 68, 76, 84–7, 139, 165

"Breath of Fresh Air, A" (*Korra* S3E01) 101, 126, 181–2

"Chase, The" (*Avatar* S2E08) 26, 28

"City of Walls and Secrets" (*Avatar* S2E14) 11–12, 14, 19–20, 83

"Coronation, The" (*Korra* S4E03) 128

"Crossroads of Destiny, The" (*Avatar* S2E20) 12, 84, 142–3, 148

"Day of Black Sun, Part 2: The Eclipse, The" (*Avatar* S3E11) 148, 156

"Desert, The" (*Avatar* S2E11) 26, 30, 141–2

"Deserter, The" (*Avatar* S1E16) 67, 89

"Drill, The" (*Avatar* S2E13) 88, 196

"Earth King, The" (*Avatar* S2E18) 148, 196

"Ember Island Players, The" (*Avatar* S3E17) 218

"Endgame" (*Korra* S1E12) 122

"Firebending Masters, The" (*Avatar* S3E13) 30, 36, 149

"Fortune Teller, The" (*Avatar* S1E10) 83

"Great Divide, The" (*Avatar* S1E11) 63

"Guide, The" (*Korra* S2E09) 123

"Guru, The" (*Avatar* S2E19) 115, 142

"Harmonic Convergence" (*Korra* S2E12) 117, 124

"Headband, The" (*Avatar* S3E02) 36, 68, 139, 157, 175, 200

"Jet" (*Avatar* S1E10) 63, 83

"King of Omashu, The" (*Avatar* S1E05) 15

"Lake Laogai" (*Avatar* S2E17) 25, 147, 196

"Last Stand, The" (*Korra* S4E13) 95, 101

"Library, The" (*Avatar* S2E10) 12, 15, 26, 30, 36, 141, 194, 196

"Light in the Dark" (*Korra* S2E14) 124–5

"New Spiritual Age, A" (*Korra* S2E10) 123

"Northern Air Temple, The" (*Avatar* S1E17) 66, 140, 197

"Painted Lady, The" (*Avatar* S3E03) 92

"Rebel Spirit" (*Korra* S2E01) 123
"Rebirth" (*Korra* S3E02) 180
"Runaway, The" (*Avatar* S3E07) 84, 86, 196, 200

"Serpent's Pass, The" (*Avatar* S2E12) 62, 86, 141, 194
"Siege of the North, Part 2, The" (*Avatar* S1E20) 25, 198
"Sokka's Master" (*Avatar* S3E04) 66
"Southern Air Temple, The" (*Avatar* S1E03) 4, 6, 82, 139, 144, 155–69
"Southern Raiders, The" (*Avatar* S3E16) 89, 149
"Sozin's Comet" (*Avatar* S3E18–21) 198–9, 213
"Stakeout, The" (*Korra* S3E09) 126
"Sting, The" (*Korra* S2E06) 123

"Storm, The" (*Avatar* S1E12) 68, 140, 144–5
"Swamp, The" (*Avatar* S2E04) 3, 6, 39–52, 121, 124

"Tales of Ba Sing Se, The" (*Avatar* S2E15) 12, 20–2, 84, 122, 139, 217
"Terror Within, The" (*Korra* S3E08) 98

"Venom of the Red Lotus" (*Korra* S3E13) 101, 127, 177

"Warriors of Kyoshi, The" (*Avatar* S1E04) 65, 76, 82, 87, 161
"Waterbending Master, The" (*Avatar* S1E18) 25, 67, 76, 87, 90
"Waterbending Scroll, The" (*Avatar* S1E09) 83
"Welcome to Republic City" (*Korra* S1E01) 99–100
"Western Air Temple, The" (*Avatar* S3E12) 201
"When Extremes Meet" (*Korra* S1E08) 214

"Zuko Alone" (*Avatar* S2E07) 3, 6, 26, 29, 31–6, 52, 198

SUBJECT INDEX

Locators followed by "n." indicate endnotes.

Aang 1–2, 4–6, 11, 14, 16–17, 19–20, 25, 28–31, 36, 40, 42, 44–8, 50–2, 54–5 n.24, 59, 62, 64–5, 67–70, 75–6, 82–5, 87–9, 91–2, 95, 97, 99, 102, 107, 115, 120–3, 193, 200, 216–18, 225, 232, 234
   traumatic experience 136–46, 148–50, 156–69, 172, 175–6
Adventures of Tintin, The 212
Adventure Time 76, 102, 191
Air Nomads 1, 5, 29, 62, 67, 84, 107, 128
   genocide 52 n.22, 122, 126, 139, 157, 161, 172, 174–5, 178
   imperial traumas 135, 139–41, 157, 159, 167, 172, 175–80
   and Tibet 5, 29, 157, 171–3, 181–2
allegory 13, 22
allusion 12–14, 17, 22, 46–7
Amon 2, 123
animation 1–6, 13–16, 22–3, 25, 27, 40, 50, 52, 53 n.2, 59, 71, 76–81, 83, 85, 88, 95, 97–103, 105, 109, 116–18, 121–2, 125–6, 129, 135–9, 145, 147, 150, 158, 169, 190–1, 197–8, 202, 208, 210–15, 218, 220, 228, 235
anime 12, 25, 27–8, 36, 102, 200, 211–12, 214, 235
anthropocentrism 3–4, 6, 41, 45–7, 50, 116, 118–19, 122
Appa (flying bison) 2, 30–1, 48, 87, 122, 147, 159
   and Aang 121, 141, 165, 168

Archive of Our Own (AO3) 5, 207–8, 212, 215–18, 220 n.2, 222 n.27
Arthur 102
Asami Sato 2, 213–14
   and Korra 95–6, 100–4, 106–9, 128, 235
As Told By Ginger 80, 99
audience
   child 3–5, 78, 81, 150
   reaction 225–35
   review 226
Avatar and *Korra* comparisons 95–9, 102, 107
   animation 212–13
   audience review 225, 229–32
Avatar State 84, 120–1, 123, 140–2, 146, 165, 167
Azula (Princess) 2, 27–8, 31, 36, 70, 76, 82–4, 144, 146, 213–14
   and Zuko 144, 146, 148
   mental illness 190, 198–202

Ba Sing Se 3, 11–23, 61, 88, 143, 148, 217–18
Big Bang Theory, The 199
Big Mouth 191
BoJack Horseman 191
Bolin 2, 101
Breaking Bad 233

camp 218–19
children's traumatic experiences 135–6
   onscreen representations 137–9
   as redemption arc 144–9
Clarissa Explains It All 99

SUBJECT INDEX

coding 3, 12–17, 20–2, 26–7, 31–2, 36, 82, 99, 106, 173, 178, 209, 232–5
Combustion Man 190, 197–8, 200–1
Covid-19 pandemic 207, 222–23 n.31
  job quitting trend 222 n.25
cultural trauma 172–77

diaspora 5, 171–3, 177–82
  Tibetan 171, 181–2
DiMartino, Michael Dante 26, 77, 95–6, 102
disability discourse
  animated television series and films 191–2
  narrative prosthesis 197–201
  supercrip 192–7
Doctor Who 199
Dragon Prince, The 191
Drama 105
Dumbo 212

Earth Kingdom 1, 3, 6, 12, 16, 20, 27–8, 30–5, 50–1, 61–3, 66, 82, 84, 88, 135, 141, 143, 156, 175, 179–80, 192, 217
  and China 13, 16–19
  fashion 3, 6, 15–23, 33
  Si Wong tribes 30–1
Earth Rumble VI 17, 189, 192, 196
ecocentrism 3, 6, 41, 45–9, 50
  characteristics 54 n.24
ecocriticism 3, 39–41, 45, 49, 52
  anthology 53 nn.1–2
  ecofeminism 3, 41–4
Empire Strikes Back, The 201

fanfiction 5, 207–8, 210–11, 215–20, 220 n.2
fan practice 226–31
fan reviews 5, 225–35
fantasy 1, 4, 11–12, 23 nn.1–2, 25, 27–9, 35, 117–18, 121, 126, 129, 191–2, 194–5, 197, 202, 203 n.5, 209
FernGully: The Last Rainforest 52
Fire Nation 1, 5, 13, 15, 27–8, 30–1, 33, 35, 47–8, 59, 62–6, 68, 70, 76, 83–9, 107, 135–6, 139–40, 143–6, 148–9, 155–7, 159–64, 166, 172, 175–6, 216, 218–19
  and Japan 12–13, 157
  imperialism 4, 33, 42–3, 156–7
Flower Drum Song 211
Footloose 36
four nations 1. *See also* Air Nomads; Earth Kingdom; Fire Nation; Water Tribe

Game of Thrones 191
Ghostbusters 225, 233
G.I. Joe: A Real American Hero 79
Good, the Bad and the Ugly, The 28
Great Train Robbery, The 27

Hamilton, Joshua 26, 37 n.12, 38 n.18
He-Man and the Masters of the Universe 79–80
Homeland 199
House of Flying Daggers 25
Howl's Moving Castle 214

imperialism 4, 33, 42–4, 50, 55, 155–69. *See also* "Southern Air Temple, The" (*Avatar* S1E03)
Internet Movie Database (IMDb) 5, 225–8, 234
Iroh (Uncle) 2, 18, 31, 49–51, 63, 66–70, 123, 158–9, 166, 198, 217
  and Zuko 144–9

Jessica Jones 199
Jet (character) 62–3, 218

Katara 1–4, 6, 11, 19–21, 25, 30, 40, 45–50, 52, 65, 67, 70, 97, 139–41, 143, 196, 216–17, 219
  gender identity 42–5, 67–8, 75–6, 82–92, 160
  romantic relationships 102, 107, 208, 217–18, 222 n.31
  traumatic experience 149, 155–7, 159–64, 166–8
Konietzko, Bryan 16–17, 77, 95–6, 99, 102

Korra 2, 4, 115, 118, 120, 122–8, 172, 182, 213–14
   Aang comparison 95, 97, 99, 102, 107, 225, 228, 232, 234
   and Asami 95–6, 100–4, 106–9, 128, 235
   gender identity 97–104, 232–5
   queer identity 100–9
Kuvira 2, 128, 179

Legend of Zelda series 46
LGBTQ+ 41, 97, 105–6, 108
looking-glass self 3, 59, 64–6, 71
Lost City of Z, The 30
Love Is Love 105

Mai 2, 76, 83
Mako 2, 101, 214
Manchu 3, 11–12, 14, 18–19, 21
Man of the West 28
material and spiritual bodies
   Cartesian dualities 115–16
   dissolution of binaries 122–7
   nonhuman and material companions 120–2
   posthumanist ontology 116–20
   theoretical concepts 115–29
Medicine Man 30
Momo (winged lemur) 2, 19, 48, 121–2, 129, 168, 218
multiplicity 118, 120, 125–7, 179, 209, 212, 214, 217–18, 229–31, 234–5
My Little Pony 79

Nausicaä of the Valley of the Wind 47, 52
Netflix 2, 78, 95, 109, 202, 207–8, 217, 220
   Zutara Week 208
Nickelodeon 1–2, 4, 7 n.2, 75–6, 78–81, 95–100, 103–10, 111 n.23, 201, 214

Ozai (Fire Lord) 2, 68–70, 82, 135, 140, 143
   and Zuko 144–6, 148–9

pastoralism 3, 41, 49–52
Persons with disabilities (PWDs) 191, 194–8, 202
Pocahontas 46
post-humanism 131 n.43. *See also* material and spiritual bodies
   binaries, dissolutions 122–8
   non-human agencies 116–17, 120–2
   performativity embodiment 118–20
   philosophical approach 115–16, 129
Powerpuff Girls, The 79
Princess Mononoke 25
The Promise 104, 171, 175–6

Qing dynasty 3, 11–12, 14, 16–19, 21

race 28–30, 39, 42, 49, 182, 190, 208–11
Raiders of the Lost Ark 30, 36
Rainbow Brite 79
Rise of Kyoshi, The 108–9
Rogue One: A Star Wars Story 194
Rotten Tomatoes 5, 226–8, 234

Shadow and Bone 191
Shane 3, 32–6, 38 n.18
She-Ra: Princess of Power 80
She-Ra and the Princesses of Power 102
Si Wong tribes 30–1, 36
Snow White and the Seven Dwarfs 78
Sokka 1, 11, 19, 21–2, 40, 42, 44–8, 50, 54 n.23, 65–7, 70, 75, 82–9, 91, 93 n.32, 97, 107, 194, 196, 198, 200, 216–19
   traumatic experience 140, 143, 155–7, 159–60, 162, 164–8
Sozin 107, 122, 135, 148, 175
Spirit World 95, 98, 100, 118, 123, 125, 172
Star Wars 30, 97, 104, 194, 201, 225
Steven Universe 102
subscription video-on-demand (SVOD) 78, 109

Suki 2, 65, 76, 87, 92, 107, 194
supercrip 5, 191–8, 202

Tang-dynasty 16, 18
Tenzin 2, 124, 172, 174–8, 180–2
Toph Beifong 2, 11, 16–21, 44–5, 67, 76, 82–4, 88, 92, 97, 190, 192–8, 202, 204 n.22, 218–19
  and Aang 44–5, 140, 143
  and Katara 82–4, 86–7, 91, 107, 140, 143, 217
  and Korra 128
  and Sokka 86, 107
Transformers 79
Tumblr 102, 108, 191, 195–6, 199, 201
Turf Wars 96, 105–8, 171, 179
Twitter 108, 208
Ty Lee 2, 76, 83–4

Undone 191

Water Tribe 1–2, 15, 27, 30, 42, 62, 65, 67, 70, 75, 84, 88–9, 91, 93 n.32, 107, 123, 125, 135, 219
  and the Inuit 12–13, 29–30, 42
Wild Thornberrys, The 80, 99
World of Strawberry Shortcake, The 79
wuxia 12, 25, 27–8, 36

xianxia 12

Yellow Peril 14

Zaheer 2, 126–8
Zhao 2, 144–5, 157, 159–61, 166, 216
Zuko (Prince) 2, 4, 18, 27–9, 31–6, 49–52, 66–70, 87, 97, 156–9, 161, 166, 208, 216–19
  and Iroh 144–9
  and Katara 208, 218, 222 n.31
  traumatic experience 136–8, 144–50, 190, 198, 200

www.ingramcontent.com/pod-product-compliance
Lightning Source LLC
Chambersburg PA
CBHW062137300426
44115CB00012BA/1956